Interpreting Kant

The Journal of Philosophy of Education Book Series

The Journal of Philosophy of Education Book Series publishes titles that represent a wide variety of philosophical traditions. They vary from examination of fundamental philosophical issues in their connection with education, to detailed critical engagement with current educational practice or policy from a philosophical point of view. Books in this series promote rigorous thinking on educational matters and identify and criticise the ideological forces shaping education.

Titles in the series include:

Interpreting Kant for Education

Dissolving Dualisms and Embodying Mind

Sheila Webb

WILEY

This edition first published 2022

Originally published as Volume 54, Issue 6 of *The Journal of Philosophy of Education*

Registered Offices
John Wiley & Sons, Inc., 111 River Street, Hoboken, NJ 07030, USA
John Wiley & Sons Ltd, The Atrium, Southern Gate, Chichester, West Sussex, PO19 8SQ, UK

Editorial Office
9600 Garsington Road, Oxford, OX4 2DQ, UK

For details of our global editorial offices, customer services, and more information about Wiley products visit us at www.wiley.com.

Wiley also publishes its books in a variety of electronic formats and by print-on-demand. Some content that appears in standard print versions of this book may not be available in other formats.

Library of Congress Cataloging-in-Publication Data

Names: Webb, Sheila (Independent scholar), author.
Title: Interpreting Kant for education : dissolving dualisms and embodying mind / Sheila Webb.
Description: Hoboken, NJ : Wiley, 2022. | Series: Journal of philosophy of education book series | Includes index.
Identifiers: LCCN 2022040971 (print) | LCCN 2022040972 (ebook) | ISBN 9781119912170 (paperback) | ISBN 9781119816478 (adobe pdf) | ISBN 9781119816485 (epub) | ISBN 9781119816461 (obook)
Subjects: LCSH: Kant, Immanuel, 1724-1804. | Education–Philosophy.
Classification: LCC LB14.7 .W425 2022 (print) | LCC LB14.7 (ebook) | DDC 370.1–dc23/eng/20220926
LC record available at https://lccn.loc.gov/2022040971
LC ebook record available at https://lccn.loc.gov/2022040972

Cover design: Wiley
Cover image: Courtesy of Johanna Nordland

Set in 11.5/12pt TimesLTStd by Straive, Chennai, India
Printed and bound by CPI Group (UK) Ltd, Croydon, CR0 4YY

C9781119912170_161222

Contents

Preface

There is perhaps no thinker in the modern world who has laid the way for the development of philosophy so influentially as Immanuel Kant. He is the towering figure in the wake of whose work philosophy finds its different directions. And it is hard to think of the philosophy of education, especially in its modern incarnations, without some sense of Kant in the background, whether as the pillar of reason, the supreme proponent of deontological ethics, or the philosopher who leads Michel Foucault to raise the question again: 'What is enlightenment?' Yet for many, both enthusiasts and detractors, Kant's ideas are encountered indirectly, with over-reliance on dominant interpretations and acquiescence in received ideas. Encyclopaedia entries, simplified exegesis, and synoptic accounts abound, and the general effect is to provide an image of the man and his ideas that readily succumbs to caricature.

It is against this background that Sheila Webb has been motivated to write the remarkable monograph that follows. On the strength of a growing suspicion of the shortcomings of so much that has been written and said about this great philosopher, and attuned to the new waves of Kantian scholarship that have recently been challenging received views, she has embarked on a ground-breaking study. Her targets are familiar interpretations in both philosophy and education, but her purpose is certainly not exclusively critical. As her title, *Interpreting Kant for Education*, indicates, her intention is to provide a more accurate interpretation, dispelling barriers to understanding, but also revealing Kant's special relevance to thinking well about education. Indeed, the motivation for the book is by no means narrowly scholarly: its author is struck by the impoverishment of so much policy and practice in education today, mired as it is in a culture of performativity and accountability, both of which are pervasive threats to what might truly be quality in education; and she is committed to the view that a new reading of Kant can do much to remedy this. As the book's subtitle—*Dissolving Dualisms and Embodying Mind*—indicates, the dismantling of the ways of thinking that have sanctioned these harmful practices involves release from the sclerotic dualisms of fact and value, subject and object, and body and mind. Through a spiralling series of arguments, the book leads the reader to an appreciation of ways in which Kant's philosophy can provide this release. Priority in this reading is given to questions of epistemology and philosophy of mind, and the pertinence of these to matters of teaching and learning is made clear by way of some vivid examples. Anyone enquiring into such matters as they bear upon the curriculum would do well to consider the insights that here come into view. It should be apparent also that the book's exposure of the harm that is done by the distortion of Kant's views reveals in turn a robust philosophy of mind, the adoption of which would put much educational research and practice onto a more secure footing.

Paul Standish
Series Editor

Author's Preface and Acknowledgements

Since starting as a teacher many years ago, I've long been interested in different ideas about mind and knowledge and how these then shape ideas about the learning process. Troubled by the impoverished conceptions in the increasing 'performativity' culture in education, I found myself agreeing with criticisms of traditional epistemology, for instance those by Richard Rorty, but unconvinced by alternative theories. I then read John McDowell's *Mind and World* which offered a very different way of thinking about mind and related concepts; as I read more of the literature around this, including Robert Brandom's *Making It Explicit* and *Articulating Reasons*, so I became more persuaded by the insights and ideas of German Idealist thought. I quickly learnt however that the Kant being referred to in this literature was radically different from the negative picture of Kant that is currently prevalent in the philosophy of education. A lack of serious engagement with his work has meant a much-criticised dualist picture continues to circulate widely. I set out to challenge this picture by drawing on contemporary Kantian exegesis and commentary, and show that Kant can be understood in a much more valuable light. Grappling with Kant's insights, and contrasting different interpretations of them, not only led me to unfamiliar conceptions of our ordinary concepts but to deeper questions about the nature of knowledge, concepts and learning, and what it is to be minded. In discussing these I have tried to draw attention to some of the exciting new ideas being developed by contemporary philosophers, as well as the significance of the German Idealist tradition for educational theorising.

In writing this book I owe a special debt of gratitude to Jan Derry, from whom I have learnt much. Her enthusiasm for the subject and generosity of spirit is apparent to everyone who knows her; so thank you, Jan, for all those lively philosophical discussions over good food and wine. My heartfelt thanks also go to Roger Marples for introducing me to philosophy in the first place, I hope in time he will be convinced of the new Kant in these pages. I am grateful to John Vorhaus for criticisms that led me to clarify my explanations, and to audiences of the Philosophy of Education Society of Great Britain for their questions and comments on papers I have given. I have also benefitted from being a member of the Hegel Society of Great Britain, where I have learnt from stimulating discussion around many rich areas of Hegelian thought. My thanks also to an anonymous reviewer for thoughtful and helpful comments, and to Paul Standish for his excellent editing of the manuscript. Any errors that remain are my own. Finally, I would like to thank my family, Sam, Jo and Jake, for enriching my life in so many ways.

Interpreting Kant for Education

SHEILA WEBB

This introduction to *Interpreting Kant for Education* begins with a puzzle. Immanuel Kant is undoubtedly one of the most important and unrivalled thinkers of modern philosophy, the influence of his work 'has been, and continues to be, so profound and widespread as to have become imperceptible' (Howard Caygill, 1995, p. 1). Yet in the philosophy of education Kant receives fierce criticisms, and his work is frequently disparaged and ridiculed. Criticism is particularly directed at alleged dualisms, intellectualism and a conception of mind as disembodied or detached from real life. This Kant in education theory stands in contrast to the Kant to be found in more careful exegesis and contemporary work in the philosophy of mind and epistemology. By contrasting interpretations of his central terms and insights, I seek to show that Kant can be understood in an altogether different and more valuable way. The focus is on some deep-seated assumptions that, I argue, are presupposed when interpreting Kant's work, leading to the dualist picture that is widespread in education. Uncovering these presuppositions and disturbing our familiar concepts by offering new understandings of Kant's terms, not only shows his philosophy in a more favourable light (with robust conceptions of mind and knowledge) but brings into view differing ideas about the nature of knowledge and concepts, cognition and rationality, prompting deeper questions about how we learn and what it is to be minded, indeed, to be human. All of these are of profound importance to educational thought, and I believe Kant has much to offer that has yet to be appreciated in the philosophy of education.

Interpreting Kant for Education: Dissolving Dualisms and Embodying Mind, First Edition. Sheila Webb.
Chapters and editorial organization © 2022 Philosophy of Education Society of Great Britain.
Published 2022 by John Wiley & Sons Ltd.

Kant's work is profound and complex, historically changing the course of philosophy. From the thousands of readings, interpretations and exegeses over the years, a particular 'picture' circulates in educational theory, and this obviously has its own history. To change this familiar picture and think of Kant's work anew would require more than one book; here a start is made by suggesting different ways to understand some of Kant's central epistemological terms, which show how mind can be understood as embodied and his subject embedded in the real world.

My interest in Kant started when looking to alternative theories and conceptions of knowledge after dissatisfaction with the increasingly 'reductive' and 'standards' culture in education, in which knowledge is all too often treated as a 'portfolio of skills'. The rising tide of scientism is increasingly reflected in educational policy and practice, despite having been the focus of a sustained critique in educational theory. I start here with two illustrations of such critique to draw attention to various dualisms that are frequently pointed out as a root of the problem. Paul Standish is a long-term critic of the reductive culture, with its preoccupation with measurement, empirical data and statistics, which are presented as 'offering hard and often incontrovertible evidence' (2010, p. 6). The push for empirical methods, evidence and measurable impact devalues conceptual work and philosophical research, the impact of which cannot be measured in quantitative terms.[1] In identifying dualisms, Standish argues that the 'hardening of the subject-object dichotomy generates crude accounts of objectivity, where objectivity is thought to be synonymous with numerical measurement' (2011, p. 3). And of the fact-value dualism, Standish quotes Hilary Putnam:

> Every one of you has heard someone ask, 'Is that supposed to be a fact or a value judgment?' The presupposition of this stumper is that if it's a value judgment it can't possibly be a [statement of] fact, and a further presupposition of this is that value judgments are subjective. (in Standish, 2010, p. 4)

Judgements are assumed to be subjective, with subjectivity understood negatively as untrustworthy and not based on fact—and in opposition to objectivity, where this is considered synonymous with numerical measurement. Kant, as I will attempt to illustrate, has quite different and less oppositional conceptions of subjectivity and objectivity.

Richard Pring is another long-standing critic of the commodification of education, arguing that despite 'the centrality of knowledge and understanding in the development of the educated person, one too often adheres to a narrow interpretation of such knowledge and understanding' (2014, p. 11).[2] Judgement, Pring argues, is 'relegated to insignificance in a world of mechanical rationalism' (2013, p. 69). In contrast, for Kant, judgement is central; he draws attention to something more fundamental than facts and propositions, and this is our human *capacity* for knowledge, with judgement at its core. Pring points to the 'wars' between two dominant paradigms of knowledge: one he characterises as naïve realism and the other as constructivism—the first 'believes in 'an objective reality'' while the other sees reality as 'a 'social construction of the mind'' (2000, p. 251). He writes:

> The division between the two has become quite sharp, reflected in their respective languages or in different logical configurations of otherwise familiar words—objective/subjectivity, reality/multiple realities, truth/consensus, knowledge/opinion, understanding/perception and so on. It is as though the Cartesian dualism has returned in a more subtle form to entrap the unwary, even those who would so roundly condemn it in its original formulation … Thus, the contrast is drawn between the objective world (out there independently of our thinking about it) and the subjective worlds (in our heads, as it were, and individually constructed); between the public discourse and private meanings; between reality unconstructed by anyone and the 'multi realities' constructed by each individual. (p. 248)

I maintain that a form of dualism does indeed 'entrap the unwary, even those who would so roundly condemn it in its original formulation', and this has shaped interpretations of Kant's philosophy in education. Kant tends to be associated with one or the other of these prevailing paradigms; either with the foundationalism of empiricism or read as a constructivist. But while Pring sees dualisms *between* these paradigms, I will point to dualist assumptions about mind and world inherent in *both* of them, revealing the extent of the (dualist) presuppositions that are reflected in typical characterisations of Kant in education.

Both Standish and Pring call on the philosophy of education to challenge such dualisms and reclaim a place for philosophy in educational research. This book responds to the challenge. A dualism between mind and the external world, mind and body, is rooted in the philosophy of Descartes, and is something Kant addresses and seeks to change with his critical philosophy. James Conant writes that 'Kant's entire theoretical philosophy aims to think through precisely this [dualist] schema as the source of a fundamental unclarity in modern philosophical thinking' (parenthesis added); indeed, Conant continues, 'it is nothing less than the primary purpose of his theoretical philosophy to dissolve the central philosophical assumption which gives rise to the standard interpretative schema in the first place—the idea that reason is added from the outside to our nature as finite sensory beings' (Conant, 2016, p. 89). Conant's remarks are indicative of the reading of Kant developed in this book, which stands in contrast to the familiar 'Kantian' picture in education, and provides the conceptual resources for rethinking the familiar dualisms referred to by Standish and Pring.

What is interesting in critique of the 'reductive' trend in education is the frequent reference to Kant as a philosophical source of it. With charges of an absolutist Reason, a mechanical rationality, a disembodied mind and a disconnect between thought and reality, Kant is routinely cast as the adversary of whatever theory is being presented. Many of the educational theories presented have been very influential and rightly so; in this book I do not engage with (or take a stand for/against) the positions these theorists take, rather I am interested in their interpretations of Kant. A look at some of the references to Kant provides a sense of his current status in educational theory.[3]

Paul Hirst tells us that it was his reading of Kant that motivated his influential *Forms of Knowledge* in the early days of modern British philosophy of education. He writes:

> to acquire knowledge is to become aware of experience as structured, organized and made meaningful in some quite specific way, and the varieties of human knowledge constitute the highly developed forms in which man has found this possible. To acquire knowledge is to learn to see, to experience the world in a way otherwise unknown, and thereby to come to have a mind in a fuller sense. (1974, p. 31)[4]

This passage is in tune with the reading of Kant developed through the chapters. However, Hirst continues by distancing himself from Kant, rejecting the idea 'that being rational in any sphere is a matter of adherence to a set of principles that are of their character invariant', and rejecting 'any elements in thought that can be known to be immune to change, making transcendental demands on us' (pp. 92–93). Hirst is resisting for his own work the idea of an ahistorical rationalism that he associates with Kant, and which fits with the conventional 'Kantian' picture in education.[5] This picture is, however, at odds with the Kant that can be found in contemporary readings and exegesis in mainstream philosophy.

Kant tends to be read as a constructivist or associated with epistemological foundationalism—which reflects the dominance of these prevailing ways of thinking about knowledge in education. For instance, Daniel Royer writes: 'Certainly much of Kant's foundationalist epistemology has been refuted or corrected in the last century' (2006, p. 61). And Wilfred Carr criticises 'Kant's "foundationalist" philosophy' with its 'absolutist and *a priori* conception of reason' and 'disembodied rational autonomous subject' (1995, p. 79). He writes of

> Immanuel Kant's attempt to provide the philosophical foundations for universal principles of rational justification that are independent of particular historical, social or cultural circumstances and that are grounded in the capacity of enlightened human reason to achieve objectivity and truth. (2006, p. 143)

Kant's subject is portrayed as disembodied, and again reason and principles are seen as independent of culture and history. Feminist theories—making significant impact on epistemology since Carol Gilligan's *In a Different Voice* (1982)—also tend to be opposed to Kant's philosophy. Claudia Card criticises Kant for his disembedded reason and disregard of particular cultural circumstances (1996), and Lorraine Code similarly gives voice to the general antagonism towards Kant's view by feminist and postmodern thinkers (2005, 2006).

While some align Kant with traditional empiricism, many more in education read Kant as a constructivist. Their criticisms, however, are aimed at the same dualisms and detached conception of mind, whether in relation to knowledge or ethics. For instance, David Carr interprets Kant as 'thoroughgoingly constructivist' with a conception of reason as disembedded and internalistic, making for a disconnect between inner thought and outer reality (2003, 2007). He argues:

> to the extent that moral judgements constitute a type of prescription that is utterly dissociated from the normal workaday motives, wants or inclinations of agents, they are entirely innocent of empirical content or any necessary connection with sensible experience. For Kant, then, morality requires to

be understood in terms of the rational *imposition* of rules or principles or pure practical reason on the rough and tumble of human practical experience. (Carr, 2003, p. 94)[6]

A disconnect between mind and sensible experience is frequently noted, as is the imposition of rules or reason onto experience. Wolff-Michael Roth also portrays Kant as constructivist and as providing 'an epistemological subject that has no hold in and on this actual world that we inhabit' (2011a, p. 23). Mind, in Kant, is 'rationalistic' and 'superior to the senses' (2011b, p. 6), submitting them to order and taking 'entire charge of the integration' (p. 45). That mind is superior to the senses, detached from the world, and imposes rules on the rough and tumble of human experience again fits with, and reinforces, the typical picture of Kant that abounds.

Not all theorists writing in education are critics of Kant; a few have appropriated this typical picture—of mind 'ordering' experience and imposing rules and meaning—for philosophical support of their positions. David Jardine, for example, writes that human reason is, 'as Kant defined it, a synthesizing faculty that, in the act of knowing something in the world, actively constructs orderliness out of the chaos of experience' (2006, p. 23). Likewise, Ernst von Glasersfeld credits Kant for the idea that mind imposes meaning onto reality, for 'we cannot even imagine what the structure of the real world might be like' (1990, p. 2). David Elkind also credits Kant for the idea that 'a child creates and re-creates reality out of his or her experiences with the environment' (Elkind, 1989, p. 115).[7] It will be argued that what these theorists who *appropriate* Kant have in common with the above *critics* of Kant is the fact that they employ the same metaphysical presuppositions that give rise to a dualism. Kant is ascribed a radical subjectivism, with mind characterised as constructing (ordering, structuring) meaning from received sense data and imposing this onto (an unknowable) reality. So, like the above critics, these theorists portray Kant's conception of mind along the lines of 'mind makes nature'—with significant consequences for theories of knowledge, perception, cognition and learning. Rather than challenge, then, these appropriations strengthen what has become the prevailing 'Kantian' picture.

What is most frequently referred to in this 'Kantian' picture is the dualism perceived to be at the heart of Kant's view. Roland Reichenbach suggests that postmodernists 'often refer to the aesthetic mode of judgement ... but, of course, they wouldn't accept Kant's strict dualism of an empirical world and a world of reason' (1999, p. 241). Two worlds are posited. David Hamlyn assumes a dualism in arguing that physical objects 'are what Kant called 'things in themselves', forever unknowable and outside our experience', giving no grounds for belief (1970, p. 170). Wilfred Carr similarly criticises the dualism 'implicit in Kant's idea of a transcendental, noumenal "self" stipulating absolute standards to which the earth-bound, phenomenal self should conform' (1995, p. 38). The 'idea of the knowing subject, disengaged from the world', he argues, 'is a myth' (1995, pp. 79, 80). 'Two-self' characterisations are not unusual; Sally Sedgwick argues that for Kant 'the empirical self is not only split off from its noumenal counterpart, but also clearly subordinated to it' (1997, p. 80). John White similarly states that 'Kant's rationale for his view depends on his "two-world" view of man as consisting of a noumenal self and a phenomenal self'; and '[d]etached from desire, the concept of reason in both Kant and Peters becomes obscure, the transcendental arguments of *Ethics and Education* leaving the reader as unenlightened as Kant's delineation of the noumenal self in the *Critique of Practical Reason* and the *Groundwork*' (2005, p. 34). Whether it be for his view of knowledge or his ethics, it appears that contempt for Kant runs deep in educational theory.

But this Kant, with its detached conception of mind, stands in contrast to the Kant to be found in contemporary mainstream philosophy. It is my view that these educational theorists are wrong to attribute the 'subject disengaged from the world' picture to Kant, instead of attributing it to the traditional empiricist (Cartesian) metaphysics from which it arises—a metaphysics that continues to implicitly prevail. The concepts and structure of Kant's arguments in his critical philosophy are complex, lengthy and sophisticated as he grapples with the metaphysics of his time, coming up with new concepts and terms to capture what he thinks is right and what wrong with this. It is the many distinctions he makes for fine-grained explanation that have been subject to dualist understandings. But read in a different light, Kant can be seen as a critic of (what has come to be known as) 'Kantianism'.[8]

In educational theory there is little exegetical work on Kant, indeed some see the notions of epistemology and metaphysics as outmoded and irrelevant. A few even have an aversion to theory itself: for instance, Wilfred Carr claims that educational theory, being deeply rooted in the foundationalist discourse of Enlightenment modernity, has run its course and should be brought to a 'dignified end' (2006, p. 150).[9] Richard Smith notes that it has become common to read of the death of epistemology, and that it has lost its place in the philosophy of education 'in the face of scepticism about the extreme version of analytical philosophy—the view of concepts as stable and susceptible to definitive mapping' (2016, p. 272).[10] But while in education Kant, along with epistemology generally, tends to be scorned or dismissed, in mainstream philosophy there has been a re-engagement with Kant and Hegel and flourishing work on German Idealist ideas. This was first prompted by John McDowell, with his *Mind and World* (1994), and Robert Brandom, with his *Making It Explicit* (1994) and *Articulating Reasons* (2000). McDowell draws on Kant to argue that the perennial dualism 'anxiety' of traditional epistemology is an illusion, for if we conceive of mind and world differently there is no dualism. This is because 'Kant—to resort to a thumbnail caricature—established that the world ... cannot be constitutively independent of the space of concepts, the space where subjectivity has its being' (McDowell, 1998, p. 306). That is to say, for Kant there is *no dualism* between mind and world—contrary to the typical 'Kantian' picture in education and the examples given above. And while the growing literature springing from fruitful exchanges between the analytic and German traditions is very varied, these theorists are not working with a view of concepts as ahistorical and stable or a disembedded rationality. When Brandom, for instance, teaches 'Kantian lessons about Mind, Meaning and Rationality' (2006), this is completely different from the 'Kantian' Kant of education. It seems to me that while the projects Smith and Carr pursue are clearly quite different from Kant's critical philosophy, they nevertheless adopt a position on the ongoing and developing thought about knowledge—what may be claimed of it, what may be argued is involved in it—in a process that is never completed. Whether comment, critique, theory or a position, worked out or suggestive, all these play a part in the open-ended process of developing ideas. My discussions through the chapters of Kant's terms and insights are at the same time an exploration of different ideas about mind, subjectivity and objectivity, perception and self as well as ideas about knowledge and concepts, and the role of education in all of these—contemporary ideas that contribute to the ongoing process in educational theory.

With his Copernican view, Kant radically shifted thought about what it is to be a knower. That is, he replaced a focus on the *success* (truth, justification) of representations, with a focus on how a representation can function at all; how can a thought come to represent in the first place, how can it have objective content, questions that are conceptually prior to those of justification. As Brandom puts it, 'Kant wants to know what it is for mental states to *be*, or to *appear to us* to be, to function for us as, *representings* of represented objects. This question is more basic than that addressed by his predecessors' (2006, p. 2). Kant shifts attention to our distinctively human *capacity* for knowledge, and *Bildung* (education) is essential to developing this.[11] Kant takes over his 'capacities' approach to knowledge from Aristotle (Engstrom, 2006). Some educationalists have turned to Aristotle for richer conceptions of rationality and knowledge than those found in the current 'reductive' culture.[12] But Kant is normally associated with the latter and portrayed in *opposition* to Aristotle[13] rather than as drawing on the *same* cognitive tradition. Despite similarities, however, there are differences, as Sebastian Rödl explains: 'Aristotle's metaphysics is not critical' like Kant's, because 'it did not occur to him that one might conceive the forms of thought he describes as projections onto a reality that in itself is alien to reason' (2012, p. 43). Coming later in history, Kant *was* faced with the (dualist) development of thought after Descartes, which he addresses with his critical philosophy. The problem, to reiterate my point, has been that the conceptual distinctions Kant makes—to capture and articulate what he takes as right and wrong with the historically existing (empiricist and rationalist) approaches of his time—have tended to be interpreted through the very dualist assumptions that his critical work is so useful for exposing.

In the Anglophone analytic tradition, with its strong 'scientific' strand of thinking, Kant has had little impact. Brandom sums this up, in his usual colourful way:

Developments over the past four decades have secured Immanuel Kant's status as being for contemporary philosophers what the sea was for Swinburne: the great, gray mother of us all. And Kant mattered as much for the classical American pragmatists as he does for us today. But we look back at that sepia-toned age across an extended period during which Anglophone philosophy largely wrote Kant out of its canon. The founding ideology of Bertrand Russell and G.E. Moore, articulating the rationale and fighting faith for the rising tide of analytic philosophy, was forged in a recoil from the perceived defects of a British idealism inspired by Hegel. Mindful of the massive debt evidently and self-avowedly owed by Hegel to Kant, and putting aside neo-Kantian readings of Kant as an empiricist philosopher of science that cast him in a light they would have found more favourable, Russell and Moore diagnosed the idealist rot as having set in already with Kant. For them, and for many of their followers down through the years, the progressive current in philosophy should be seen to have run directly from Locke, Leibniz, and Hume to Mill and Frege, without any dangerous diversion into the oxbow of German idealism. (2013, p. 107)

But while on the one hand there is growing appreciation of German idealism in mainstream analytic philosophy, on the other hand, there is the growth of scientific naturalism. This science-based approach dispenses altogether with the dualism problem (of how to fit a non-material mind into an external material world) for the concept of mind is eliminated entirely from explanations, which are given using the concepts of the natural sciences. Naturalism has become an orthodox approach: 'Naturalism has become a slogan in the name of which the vast majority of work in analytic philosophy is pursued' (Mario de Caro and David Macarthur, 2004, p. 2). For examples, see the work of Jerry Fodor, Paul and Patricia Churchland, Daniel Dennett and Mario Bunge.[14] However, Robert Hanna argues that this scientific trend is a 'disastrously regressive turn in philosophy', which amounts to 'the *Copernican Devolution*, a retrograde evolution in philosophy that brings us back, full circle, to naïve, pre-Kantian, pre-critical conceptions of mind, knowledge, and world' (2016a, p. 2). Like Brandom, he argues for the need to learn Kant's lessons.

There are of course scholars of Kant in the analytic tradition; these include Henry Allison, Karl Ameriks, Paul Guyer, Allen Wood, David Velleman, Christine Korsgaard, Onora O'Neill, to name a few. Peter Strawson's reading remains very influential, as does Richard Rorty's profound critique.[15] Also, Wilfred Sellars criticises foundationalist epistemology with a powerful 'Myth of the Given' argument that mirrors Kant's own (1956, 1967). In the contemporary literature I draw on, there are references to Anglophone interpretations of Kant that are referred to as dualist or 'two-world' readings. Robert Greenberg, for instance, argues that 'almost without exception', Kant is read as being concerned with the conditions for possible experience, or the possibility of empirical knowledge, and contends that 'this view of the *Critique* reflects a fundamental misunderstanding of the work' (2001, p. 4). Pirmin Stekeler-Weithofer also argues that '[t]here are widespread misreadings of Kant's philosophy, especially in Anglophone traditions' (2010b, p. 5). Kant's sources of knowledge (intuition and spontaneity, or sensibility and the understanding) tend to be read as two separate entities or two worlds (Rüdiger Bubner, 2002; Andrea Kern, 2006, 2017; Stephen Engstrom, 2006; James Conant, 2016). Graham Bird writes of the traditional tendency to 'ascribe to Kant an exhaustive idealist dualism of mental states, "ideas," and transcendent things in themselves and then note the inevitable tensions and contradictions which arise from Kant's apparent attempts to escape from that tradition' (2006, xii). Bird urges us 'to abandon the temptation to understand Kant in a traditionalist way' and to avoid the 'Cartesianism which still haunts contemporary philosophy' (p. xiii). Dualist readings 'cannot be squared', Stephen Engstrom similarly argues, 'with what Kant actually says about theoretical cognition and the way understanding and sensibility cooperate in it' and claims that a 'proper appreciation' of the capacities 'eliminates the appearance of dualism' (2006, p. 2). In this literature, it is the *unity* of thought and reality, mind and world that are apparent. For instance, Dieter Henrich (an eminent Kant scholar) talks of the 'indissoluble' correlation between the unity of thought and unity of reality (1994). Rödl argues that 'a substance and its form enter thought together' (2012, p. 205), and Stekeler-Weithofer makes it clear that 'our social conceptual distinctions and our (joint) perceptual access to the object are "grown together", and embedded in our practices' (2010a, p. 15). Understanding Kant's terms differently not only eliminates the appearance of a dualism, as Engstrom says, but offers to educationalists a different way of thinking about concepts, knowledge and mind (and related concepts such as subjectivity and objectivity, and cognition).

Some of these new developments in mainstream philosophy are beginning to make inroads into educational theory, particularly through the ongoing work of Jan Derry and David Bakhurst. Derry, for instance, draws on Brandom and McDowell for her work on inferentialism, which she brings to bear on educational issues (2009, 2014, 2016, 2017; Derry and Bakker, 2011). And McDowell is an important influence on David Bakhurst whose significant contributions to education include *The Formation of Reason* (2011) and a variety of papers and seminars (2009, 2014, 2016). This work, however, draws principally on Brandom and McDowell; there has not been a focus on Kant *per se*—so in educational theory, as far as Kant is concerned, the dualist 'Kantian' picture remains in force.

In order to make explicit some of the presuppositions through which, it is argued, Kant has typically been read and portrayed in education, some philosophy at a metaphysical level is necessary. This is the work of Part One of this book. McDowell is used to expose the conceptual errors that give rise to the dualism 'anxiety' inherent in the traditional way of thinking about knowledge. While McDowell argues that the dualism rests on an illusion, he also writes that '[i]t matters that the illusion is capable of gripping us' (1996, p. xi). This is why I give much attention in the course of these chapters to loosening this grip by introducing different ways to think about Kant's central concepts. The reading that is developed through Part One is then used in Part Two to challenge the widespread 'Kantian' picture in education and address criticisms of intellectualism and a detached mind. At the same time, Part Two further elaborates the reading being presented to show how Kant's conception of mind can be understood as embodied, with his subject always immersed in and responsive to a particular context.

Reading Kant anew means setting aside some deep-seated assumptions as well as familiar understandings of concepts, and thinking of them in a different way. This is no easy task. In fact, this is an extremely difficult task, as our ordinary English understandings of such words and concepts naturally come to mind. We understand what we read or hear through our prior understanding of what these concepts capture (even when reading unfamiliar text), and this is perfectly natural. But what can get lost are different understandings of what a concept *can* capture, which can vary in different languages and traditions. An example of this is given by Standish, who talks of the dominance of the English or Anglophone understanding of the term 'science', and the richness that is lost in translation from German:

> In the increasingly internationalized space of educational research, in which English as a foreign language is widely spoken, the term 'science' becomes all the more equivocal. As this is the most familiar translation of *Wissenschaft*, the native speaker of German is likely to assume that the term will carry a similarly rich range of reference, and she will perhaps speak unselfconsciously of 'scientists' in disciplines where the more natural English expression might be 'researchers' or perhaps, better, 'academics'; the same point applies, of course, with terms comparable to *Wissenschaft* in other languages (the French term *science* included). Now it might be hoped that the

broader understanding of enquiry and understanding that the German term captures would then favourably affect the usage of the English term, and that this would be a corrective to scientistic tendencies. But the dominance of the research space by Anglophone practice—especially that of the UK and the US, with their philistine aversion to theory in general—means that physical science is indeed taken as the model, and the richer understanding that *Wissenschaft* might suggest is effectively colonized by the English term and its associations. (2007, p. 339)

Whether or not scientistic tendencies are to blame, the point remains that something is lost in translating the German term *Wissenschaft* into the English word 'science'. The same is the case with Kant's terms, which have (naturally) been prone to English understandings in the Anglophone world but can be understood in different ways. For example, '[w]e are apt to misunderstand Kant', Conant writes of the Deduction section of Kant's first *Critique*, 'if we take ourselves already to understand what terms such as "critique" and "deduction" are supposed to mean independently of our being about to make sense of why his text comes in the very particular shape—with all its initially puzzling twists and turns—that it does' (2016, p. 76). A proper understanding, Conant explains, 'requires reading Kant's book in a very different way than it has usually been read. It requires getting fully into view that the structure of a work of critique must be dialectical from the start' (p. 96). We must be prepared to change our understanding of even familiar terms.

To bring into view an unfamiliar picture of Kant, as stated above, lies outside the scope of one book, so I first of all restrict my focus to Kant's epistemology, his *Critique of Pure Reason (1787)*.[16] This is because his epistemology informs his thinking on ethics and practical knowledge: 'the fundamental theorems of the first *Critique* remain unchanged and serve continuously as premises in all of Kant's subsequent work' (Henrich, 1992, p. 6).[17] Accordingly, different understandings of Kant's epistemological terms allow different understandings of his ethics and practical knowledge, which currently also receive much criticism in educational theory. But even an adequate account of Kant's epistemology would involve already having different understandings of the terms being used; my aim, more simply, is to focus on aspects of contemporary readings that challenge the conventional picture in education. While this would seem to limit the scope, it involves discussing and thinking differently about a whole range of concepts of knowledge because their inter-relatedness means they can only be understood with reference to each other (Kant's systematicity is one of his strengths). As different understandings for an array of concepts cannot be discussed all at once, they are introduced in each chapter in Part One with a spiral effect, and continue to be elaborated throughout Part Two, and this demands a certain level of 'going with the flow'. Nevertheless, I make an attempt to revise the typical 'Kantian' picture in education and present enough contemporary readings of Kant to show how his Copernican view can be understood in a very different way. At the same time, discussions bring to light new ways of thinking about many familiar educational concepts.

In the current educational climate—with an emphasis on empirical research and measured impact on the one hand and postmodern scepticism towards Kant and grand narratives on the other—contemporary references to Kant's work are often fleeting or cursory. This makes it difficult to discuss interpretations or respond to critics in a meaningful way, so much of the philosophical work through the pages is at a metaphysical level—identifying and discussing presuppositions and attempting to articulate Kant's complex terms. However, Standish urges us not to shy away from engagement with mainstream philosophy but to draw on this to open up our thinking and understanding. He questions the benefit of theories that give merely a 'professional gloss to otherwise highly technicized practice, a protective theoretical veneer' (2007, p. 336).[18] And if exploring the thought of major philosophers seems too abstract and theoretical to be of help for 'impact' or practical concerns in the classroom, Standish reminds us that metaphysics derives from and returns to socially concrete and practical matters:

It is a characteristic of educational problems that they involve the most complex and profound questions about human beings and the good life. Push those practical problems hard enough, and you come to questions of ethics and metaphysics, and some of the richest, most far-reaching ways that these have been examined are to be found in the often difficult work of major philosophers, and not just, please note, of philosophers of education. Are we to shy away from this? Let us remember that what we are talking about here has implications for the practical domain. In a serious sense these are practical matters. (Standish, 2007, p. 337)

And Kant's view is certainly far-reaching: 'from metaphysics and epistemology through philosophy of science, philosophy of history and aesthetics to ethics, philosophy of law and political philosophy', and with 'a unity of conception and execution' writes Günter Zöller (2010, p. 66). I believe these far-reaching insights, freed from the 'Kantian' picture's often crude caricatures, offer a range of rich resources yet to be fully explored in the philosophy of education. I hope the more friendly Kant of this book goes some way in prompting renewed interest in his philosophy.

NOTES

1. See Paul Smeyers *et al.* (2014), who argue that the emphasis on quantitative measuring of scholarly output of academics disadvantages philosophers of education.
2. In asking what counts as an educated person, Pring refers to Bruner: 'Jerome Bruner took up this theme of education as being an introduction to the distinctively human life. Learning to be human was at the centre of his educational enterprise' (2014, p. 14). In very many ways, the reading of Kant I present in this book resembles Bruner's emphasis on a distinctively human life.
3. The examples noted here are discussed in Part Two.
4. Hirst famously argued for around seven distinct domains or forms of knowledge, and his work was enormously influential in late 20th-century educational philosophical theory, policy and practice in education (see 1963, 1973, 1974).
5. Hirst later tells us that he has moved away from his 'Kantian inspired' propositional view of knowledge for an emphasis on practical knowledge (2008). But contemporary readings of Kant show that action and practical reason are incorporated in Kant's overall view of knowledge in a way I believe Hirst is looking for.
6. Carr acknowledges that Kant's *epistemology* is less radically constructivist, as it involves rational principle *and* sensory input; but I hold that his moral theory grows out of his epistemology and that these are not incompatible.
7. Again, the examples in this introduction are discussed more fully in Part Two.
8. This is taken from Conant's (2016) paper entitled 'Why Kant is not a Kantian', discussed in Chapter Eight.
9. Carr argues for the 'future emergence of a "dephilosophized" or "post-philosophical" strategy for educational inquiry' premised 'on very different assumptions' from those of the Enlightenment (2001, p. 440). Also see Robin Usher and Richard Edwards (1994), who question the very purpose of education for being founded on Enlightenment ideals (of a self-directing and rational subject), which they see as obsolete.
10. In light of this, attention has shifted, Smith writes, from knowledge and truth to virtue epistemology, with a focus on what it is to be a good knower. Smith questions this and wants to give judgement a central role.
11. The German concept *Bildung* is also subject to different interpretations. Most commonly translated as 'education' (a broad term itself), it is far more than 'schooling' and more like 'experience', a lifelong process of personal growth and cultural development. Some useful English texts on this are: Allen W. Wood (2016), *The German Bildung Tradition* (available at: http://www.philosophy.uncc.edu/mleldrid/SAAP/USC/pbt1.html) and the introduction to *Bildung and the idea of liberal education*, by Lars Løvlie and Paul Standish (2002); also see *Theories of Bildung and Growth*, (eds.) Pauli Siljander, Ari Kivelä and Ari Sutinen (2012);

and Yotam Hotam's *Bildung: Liberal Education and its Devout Origins* (2019). Also, for a different approach to *Bildung*, see Jennifer Herdt's *Forming Humanity: Redeeming the German Bildung Tradition* (2019).

12. An example is Joseph Dunne's *Back to the Rough Ground* (1993), which has been enormously influential. Many have taken up Aristotle's concept of *phronesis* as educationally significant.

13. See, for instance, David Carr's work on Aristotle (2003, 2007) and Jane Green (2011).

14. Paul Redding, writing on the history of analytic philosophy, writes that there are two directions for the analytic tradition to take: naturalism or idealism. He concludes by recommending that the contemporary idealism brought into the analytic tradition, 'with its insistence on the irreducibility of the normative, looks better equipped than contemporary philosophical naturalism to answer' the 'problems that have plagued modern philosophy' (2010a, p. 288, see also 2010b).

15. Rorty's reading is discussed in Chapter Six and Strawson's in Chapter Eleven.

16. All references are to Kant's second edition of *Critique of Pure Reason* (1878), from the classic Norman Kemp Smith translation (2007 edition).

17. That is to argue that Kant's individual works, including his *Groundwork*, should not be read as standing alone, but understood within his wider epistemology.

18. This compares with Continental Europe where, Blake *et al.* write, 'philosophy of education developed out of the educational thought of Kant and Herbart. Here the approach to philosophy of education was always academically more securely rooted in the philosophical canon' (2003, p. 9).

1

Empiricism and Dualisms

SHEILA WEBB

As exemplified in the introduction, Kant is frequently criticised in educational theory for being intellectualist and dualist, with a conception of mind as detached from real life. I argue in this book that some deep-seated presuppositions about mind and world have influenced the way Kant is typically understood, and that, in light of contemporary work in the philosophy of mind and epistemology, Kant can be read in a much more friendly way. This first chapter identifies these presuppositions about mind and world. It looks at some empiricist epistemology, starting with a recent defence of a mind-independent view of knowledge, before introducing the work of John McDowell to expose the conceptual problems with this traditional way of thinking. McDowell draws on Kant's philosophy to show how a perceived dualism is an illusion, bringing to light a reading of Kant that contrasts with the familiar one that is widespread in educational theory, and which will be elaborated through the chapters.

Empiricism is of course far from a homogeneous theory, but a thread that runs through what is loosely called the analytic tradition is the idea of mind-independent knowledge. This way of thinking about knowledge embeds a conception of the relation between mind and world (as separate) that is understood to make knowledge objective. To be clear, my concern here is with the metaphysics of traditional empiricist epistemology; this is very different to everyday discourse about empiricism in education, including what is typically understood as empirical knowledge, empirical methodology, empirical research etc. I emphasise that empirical knowledge

Interpreting Kant for Education: Dissolving Dualisms and Embodying Mind, First Edition. Sheila Webb.
Chapters and editorial organization © 2022 Philosophy of Education Society of Great Britain.
Published 2022 by John Wiley & Sons Ltd.

(knowledge from observation) is not an issue; what is at issue is different *accounts* or theories of knowledge, and at the heart of different accounts tends to be different conceptions of mind, world and their relation. A closer look at traditional (mind-independent) epistemology reveals an inherent dualism between mind and world or thought and reality, which, it will be argued in Part Two, has influenced interpretations (and criticisms) of Kant in education.

In order to help make explicit such conceptions of mind and world, a fairly recent defence of a mind-independent account of knowledge will be discussed. This is Paul Boghossian's book *Fear of Knowledge: Against Relativism and Constructivism* (2006), in which he makes a spirited attack on constructivism. My intention is not to critically engage with the arguments of the book and agree or disagree, rather I use this account of knowledge to highlight central commitments for discussion. Boghossian begins:

> It is rare for a philosophical idea to command widespread acceptance in the broader intellectual community of the academy; philosophy, by its nature, tends towards claims of a scope and generality that invite controversy.

> Over the past twenty years or so, however, a remarkable consensus has formed—in the human and social sciences, even if not in the natural sciences—around a thesis about the nature of human knowledge. It is the thesis that knowledge is socially constructed.

> Although the terminology of social construction is relatively recent, the underlying ideas ... engage long-standing issues about the relation between mind and reality. (2006, p. iv)

This rightly identifies the underlying ideas about the relation between mind and reality as the root of different views of knowledge. How these are understood then shapes other concepts—subjectivity, objectivity, truth, judgement, and conceptions of self—all of which affect educational thought, from theories of learning, teaching and assessment to curriculum design and the educational process itself; thus, these underlying ideas are important.

Boghossian starts by criticising postmodernist relativism in social constructivist conceptions of knowledge, and appeals to the 'standard, widely accepted Platonic definition of knowledge' as *justified true belief* (p. 15). He characterises the social constructivist conception of knowledge as 'the doctrine of Equal Validity: there are many radically different, yet "equally valid" ways of knowing the world, with science being just one of them' (p. 2).[1] Boghossian says of this doctrine:

> Equal validity ... is a doctrine of considerable significance, and not just within the confines of the ivory tower. If the vast numbers of scholars in the humanities and social sciences who subscribe to it are right, we are not merely making a philosophical mistake of interest to a small number of specialists in the theory of knowledge; we have fundamentally misconceived the principles by which society ought to be organized. There is more than the usual urgency, then, to the questions whether they are right. (p. 5)

Again this reflects the significance of the debate. Metaphysical reflection on mind and reality is relevant not only to epistemologists but to the wider society more generally—and, I will argue, to interpreting Kant.

Boghossian's 'Equal Validity doctrine', however, constitutes a 'straw man' version of relativism, and while some constructivists may well embrace this, not all would argue for the more radical consequences of this doctrine. Even a sympathetic reviewer of Boghossian's book writes:

> his consistent ignoring of large swathes of relevant literature and arguments will make Boghossian's book frustrating to philosophers who work in this area. Equally frustrating are Boghossian's concentration on Rorty, and moreover his attention to only a relatively narrow (if admittedly central) portion of Rorty's work, ignoring other portions in which Rorty is careful to distance himself from certain forms of relativism. (Siegel, 2007)

But again, what makes this work relevant here are the conceptual commitments that exemplify mind-independent views of knowledge. When Boghossian writes 'there is broad consensus among philosophers' about the objectivity of facts and justification (p. 19), he means scientific conceptions, on which objectivity is associated with the real material world which is *separate from* (an inner and unreliable) subjectivity. He argues that constructivist knowledge is *anti*-objectivist, and receives support from such analytic philosophers as Richard Rorty, Ludwig Wittgenstein, Thomas Kuhn and Hilary Putnam, and that these in turn could appeal to Kant, Hume and Nietzsche. While there is much to debate in this, what is central to this approach to explaining knowledge is that mind is seen as separate from (a mirror of) the objective world so that beliefs can be checked against it for correctness.[2]

On this traditional 'correspondence' picture of knowledge, a deeply ingrained presupposition is that reality is the natural world that science describes—only physical and material things are understood to be real. With this ontological commitment, all normative phenomena, such as mind and thought, are excluded from what is considered 'real'. Not part of physical reality, mind is often considered immaterial and mysterious.[3] This way of thinking gives rise to a dualism between the subjective realm of thought (mind, consciousness etc.) on the one hand, and objective reality on the other, against which knowledge claims are compared for their truth. That mind is separate from the physical world is important on this traditional approach if knowledge is to be seen as objective, reliable and mind-independent. But this way of thinking raises the conceptual problem of how a separate mind fits into the external world, what is the relation? This has been a philosophical 'anxiety' since Descartes, which Kant took himself to have resolved with his Copernican thinking, breaking from the traditional metaphysics that were dominant in his time. However, if read through the existing traditional metaphysics, he can be seen as failing in this attempt, continuing to embed a dualism of subjective mental states and real things in themselves. It is the presuppositions of a physicalist conception of reality and a separate mind that are at the heart of different interpretations.

Boghossian, with his mind-independent view, critiques Richard Rorty, whose 'mind-dependent view' sees knowledge as made or constructed rather than found or mirrored—making it, in Boghossian's view, 'anti-objectivist'. In his enormously influential *Philosophy and the Mirror of Nature*, Rorty famously works towards discrediting the traditional empiricist theory of knowledge as being 'a whole set of terms and assumptions which center around the image of mind as mirroring nature, and which conspire to give sense to the Cartesian claim that the mind is naturally 'given' to itself' (1979, p. 97). In contrast, Rorty sees knowledge as arising from social agreement and the linguistic practices that constitute our human lives; he believes there *is* an independent world, but this cannot be *known* without essential reference to language and social solidarity. Boghossian illustrates what he calls Rorty's 'relativistic constructivism', by quoting Rorty as follows: '[I]t is not clear that any of the millions of ways of describing the bit of space time occupied by what we call a giraffe is closer to the way things are in and of themselves than any of the others' (2006, p. 30). That Rorty sees knowledge arising from social practices and agreement, and not from the object itself, is a significant difference between them.[4] Boghossian responds:

> It is one thing to say that we must explain our acceptance of certain descriptions in terms of our practical interest rather than in terms of their correspondence to the way things are in and of themselves; and it's quite another to say that there is no such thing as a way things are in and of themselves, independently of our descriptions. (2006, p. 31)

Boghossian commits to 'a way things are in and of themselves', and appeals to common sense: 'if I were to call the chunk of space-time occupied by the giraffe a tree, or a mountain, or a dinosaur or an asteroid—all of those descriptions would simply be false by virtue of not corresponding to the way things are' (pp. 31–32). This is of course right; if we call a giraffe a tree, we are wrong. The suggestion is that Rorty might be happy to call the giraffe a tree, or mountain or dinosaur. Boghossian expresses a widespread anxiety that if we lose the idea of a foundation and the way things are in themselves independently of mind, then we lose objectivity and truth, and without these anything goes, and we can call a giraffe whatever we like. Competing ideas about the mind dependency or mind independency of knowledge then shape conceptions of objectivity, perception, justification etc. Both agree that there is a way things are, necessitating constraints on what we can say, but for Rorty these normative constraints are linguistic and social—if we are wrong, our peers will correct us. For Boghossian, the way things are is independent of how we talk about them, and the validity of a claim is warranted by observation, by its correspondence to external reality, not by what others say.

Significantly for Boghossian—and reflected in the current educational climate of prioritising 'scientific' approaches—some descriptions do get closer to the way things are in and of themselves, and these are scientific descriptions. He explicitly commits to the knowledge and methods of the natural sciences as exemplars of truth and objectivity. Although his book is concerned with metaphysics—philosophical differences in conceptions of knowledge—Boghossian insists that the only legitimate ways of forming rational beliefs are by the methods of science:

> we *defer* to the deliverances of science: we assign it a privileged role in determining what to teach our children at school, what to accept as probative in our courts of law and what to base our social policies on. We take there to be a fact of the matter as to what is true. We want to accept only what there is good reason to believe true; and we take science to be the only good way to arrive at reasonable beliefs about what is true. (p. 4)

Boghossian expresses a widely held concern: 'if science wasn't privileged', he argues, 'we might well have to accord as much credibility to archaeology as to Zuni creationism' (pp. 4–5).[5] Again, the idea of mind as separate from nature is what is seen to give this way of thinking about knowledge its 'scientific' credentials. A quick look at some past accounts of the relation between mind and world helps illustrate this idea.

The scepticism of René Descartes in the early 17th century has had a lasting effect. Searching for certainty, Descartes famously believed that the only thing about which he could be absolutely certain, beyond doubt, was that he existed, because he was a thinking being (a *res cogitans*), captured in his famous phrase '*cogito ergo sum*'. Everything else *could* be doubted—body, world, objects—but the 'I' who does the doubting or thinking must exist. Conceiving the body as material, a machine, Descartes saw the mind as nonmaterial or immaterial ... and a mind–body or mind–world relational problem has been a concern of philosophers ever since. Descartes was a rationalist, but it was the British empiricists—John Locke, David Hume and George Berkeley—who shifted thought to a more 'scientific' or naturalist direction. In these early views, knowledge was seen to be derived directly from objects via the senses; Locke, for instance, conceives of mind as a 'blank slate' on which experience is 'written', or upon which a 'bundle of perceptions' from experience is 'inscribed'. Hume's naturalist approach was significant at the time, moving against the dogma of religion and dominance of Rationalism; he explains human nature and human knowledge along the lines of the natural sciences. He famously introduces an is–ought distinction arguing that there is no valid inference from descriptions of fact, what *is*, to how things *ought* to be, thereby separating the normative from the factual and introducing the idea of a fact–value dichotomy (Kant tells us it was Hume who first prompted his critical thinking). The logical positivism of the Vienna Circle reinforced these 'scientific' ways of thinking about mind and knowledge with their rejection of metaphysics and use of the 'verificationism' principle, which only endorsed statements that could be verified empirically (with value statements seen as cognitively meaningless).

Such scientific approaches to explaining knowledge influenced the early thinkers of the analytic tradition of Anglo-American philosophy. For instance, Bertrand Russell and G. E. Moore, recognised as founders of this tradition, also reject idealist philosophy; Russell puts forward an account of knowledge derived solely from the senses—we receive 'bundles' of 'sense data' or impressions from material objects.[6] According to this way of thinking, the causal impact from outside of mind is taken as a warrant, a 'tribunal' from objective reality, for beliefs to count as knowledge. Sense experience is conceived as a (mechanically) causal relation between mind and reality, with sense data or impressions resulting in beliefs. This 'causal' conception is seen to play a central role in gaining *objective* knowledge, for the immediate 'given' of sense data is seen as ensuring it is *value free*. Claims can be checked for validity against material objects, which are unequivocally there for all to see, independent of mind. The knowledge that results is seen to be neutral, objective and valid *because* justification lies in the mind–external empirical world. However, a conceptual consequence of this 'empiricist' way of thinking about knowledge is that mind is left looking 'mysterious' because if it is not part of the material world, then how does it fit into it at all?[7]—there is an ontological gulf between mind and world. While naturalist approaches characterise much of the work carried out in the analytic tradition, there are of course very different strands too, developed from the work of Frege, Wittgenstein, Quine, Lewis, Kuhn and Dennett, to name only a few. However, what have *implicitly* remained widespread with respect to knowledge are the assumptions about mind and an external world, making for a dualism between thought and reality, subject and object.

Indeed, Rorty famously critiques philosophy itself for this basic picture of mind as 'mirror' of mind-independent nature, and he disparages the priority accorded to science. For Rorty however, Kant is the principal target of his whole critique; he associates Kant, and Enlightenment thought in general, with the foundationalism and 'representationalism' of the empiricist tradition because he sees them as sharing the same idea of mind as mirror of a mind–external nature—a picture he rejects entirely. Rorty and John McDowell have very different readings of Kant (which are contrasted in Chapter Six) but they share a recognition of the errors of traditional empiricism. Their responses to these problems, though, differ. 'Like me', Rorty writes, 'McDowell regards himself as a therapeutic philosopher. He hopes, as I do, to create a "frame of mind in which we would no longer seem to be faced with problems that call on philosophy to bring subject and object back together again"' (1998, p. 142). But, Rorty continues, 'McDowell believes, as I do not, that "a real insight is operative in seeming to be faced with that obligation." So he thinks that empiricism, expelled with a pitchfork, will return again through the window' (*ibid.*). So while Rorty rejects empiricism and moves on, McDowell recognises the need to 'explain away' the conceptual dualism problem of empiricism to prevent it being 'a source of continuing philosophical discomfort' (*ibid.*).[8] This is why McDowell's work is so important here, for he not only makes explicit the assumptions that give rise to the (perceived) dualism—that continues to pervade much philosophical thinking—but in doing so he draws on Kant's philosophy, thus bringing to light a reading of Kant that is very different to the unpopular Kant of education. That is, McDowell sees the task of bridging 'an ontological and epistemological gulf' between mind and world as the 'basic misconception of modern philosophy' (1998b, p. 409), and draws on Kant's framework to 'exorcise' the 'seeming task' of bridging the epistemological gulf, by thinking differently about mind and world.[9]

McDowell (1996) articulates the conceptual inconsistencies in traditional empiricist epistemology by drawing on Wilfred Sellars's 'Myth of the Given' argument in his *Empiricism and the Philosophy of Mind* (1956).[10] The Myth of the Given is a powerful argument that mirrors Kant's own critique of empiricism; it highlights the *normative* aspects of knowledge that are missing in (mechanically conceived) *causal* conceptions. McDowell argues: 'In characterizing an episode or a state as that of *knowing*, we are not giving an empirical description of that episode or state; we are placing it in the logical space of reasons, of justifying and being able to justify what one says' (1996, p. xiv). He explains:

> the logical space in which talk of impressions belongs is not one in which things are connected by relations such as one thing's being warranted or correct in the light of another. So if

we conceive experience as made up of impressions, on these principles it cannot serve as a tribunal, something to which empirical thinking is answerable. Supposing that it can would just be a case of the naturalistic fallacy. (p. xv)

Sellars's 'space of reasons', the normative space in which justification belongs, is a metaphor of which McDowell makes much use in order to contrast it with the mechanical 'causal' relations investigated by the natural sciences, usually expressed as the 'laws of nature'. The Myth of the Given argument criticises the idea that if experience is conceived as an impression by the world on our senses ('caused' in us), it cannot at the same time function as a *justification* for a belief:

What happens there is the result of an alien force, the causal impact of the world, operating outside the control of our spontaneity. But it is one thing to be exempt from blame, on the ground that the position we find ourselves in can be traced ultimately to brute force; it is quite another thing to have a justification. In effect, the idea of the Given offers exculpations where we wanted justifications. (p. 8)

As tempting as this picture is, McDowell argues, it is 'in fact useless for its purpose ... [t]he attempt to extend the scope of justificatory relations outside the conceptual sphere cannot do what it is supposed to do. [For this would be] a move from an impression, conceived as the bare reception of a bit of Given, to a judgement justified by the impression' (pp. 7–9). The 'causal' conception of acquiring knowledge does not account for judgement (or normativity, intentionality, rational freedom). That is, if it is 'impressed' or 'caused' in us, we cannot help but think it, so how do we know if we are right or wrong? This mechanical picture does not allow for normativity: *for our claims to be right or wrong*, or for us to take responsibility for what we say and do.[11] Furthermore, McDowell argues that although Sellars is talking about knowledge, a normative context is necessary 'for the idea of being in touch with the world at all, whether knowledgeably or not' (p. xiv).

The Myth argument reveals the conceptual incoherence of mind-independent accounts of knowledge. A dualism is inherent in traditional empiricist epistemology, for how does a separate and immaterial mind (thought or reason) connect with the material world?[12] If sense data are seen as a ladder between an outer world and an inner mind, this mechanical or causal contact (impressed on the mind) does not allow for the rightness or wrongness of knowledge claims (for judgement), because we cannot help but think what we do. McDowell writes of:

> the tendency to picture the objective world as set over against a 'conceptual scheme' that has withdrawn into a kind of self-sufficiency. The fantasy of a sphere within which reason is in full autonomous control is one element in the complex aetiology of this dualism. The dualism yields a picture in which the realm of matter, which is, in so far as it impinges on us, the Given, confronts the realm of forms, which is the realm of thought, the realm in which subjectivity has its being. (1998b, p. 408)

Reason as 'detached from the world' and 'self-sufficient', in full autonomous control, mirrors typical criticisms of Kant in education. I argue that it is the picture from this traditional way of thinking about knowledge, with assumptions about mind as separate from reality, that has influenced the widespread 'Kantian' picture in education and led to charges of intellectualism and a detached mind. It is a picture McDowell urges us to reject: 'this picture is hopeless; it is the source of the basic misconception of modern philosophy, the idea that the task of philosophy is to bridge an ontological and epistemological gulf across which the subjective and the objective are supposed to face one another' (p. 409). Objectivity and subjectivity are understood as located in different places. Our senses are seen to bridge this gap and provide knowledge, but how can we rely on our senses to provide objective knowledge (through impressions on our mind/brain) when they may mislead us? How do we know if we are right or wrong? What if the external world is an illusion? Such scepticism is inherent in traditional empiricist epistemology (the vast literature on the 'argument from illusion' in the analytic tradition is testament to this enduring problem). The 'Myth of the Given' argument exposes the conceptual problem: if our contact with the world—our experience—is conceived in merely mechanical *causal* terms, as an impression on mind by the world, it cannot at the same time function as a *justification* for knowledge, for—again—if it is 'caused' in us, how do we know if and when we are right or wrong?

McDowell shows that by thinking differently about mind and world, this dualist problem of knowledge is 'exorcised'. But this entails rethinking the long-standing conception of the world as the mere physical reality as described by the natural sciences, and also rethinking how we picture mind (thought, subjectivity, reason). We should not think of mind as the brain, which is a position some philosophers hold (and some educationalists have adopted).[13] McDowell writes that he intends:

> not just to reject a more specific spatial location for someone's mind than that it is where its possessor is. It is to reject the whole idea that the mind can appropriately be conceived as an organ: if not a materially constituted organ, then an immaterially constituted organ … the cash value of this talk of organs is the idea that states and occurrences 'in' the mind have an intrinsic nature that is independent of how the mind's possessor is placed in the environment. (1998b, p. 281)

This is a prejudice, McDowell argues, that should be discarded. While a brain is necessary, '[m]ental life is an aspect of *our* lives':

> the idea that it takes place in the mind can, and should, be detached from the idea that there is a part of us, whether material or (supposing this made sense) immaterial, in which it takes place. Where mental life takes place need not be pinpointed any more precisely than by saying that it takes place where our lives take place. And then its states and occurrences can be no less intrinsically related to our environment than our lives are. (*Ibid.*)

This is a mind embodied and embedded in the environment in which we live our lives. And it is a conception of mind that McDowell draws from Kant, because for Kant, McDowell writes, the world 'cannot be constitutively independent of the space of concepts, the space where subjectivity has its being' (1998a, p. 306). McDowell is using Kant to argue *against* this dualist picture of knowledge because, for Kant, mind is intrinsically related to the world it knows with no dualism. This shows Kant in stark contrast to the dualist Kant found in educational theory, and it is this more valuable Kant that is developed through the chapters.

We can say that mind is in touch with the world through the senses, and while existing independently, the world we know is not independent of mind.[14] McDowell insists 'thought and the world must be understood together. The form of thought is already just as such the form of the world. It is a form that is subjective and objective together' (2009a, p. 143). Dieter Henrich too emphasises their unity, writing that Kant reveals their 'indissoluble mutual correlation' (2003, p. 22), he tells us that Kant, after being initially drawn to empiricism, later regarded empiricism 'as the corruption of all fundamental philosophy' (1993, p. 100). Hume 'awoke' Kant from his 'dogmatic slumbers' and started his critical thinking. Sebastian Rödl also stresses the unity of mind and world, thought and reality, and criticises empiricist assumptions about knowledge:

> [w]ithout the notion of spontaneous knowledge of the material nexus to an object by which one gains receptive knowledge of it, epistemology remains stuck in the antinomy of internalism and externalism. This is a fair price for isolating the theory of knowledge from the theory of self-consciousness. (2007, p. 145)

The debate about internalism and externalism has grown out of the presupposition of an inner mind, separate from the external world—the question becomes where does the mind stop and the world begin?[15] Rödl argues that the antimony of internalism and externalism can be 'dissolved' with an idealist account of knowledge which 'removes the error that is the source of that opposition' (2007, p. 145).[16] Many theorists I draw on point to the same passage by Kant to emphasise this unity: 'The same function which gives unity to the various representations *in a judgment* also gives unity to the mere synthesis of various representations *in an intuition*' (Kant, 1787, B104-5). That is, the unity of self-consciousness (mind, our conceptual capacities, the knowledge we have gained) is the same as (indissoluble from) the objective unity that we perceive and experience. As Rödl says, knowledge of the particular (in experience) is possible only through knowledge of the general because 'it is only through general knowledge that sense perception gives rise to knowledge of particulars' (Rödl, 2012, p. 13).[17] The *unity* of the general and particular, thought and reality, mind and world and subject and object is emphasised in each chapter to argue that for Kant, mind can be understood as integrally related to the world (McDowell), in a material nexus with objects (Rödl), making for an indissoluble mutual correlation between mind and world (Henrich). This stands in contrast to the widespread dualist characterisations of a detached and disembodied mind found in educational literature.[18]

   To conclude, attention has been drawn to some central commitments and assumptions about mind and world in traditional empiricist epistemology that, it will be argued, extend beyond this paradigm, shaping the way Kant's terms have typically been understood in educational theory. Mind-independent accounts of knowledge tend to be considered more 'scientific'—objective and reliable—than mind-dependent views, but McDowell's work was introduced to show, through the Myth of the Given argument, that this way of thinking is problematic in virtue of the conceptual dualism between mind and the external world. By thinking differently about mind and world, their seeming gap 'dissolves'. In the next chapter, some of Kant's key terms are discussed in order to begin the ongoing process of disentangling them from familiar Anglophone understandings and introducing different interpretations that give quite a different shape to Kant's work.

NOTES

1. See Kukla (2000) for a discussion of relativist concerns about some educational theories of knowing the world.
2. Judgements and knowledge claims also depend on how things are in the world for their correctness on Kant's view, but this entails different conceptions of objectivity, mind and world, that are introduced through the chapters.
3. A ghost in a machine, as Ryle characterises it (1949).
4. Rorty's position and reading of Kant is specifically discussed in Chapter Six.
5. I emphasise that this discussion does not entail an argument against science or empirical enquiry. As John McDowell points out, the 'role of science in our culture is not immediately the explanation. Science does not itself lay claim to enshrining metaphysical truth; it takes philosophers to make such claims on its behalf' (1998a, p. 181). More on this in Chapters Four and Five.
6. Bertrand Russell uses expressions like 'bundles' of 'sensibilia' or 'sense data' to describe the impressions or sensations on our senses by the natural world; see Russell (1905) and (1914).
7. That mind looks 'mysterious' is not to say that these philosophers allow anything mysterious into their scientific accounts, quite the contrary; mind appears 'mysterious' ('a ghost in a machine') because its place in the material world remains conceptually unaccounted for.
8. Again, these exchanges between Rorty and McDowell are further discussed in Chapter Six.
9. McDowell draws on other philosophers (Hegel, Wittgenstein and Aristotle, amongst others) but I focus on McDowell's use of Kant, for Kant is the topic here.
10. In his *Empiricism and the Philosophy of Mind*, McDowell writes, Sellars offers 'the outlines of a deeply Kantian way of thinking about intentionality—about how thought and language are directed towards the world'; but while McDowell shares the belief 'that there is no better way for us to approach an understanding of intentionality than by working towards understanding Kant'; he also writes, 'I think a fully Kantian vision of intentionality is inaccessible to Sellars, because of a deep structural feature of his philosophical outlook' (2009a, pp. 3, 4)
11. This 'mechanical' relation is contrasted with Kant's different conception of the relation between mind and world as we proceed.
12. Again, conceptions of the relation between mind and world (as our contact with the world) underlie different accounts of knowledge and are central to discussions of Kant. Specific

attention is given in Chapter Eight in contrasting the layer-cake conception of human mind-edness with Kant's 'transformative' conception (Conant, 2016, 2017).

13.   Chapters Four and Five discuss this. It is relevant to understanding how a conceptual dualism between mind and world is thought to be 'resolved' (by collapsing one side of the dualism into the other) and is contrasted with Kant's philosophy in order to bring the latter into sharper relief.

14.   Following McDowell, I have used in this book the language of mind being 'in touch with' or 'connected with' and 'in a rational relation with' the world. In a way this is inappropriate, for it suggests the incorrect idea that mind is in a different place to world and that they are 'connected' (through the senses). This is not the right picture, for they should be understood 'together' and not in any way as ontologically or epistemologically separate. However, to say mind and world (subjectivity and objectivity, thought and reality) should be understood together, in an indissoluble unity, may be difficult to conceive of, and given the ingrained presupposition that they are separate, I believe a step towards comprehending their unity is first to picture them as related, connected. Sebastian Rödl too writes of an internal connection, a material nexus. So I borrow these expressions as a first move towards an understanding of their indissoluble unity.

15.   The influential work of Andy Clark (1997) and his work with David Chalmers (1998) on 'the extended mind' illustrates this opposition.

16.   A proper discussion of internalism versus externalism lies outside the scope of this chapter, for both sides of the debate presuppose a conception of mind as 'bounded', as falling short of the world; see Rödl (2007) on this.

17.   Rödl's arguments on this are elaborated in Chapter Nine.

18.   Again, particular interpretations and criticisms of Kant by educationalists are examined in Part Two, drawing on understandings of Kant's terms that are introduced and elaborated in Part One.

2

Dualisms, Distinctions and Unity

SHEILA WEBB

Chapter One looked at some empiricist epistemology in order to draw attention to a conceptually problematic dualism between mind and the external world that is inherent in mind-independent accounts of knowledge. It will be argued that presuppositions from this traditional way of thinking about knowledge have shaped interpretations of Kant in contemporary educational theory, prompting much criticism, particularly for intellectualism and a detached conception of mind. McDowell's work was used—with Sellars's Myth of the Given argument—to make explicit some conceptual inconsistencies in this approach to knowledge. With different conceptions of mind, world and their relation, the perceived dualism is 'exorcised', and McDowell draws on Kant's philosophy to show this.

Chapter Two introduces and discusses some of Kant's key terms, suggesting unfamiliar understandings and distinguishing his view from empiricist epistemology as a way to bring clarity to these terms. Kant makes many distinctions in formulating his view, most notably between spontaneity and intuition, sensibility and the understanding, things in themselves and appearances, and receptive and spontaneous knowledge. Such distinctions are typically read as dualisms in educational theory; for instance, sensibility and the understanding are read as separate entities getting together to produce knowledge, and appearance and thing in itself as ontologically distinct objects. It will be argued that these can be understood quite differently. This chapter starts by looking at Kant's conception of experience and then at some of these distinctions. Different understandings are introduced, which will be revisited and elaborated through the

Interpreting Kant for Education: Dissolving Dualisms and Embodying Mind, First Edition. Sheila Webb.
Chapters and editorial organization © 2022 Philosophy of Education Society of Great Britain.
Published 2022 by John Wiley & Sons Ltd.

chapters, making for a different overall picture when contrasted with the widespread 'Kantian' one in education.

First, I want to point out that concepts such as spontaneity, understanding, reason and imagination carry particular meanings in Kant's work; also 'mind', 'reason', 'thought' and 'subjectivity' are variously used by Kant and by Kantian theorists. Here, however, for the ease of discussing Kant's complex insights, I will often use 'mind' as a general (shorthand) term, but sometimes specific terms will be used as the context demands. Referring to different concepts of mind, Kant writes:

> We have already defined the understanding in various ways: as a spontaneity of knowledge (in distinction from the receptivity of sensibility), as a power of thought, as a faculty of concepts, or again of judgments. All these definitions, when they are adequately understood, are identical. (A126)[1]

As Kant says, with adequate understandings, some of the concepts he uses can be understood as identical; he distinguishes them for explanatory purposes.

An attraction of empiricism is the common sense thought that we know something through the senses, through experience. This is right, and Kant accepts this too; however, 'experience' and 'sensibility' can be understood in different ways, and as our contact with reality (the relation of mind and world, thought and reality) how they are conceived shapes pictures of perception and cognition, and other related concepts—as well as affecting how Kant is understood. As previously discussed, in traditional empiricist epistemology 'causal' impressions are seen to play an essential role in providing *objective* knowledge, as this mechanical 'causal' relation (between mind and world) is taken to provide mind-independent knowledge. But the 'Myth of the Given' argument exposes the conceptual problem with 'causal' accounts of gaining knowledge, for if 'experience', as our contact with the world, is conceived of in merely mechanical terms as an impression on mind by the world, it cannot at the same time function as a *justification* for knowledge. For if it is 'caused' in us, how do we know if and when we are right or wrong? This does not allow for judgement or normativity. Engaging with the range of ideas and metaphysics of his time, and also with those of his predecessors going back to Aristotle and Plato, Kant comes to see empiricism as flawed because it recognises only one of our two 'sources' of knowledge—the senses.

Kant does not doubt the importance of experience in gaining knowledge. Indeed, he insists: 'all knowledge begins with experience. For how should our faculty of knowledge be awakened into action did not objects affecting our senses partly of themselves produce representations' (B1).[2] However, Kant continues: 'though all our knowledge begins with experience, it does not follow that it all arises out of experience' (*ibid.*). He famously holds that the 'spontaneity' of mind is also a source of knowledge. For Kant, mind is a *power*, a faculty or *capacity* for knowledge—accounting for the self-conscious nature of our thinking. That mind (or what we can call our rational capacities, as the knowledge we have accumulated) is exercised in experience makes Kant's view fundamentally different from mind-independent 'causal' accounts (impressions on the brain/mind). It also contrasts with the familiar 'Kantian' picture in education, in which mind orders or structures the raw data from the senses and imposes meaning or rules onto reality. What is important to the reading being presented is that rational capacities be understood as passively exercised *in* experience; sensibility is transformed by them (it is not merely delivering sense data to the mind to be structured). This conception of what Kant sees as our distinctively human contact with the world can be described as a 'rational' relation because it implicitly draws into play our previously acquired knowledge, in contrast to the mechanical 'causal' relation and active 'imposition' interpretations.

Kant makes some conceptual distinctions in order to capture what he takes as right and what he takes as wrong in the empiricist and rationalist traditions of his time. One of these is intuition and spontaneity. *Intuition*, he says, is the capacity for receiving representations (content) through which 'an object is *given* to us', while the *spontaneity* (or the understanding) is 'the power of knowing an object through these representations', the power through which 'the object is *thought* in relation to that [given] representation' (B74). Kant, in his critical philosophy, sees the error in each of the prevailing traditions of the time—empiricism and rationalism—to lie in their recognising only one of these two sources of knowledge. He insists that it is the *unity* of the sources that provides knowledge:

> Our nature is so constituted that our *intuition* can never be other than sensible; that is, it contains only the mode in which we are affected by objects. The faculty, on the other hand, which enables us to *think* the object of sensible intuition is the understanding. To neither of these powers may a preference

be given over the other. Without sensibility no object would be given to us, without understanding no object would be thought. Thoughts without content are empty, intuitions without concepts are blind... Only through their union can knowledge arise. (B75)

Read through the dualist presuppositions discussed in Chapter One—where mind is understood as separate from the material world—it can look as if intuition and spontaneity are two distinct realms, getting together to produce knowledge. Despite insisting on their *unity*, Kant's use of separate terms can fuel dualist readings. But if we accept that Kant distinguishes these terms *conceptually* (not ontologically) to explain the *functions* of these capacities, and if we set aside some of our familiar understandings, this passage can be appreciated in a different way. Kant's concept of intuition is not the causal sense data of traditional empiricism; it is perhaps the most overlooked aspect of Kant's philosophy in educational interpretations (which mainly focus on mind), and for this reason it is something to which we will keep returning.

Intuition is a rich concept and one not easy to explain. While intuition is the English translation of the German *Anschauung*, much is lost in translation. The English language *Merriam-Webster* dictionary defines intuition as 'a natural ability or power that makes it possible to know something without any proof or evidence: a feeling that guides a person to act a certain way'. This subjective feeling or inner state stands in stark contrast to Kant's use of *Anschauung*: intuition accounts for the *objective* aspects of knowledge. McDowell warns that in thinking about *Anschauung* 'we need to forget much of the philosophical resonance of the English word intuition' (2009a, p. 260). In educational theory, Kant's notion of intuition or sensibility is standardly interpreted as a matter of brute impressions or empiricism's sense data,[3] but we need a different understanding of sensory perception.

In *Mind and World*, McDowell writes: 'We should understand what Kant calls "intuition"—experiential intake—not as a bare getting of an extra-conceptual Given, but as a kind of occurrence or state that already has conceptual content' (1996, p. 9).[4] More recently, McDowell writes: Kant 'insists that in intuitions forms required by the understanding come into play without activity on the part of subjects' (2009a, p. 191); and that intuitions 'directly bring objects into view through bringing their perceptible properties into view' (p. 268). Sebastian Rödl argues that thought is *only possible* by relating directly or indirectly to intuition. He describes it as 'sensory content': 'By "content" Kant means content taken in through the senses. What is taken in through the senses—a sensory content—is what we perceive when we perceive something; Kant calls such a content an intuition' (2012, p. 55). 'Thoughts without intuitions are empty: the human, discursive intellect depends on its being given an object through the senses', Rödl explains, '[t]hus it is *finite*: it is conditioned by what it represents' (p. 57). This is to argue that the intellect is intuition-dependent for empirical knowledge (sensory content) making it finite (which contrasts with an 'infinite' mind—such as a 'divine' will—which is the source of the *existence* of its objects).[5] These theorists are articulating how we experience the world. McDowell asks, 'How is empirical content so much as possible' and argues that the 'question whether some of our thinking puts us in possession of knowledge cannot even arise unless this prior condition, that our thinking can have empirical content at all, is met. I use the word "transcendental," in what I hope is sufficiently close to a Kantian way, to characterize this sort of concern with the very possibility of thought's being directed at the objective world' (2009b, p. 243). Kant uses intuition to capture the *content* of thought, and this helps picture mind as embodied and embedded, because the content of our empirical thought comes from our concrete standpoint, the actual experience in which are at any moment immersed.

While intuition can be understood as providing the material or worldly *content* of thought (*what* is intuited is what is perceived or thought), intuition is also used to describe a capacity, an ability or power. This *ability to* intuit can thus be distinguished from *what* is intuited.[6] Importantly, when Kant says intuition is a capacity through which 'an object is *given* to us', he is working with a different understanding of 'given' to the 'Given' of empiricist epistemology; it is a straightforward sense of given and not subject to the Myth. McDowell writes: 'The idea of givenness becomes mythical—becomes the idea of Givenness—only if we fail to impose the necessary requirements on getting what is given ... Avoiding the Myth requires capacities that belong to reason to be operative in experiencing itself, not just in judgements in which we respond to experience' (2009a, p. 258). This is a significant point. For Kant, not only are our rational capacities exercised consciously—such as in making judgements, reasoning and in discursive activities—but they are also exercised *passively* in ongoing experience and perception. This passive aspect to experience is obscured in portrayals of Kant in educational theory, which tend to focus on the active nature of mind (typically as ordering, structuring or making sense of what the senses deliver). Sensibility for Kant is not blind data but is permeated by our rational capacities, which are operative in experience. While experience and perception draw on what we already know, this knowledge is constituted by partial and opaque concepts, feelings, memories, as well as more factual and propositional knowledge.

While this mind-dependent conception of experience differs from mind-independent accounts, it does not lose objectivity. Pirmin Stekeler-Weithofer draws our attention to the objective and factive aspects of Kant's view. 'A proper understanding of the notion of *Intuition* is of highly systematic importance for understanding the possibility of reference and of world-related content not only of judgements about things present to us but all things in the real world at large' (2010b, p. 2). Stekeler-Weithofer also brings out the social and practical aspects of this objectivity. It is 'a practical form of identifying real objects in actual experience' (2010a, p. 10). Embedded in actual experience, it involves interpersonal activity with shared relations to objects, and this contrasts with mind-independent accounts of individual sense data that the mind then works on:

> Our knowledge does not rest on the ground of phenomenal sense data. Rather than with individual sense data, any knowledge begins with an apperception of things in my or your or our present and object-related *Anschauung* that I can share with you and others, on the ground of some transformations of perspectives and on the ground of joint conceptual distinctions. (Stekeler-Weithofer, 2008, p. 14)

As a human capacity, Stekeler-Weithofer emphasises the interpersonal and cooperative norms involved in joint perception, which provide objectivity.[7] An educational point here is that this ability is socially learnt rather than simply a genetic development in children's perception of the world; this compares with, say, Piaget's genetic conception of cognitive development. Intuition is a rich notion, and its almost complete obscurity in educational interpretations means important areas of Kant's philosophy, such as objectivity and sociality, have not been sufficiently appreciated.[8]

What of Kant's concept of spontaneity? The spontaneity or power of mind can be contrasted with empiricist epistemology in which mind tends to be presupposed as an object—a brain, a blank slate, a mirror, a recipient of impressions. 'Reason has no power to produce anything outside its representations' in empiricism, Stephen Engstrom writes, 'but serves merely to achieve a true representation of things that are there anyway. It simply tracks reality' (2013, p. 138). Kant's conception of mind as a *power*—an energy—is captured by 'spontaneity', and as a power it can be the 'causality' of our actions, in that we are not merely pushed around by external forces (determined from without); rather the power of thought *itself* can move us to act. McDowell argues that we act in the light of reasons, and reasons have a certain grip or hold on us, the authority of which comes from spontaneity. Rödl points out that, '[a]s is traditional, "light" here signifies knowledge: acting in the light of reasons is not just acting in accord with reasons, but from recognition of those reasons' (2016, p. 85). In the same vein, Christine Korsgaard writes that 'reasons direct, guide, or obligate us to act or judge in certain ways' (2003, p. 226). Douglas Lavin similarly argues that 'the way in which agents are directed by principles is radically different from the way in which mere bits of stuff are directed by physical laws' (2004, p. 444). It is the spontaneity (the autonomy, self-determination) of mind that is being expressed by these Kantian interpreters. It is a term Kant uses to capture what he takes as lacking in the traditional metaphysics of his time—both empiricist and rationalist epistemology.[9]

Descartes, as a rationalist, also recognised the activity of mind, the 'I' who thinks, but, unlike Descartes' conception, Kant's is not dualist in that his "I" is not a source of knowledge that stands alone, separate from body and world, but is embodied and embedded in real life through *actual experience*. Kant refers to rationalism as 'dogmatic metaphysics', which he describes as 'a completely isolated speculative science of reason, which soars far above the teachings of experience, and in which reason is indeed meant to be its own pupil' (Bxiv). This sounds familiarly like criticism of Kant in education, but here it is Kant himself who is the critic, and rationalism is his target. James Conant describes Kant's purpose in his *Critique*:

> Kant is conducting an argument on two fronts—one directed at the empiricist and one at the rationalist—while waging a campaign against what is ultimately to be unmasked as a single enemy. The aim is to show that what is philosophically fatal in each of the two traditionally opposed philosophical approaches flows from a single assumption—one that they share. (2016, p. 85)

What they share is the erroneous assumption that their chosen single capacity (the senses or the understanding) is intelligible as a *self-standing capacity*. In contrast, for Kant each capacity can be made sense of only in light of the other, as both are exercised together—in unity—in experience.

The distinction between intuition and spontaneity (again, a conceptual distinction) has typically been interpreted in educational theory as a form of dualism, as is the case with Kant's other distinctions. That is, sensibility and the understanding are interpreted as two distinct entities, each able to produce representations.[10] Sensibility (and intuition) tend to be understood as empiricist sense data, while the understanding (and spontaneity) are associated with a separate, inner mind—hence, the many criticisms of Kant as a dualist with a detached conception of mind. But there are other ways of understanding the capacities. Stephen Engstrom, for instance, argues that dualist readings 'cannot be squared' with 'what Kant actually says about theoretical cognition and the way understanding and sensibility cooperate in it' (2006, p. 2). McDowell writes of the supposed dualism:

> It [dualism] is taken for granted in the empiricist tradition, but in this dialectical context that would be an unimpressive basis for defending it. So much the worse for the empiricist tradition, we might say. Resting content with a dualism of the sensory and the intellectual betrays a failure of imagination about the possibilities for finding the rational intellect integrally involved in the phenomena of human life. We should argue in the other direction. Actualizations of conceptual capacities, capacities that belong to their subject's rationality, can present things in a sensory way, and that gives the lie to the dualism. (2011, pp. 10–11)

Different understandings of what tend to be referred to simply as the capacities can reveal Kant's conception of mind as embodied, situated and continually engaged in ongoing experience.

To help bring this into view, I turn to a related distinction Kant makes between 'things in themselves' and 'appearances'. As with other distinctions, this contrast has typically been read as a form of dualism, often with the 'thing in itself' understood as objective reality and appearance as something in the head. For instance, David Carr writes:

> Kant's epistemology maintained that if the subjective experiences of agents were to be sources of genuine

knowledge, such knowledge claims would need to correspond to an objective reality lying beyond experience which
he called the *noumenon* or thing-in-itself. (2003, p. 187)

The idea of the thing in itself is associated with objective reality,
and this objective reality cannot be known for it lies beyond our
subjective experience. Carr writes that Kant 'feels compelled to
say that something 'behind' appearance is needed to secure the
complete objectivity of accurate perceptions' (p. 104). This fits with
the 'Kantian' picture that is widespread in educational theory. That
we can never attain knowledge of things in themselves is understood
to mean that our knowledge is restricted to appearances and we are
denied knowledge of objective reality itself, of things as they really
are. However, as Kantian Graham Bird writes, such a doctrine would
seem 'to legitimize only a subjective experience and to reject the
very objectivity which Kant claimed to establish. Kant himself was
adamant that no such conclusions could be drawn from his account.
For him appearances themselves provide the required objectivity
while the claim to know things as they are in themselves is no more
than an illusion' (2006, p. 2).

What contributes to dualist interpretations is the often found
rewording of 'things in themselves' as 'things as they are in
themselves', or even as 'the way things are in and of themselves'
(Boghossian, 2006, p. 31). With this understood as objective reality,
it is then contrasted with appearances, which are presupposed as
something in the head—and we have a dualism. As with Kant's other
distinctions, the traditional empiricist picture of mind as separate
from the external world can be seen to shape interpretations; but
these distinctions can be understood differently, for as Bird says,
for Kant appearances themselves provide objectivity. McDowell
too argues that Kant does not posit two distinct realms, 'one
knowable by us and one unknowable by us', because this does not
acknowledge 'Kant's insistence that appearances, things as they
appear, *are the same things* that can also be conceived as things in
themselves' (2009a, p. 64, emphasis added). McDowell explains:

> When we speak as philosophers, we do not start to speak of a
> new range of objects, genuinely real as the objects of the man-
> ifest image were not. We speak of the same objects, under a
> special mode of consideration in which we abstract from the
> way in which the objects figure in our world view. (2009a, p. 42,
> footnote 30)

He argues that what Kant is insisting on when he speaks of the distinction is:

> an identity of things as they appear in our knowledge and 'those same things as things in themselves'; not 'those same things *as they are* in themselves'. (This latter wording pervades …). Things in themselves are the very things that figure in our knowledge, but considered in abstraction from how they figure in our knowledge. That is not to say: considered as possessing, unknowingly to us, other properties than those they appear as possessing in our knowledge of them. (*Ibid.*)[11]

So why does Kant make the distinction? For one thing: to clarify his view and differentiate it from the 'school metaphysics' of his day. It is the *claim to know* things as they are in themselves (independently of mind) that is an illusion, a version of the Myth of the Given.

The distinction comes into play when we think of knowledge of ourselves, knowledge through spontaneity. This involves another of Kant's distinctions, between 'receptive knowledge' and 'spontaneous knowledge' (or self-knowledge). Through sensibility we acquire empirical knowledge of the world. Kant describes this as receptive knowledge, acquired *a posteriori* through the senses. (It shares with empiricism the idea that the senses are a source of knowledge, but spontaneity is also involved.) Self-knowledge stems from spontaneity; it is not acquired through the senses, and includes knowledge of ourselves as self-conscious thinking beings. This knowledge can be seen as knowledge of ourselves as a thing in itself; it is not receptive knowledge of a separate object. We cannot know a separate object as a thing in itself, only as it appears to us, but as human beings we can know ourselves as thinking and intentional agents, as a thing in itself as well as an object to be observed. This is related to Kant's 'realm of freedom'. Kant first writes that we can 'have no knowledge of any object as thing in itself, but only in so far as it is an object of sensible intuition, that is, an appearance', and so 'it does indeed follow that all possible speculative knowledge of reason is limited to mere objects of *experience*' (Bxxvi). But as we know, Kant's insight is that knowledge is not exhausted by knowledge through the senses, we also have knowledge from spontaneity. As rational beings, we are on the one hand subject to the laws of nature as described by the sciences (for example illness, maturation, things that we cannot change), but at the same time what makes us distinctively human is spontaneity (the realm of freedom), which can itself be a 'cause' of action. Another way to put this is that being autonomous we are subject not only to the mechanical laws of nature but to the 'causality' of freedom, the power of thought to move us to act. So when it comes to understanding ourselves as humans and intentional agents, we can know ourselves, Kant writes, '*in a twofold sense*, namely as appearance and as thing in itself'; we are 'necessarily subject to the law of nature, and so far *not free*, while yet, as belonging to a thing in itself, [we are] not subject to that law, and [are] therefore *free*' (Bxxvii). We can know ourselves through spontaneity (self-conscious awareness of what we are doing or intend to do) and also through observation (looking in a mirror). Rödl gives voice to this insight—that self-knowledge springs from spontaneity and is not receptive knowledge:

> Kant states that, insofar as we are under the causality of freedom, we know ourselves not as appearances, but as things in themselves. He means that, as subjects of intentional action, we do not know ourselves receptively; our knowledge in this case does not depend on a faculty of sensibility that mediates between ourselves and the objects we know. Since 'appearance' refers to an object known by means of a receptive faculty, our knowledge of ourselves as agents is not knowledge of appearances. The power of this insight has been underestimated. (2007, p. 122, footnote 20)

We can know ourselves as thing in itself, as an intentional and thinking agent, as well as empirically through appearance, and as Rödl says, the power of this insight has been underestimated. Read implicitly through dualist presuppositions, interpretations have tended to obscure Kant's explanatory reasons for the distinction and reinforced the typical 'dualist' picture.[12]

The recognition of spontaneity differentiates Kant's view from empiricist epistemology in two important ways; first, spontaneity is understood as a source of knowledge itself, and second, spontaneity is understood as being involved even in acts of knowing through the senses. This 'rational' relation between mind and world contrasts with the mechanical 'causal' conception of mind-independent accounts, in that rational capacities are exercised even in receptive empirical knowledge. For while we can know *what* we perceive from receptivity, as Rödl argues, we know *that we perceive* from spontaneity:

> Knowing from receptivity that something is the case is an act of a self-conscious power, a power whose acts are known by their subject from spontaneity ... She who receptively knows something knows that she does, not from receptivity, but from spontaneity. (p. 134)

If I see a glass on my desk, I know *what* I perceive (the glass) from observation (from the senses, intuition), but I know *that* I perceive the glass from seeing it. Rödl writes: 'Unmediated first person thoughts articulate knowledge I possess, not by *perceiving*, but be *being* their object. If I know without mediation that I am F, then I know it, not by perceiving that I am F, but by being F' (p. 9). For example, if I am feeling thirsty, I know this by being thirsty. Spontaneous knowledge is 'of oneself as oneself' as opposed to receptive knowledge 'of an independent object and is of something as other' (p. 145). Knowing ourselves to be thinking, deciding or doing something does not arise from observation. Rödl develops Kant's insight, arguing that while first-person knowledge is non-receptive and non-empirical, it is nevertheless of a material reality, for it shows 'the subject of action and the subject of belief to be, *in such a way as to know herself to be*, material, which knowledge is first personal and not empirical' (p. 14). Mind is not detached but materially embodied, and a subject knows this from spontaneity. 'The concept of spontaneity is broad; it applies to the sentient life of animals and perhaps even to the vegetative life of plants', Rödl writes, but the 'spontaneity of thought is of a special kind: it is a spontaneity whose acts are knowledge of these very acts [...] such is the spontaneity of *reason*' (2007, p. 14).[13]

Rödl points out that it is 'the principle thought of German Idealism that self-consciousness, freedom, and reason are one' and form the starting point of any investigation into knowledge (p. 105). He writes:

> If we inquire into the nature of knowledge, we inquire into our own nature ... The science of man, of which the theory of knowledge forms a part, is not an empirical science. It is pursued not by observing men and drawing inferences from these data but by articulating what we know of man by being men. (p. 164)

The nature of knowledge is best investigated through reflection, philosophical enquiry.

Kant makes the distinctions he does (between receptive knowledge from the senses and knowledge from spontaneity, between thing in itself and appearances, intuition and spontaneity) for fine-grained explanations of his view that he takes to be a complete break away from the traditional (Cartesian) metaphysics that had long prevailed. At the time Kant complained that he was being read by critics through the very tradition he was rejecting; it is argued that the same dualist metaphysics continue and have influenced the 'Kantian' picture that is widespread. Portrayals of Kant's view in educational theory are often simplistic and obscure the sophistication of his view and reasons for his many distinctions. This chapter has discussed a number of them, suggesting different understandings, and argued that for Kant our conceptual capacities are exercised unreflectively in experience as well as consciously in thinking and reasoning. The above begins to articulate a picture of Kant that sees mind as embodied and continually engaged in ongoing experience. The next chapter continues to develop what has been discussed here, but in relation to Kant's 'Copernican revolution'.

NOTES

1. This is the only reference to the A edition of Kant's *Critique of Pure Reason (1878)*, all other references are to the B edition.
2. This point is particularly important for discussions in Part Two.
3. For instance, David Carr writes that for Kant, moral judgements are 'a matter of active imposition of meaning-constitutive rules and principles on the brute data of sensory perception' (2003, p. 100).
4. McDowell's early characterisation of intuition in *Mind and World* provoked response in Kantian exegesis. For instance, Günter Zoller (2010) argues that McDowell's intuitions being content-laden or propositional is a relapse into the Myth of the Given. McDowell has since reread Kant's first *Critique* and changed his position (discussed in Chapter Eleven). He tells us that he used to assume experiences have *propositional* content but now sees content as *intuitional* in Kant's sense (see 'Avoiding the Myth of the Given', 2009a, pp. 258–261).
5. While the human intellect is 'finite' (it is connected with reality and thus conditioned by empirical objects), its *spontaneity* (the realm of freedom) means it can think freely, including about non-empirical concepts such as infinity and abstract mathematical ones.
6. That is, intuition *describes* our human capacity to receive representations (in perception and experience) but we can also talk about *what* is perceived (the content of perception and experience); see Rödl (2007).
7. Stekeler-Weithofer's work is particularly helpful in making many of Kant's difficult terms accessible; it is used in many of the chapters.
8. As with all the terms discussed in this chapter, the 'capacities' (intuition and spontaneity, sensibility and the understanding) will be revisited in the chapters to come.
9. Eighteenth-century classic empiricism was largely from Hume, Locke and Berkeley, while the rationalism Kant inherited came mostly from theological thinking.
10. The examples from educational literature are discussed in Part Two, once different ways of understanding Kant's terms have been introduced.

11. McDowell is referring to a reading of Kant by Sellars who, he maintains, 'reads Kant as a scientific realist manqué; in Sellars's view, had Kant only been sophisticated about the possibilities for scientific concept-formation, he would have cast the objects of the scientific image in the role of things in themselves. But for Kant, objects as they appear in the scientific image would be just another case of objects as they appear, with a transcendental background for that conception just as necessary here as anywhere. Sellars's attempt to be responsive to Kantian transcendental concerns goes astray in his idea that an appeal to science could do the transcendental job; here Sellars's scientism is seriously damaging' (McDowell, 2009a, p. 42, footnote, 30).

12. Kant also uses the idea of thing in itself to show the limit of the senses, compared with the freedom of spontaneity, discussed in Chapter Eight.

13. Rödl's argument here is developed in later chapters.

3

Kant as a Revolutionary

SHEILA WEBB

Attention has been drawn to some deep-seated assumptions about mind and world that, it is argued, have influenced the familiar 'Kantian' picture in educational theory, a picture that draws much criticism for its dualisms and detached conception of mind. The previous chapter introduced alternative interpretations of some of Kant's terms in order to begin to bring a more favourable picture into view. This chapter continues the process through a discussion of Kant's Copernican 'revolution', contrasting aspects of Kant's view with empiricist and rationalist ideas for clarity.

Kant took himself to have broken away from the traditional metaphysics of his time, seeing his achievement as a revolution in thinking (Bxxii).[1] With his radically different view, Kant introduced a powerful new description of the human condition. What is distinctive about us, as 'discursive' creatures, is what we can call our 'rational capacity' (spontaneity, free will, intentionality, judgement), which makes us *self*-determining. That is, we act and experience the world in light of the knowledge and norms we have learnt and are not solely determined by external forces, whether these be the causal laws of nature or a Divine Will. This was a new way of thinking; the 'power' of mind is part of our nature as human beings. Howard Caygill, in an introduction to Kemp Smith's classic translation, writes:

> Kemp Smith interprets Kant as offering a 'fresh start' to 'modern philosophy', one that freed it from the tension between 'naturalism' and 'spiritualism'. His reading of Kant emphasises the totality of experience, and situates such apparent oppositions

Interpreting Kant for Education: Dissolving Dualisms and Embodying Mind, First Edition. Sheila Webb.
Chapters and editorial organization © 2022 Philosophy of Education Society of Great Britain.
Published 2022 by John Wiley & Sons Ltd.

as 'self and not-self', 'inner and outer', and 'phenomenal and noumenal' as 'relative' distinctions *within* experience'. (2007, p. vii)

Kant took inspiration from mathematician/astronomer Copernicus, writing: 'Failing of satisfactory progress in explaining the movements of the heavenly bodies on the supposition that they all revolved round the spectator, he tried whether he might not have better success if he made the spectator to revolve and the stars to remain at rest' (Kant, Bxvi). Kant brought this to bear on his thinking about knowledge and the relation between object and subject. 'Hitherto it has been assumed that all our knowledge must conform to objects', he writes, but, this ending in failure, he wonders 'whether we may not have more success in the tasks of metaphysics, if we suppose that objects must conform to our knowledge' (Bxvi).

Most in education will be familiar with Kant's Copernican revolution. However, what is less familiar in education are discussions on what Kant *means* by saying that objects conform to our knowledge. This is typically interpreted as a subjectivist or constructivist move, which leads to regular characterisations of Kant as a constructivist. Influence from empiricist epistemology is evident in that intuition and sensibility are routinely interpreted as empiricism's sense data; however, in *contrast* to empiricism (which prioritises the senses in providing knowledge), the capacities are inversed and it is mind that is prioritised in constructivist readings of Kant's Copernican view. That is, Kant is typically ascribed a radical subjectivism; mind becomes reified as it orders and structures the sense data it receives, imposing meaning or maxims onto the world (the objective world itself is frequently portrayed as unknowable). Such interpretation is widespread and is what I refer to as the typical 'Kantian' picture in education. I argue that such subjectivist interpretations exaggerate the activity of mind, and under-appreciate the objectivity in Kant's view, obscuring the idea of objective constraints. While this will be discussed in later chapters, some quick examples here help illustrate the tendency in education to interpret Kant's Copernican view in subjectivist or constructivist terms. 'The first telling theme for educators in Immanuel Kant's epoch-making *Critique of Pure Reason*', writes David Jardine, 'is the conceiving of knowledge as an active, constructive, orderly and ordering, demand made upon things ... [T]o know is "to impose structure"' (2005, p. 40). 'Imposition' characterisations are all-pervasive. David Carr reads Kant as a 'thorough-going constructivist', whose basic insight is 'a matter of active imposition of meaning-constitutive rules and principles on the brute data of sensory perception: this is the basic Kantian insight that "intuitions without concepts are blind"' (2003, p. 100). Intuitions and the senses are read as empiricism's 'brute data', and all attention is given to the activity of mind, imposing rules and principles. Similarly, Ernst von Glasersfeld interprets Kant's 'manifold' as 'the raw material, the stuff on which constructive perception and reason can operate' (1995a, p. 40). Subjectivist readings come not only from educational theorists but from some analytic philosophers too, the most influential perhaps being that of Peter Strawson (1966).[2] The theorists I draw on read Kant in a very different way. Karl Ameriks—from his *Kant's Theory of Mind* (1982) through to his *Kantian Subjects* (2019)—has long critiqued certain interpretations of Kant and 'numerous *unfortunate caricatures* that define the Critical philosophy in hopelessly subjectivist, monological, or anti-natural terms' (2019, p. 4). As Stephen Engstrom insists, a 'proper appreciation' of the capacities helps allay a 'concern that Kant's distinction would taint our cognition with an unacceptable subjectivism' (2006, p. 2).

The problem with any revolutionary way of thinking is that it naturally tends to be understood through existing traditions. Kant himself makes it clear he doesn't intend his work to be understood in a subjectivist (psychological idealist) way. After his first *Critique*, he said that he was being misunderstood with his work being read through the very tradition, the very metaphysics, he was rejecting. Graham Bird, in his extensive work on Kant since his *Kant's Theory of Knowledge* (1962), has long argued that Kant was more radical than has previously been appreciated (by analytic philosophers). He recommends more 'revolutionary' readings of the *Critique*, in contrast to what he calls 'traditionalist' accounts that 'ascribe to Kant an exhaustive idealist dualism of mental states, "ideas," and transcendent things in themselves and then note the inevitable tensions and contradictions which arise from Kant's apparent attempts to escape from that tradition' (2006, p. xii). One such early critic of Kant was Christian Garve; Bird writes:

> Garve's claims stand as an example of traditionalism in virtue of their inherent and exhaustive dualism of 'subjective' sensations and real independent things (in themselves) which must be 'created' or 'postulated' but remain problematic. In what must be one of the first occasions of its use, Garve's phrase 'the mind making nature' is intended to capture that traditional dualism as Kant's basic position. (p. 3)

Both the 'mind making nature' picture and the 'traditional dualism' are the most frequently found criticisms of Kant in contemporary educational theory; but they are charges Kant himself denies, as illustrated in his hostile response to Garve, who 'cannot escape from a routine school metaphysics which the Critique questions' (Bird, 2006, p. 7). 'In rejecting all previous metaphysics', Bird writes, 'Kant denies that he is working within that assumed traditional framework so that Garve has simply failed to appreciate the extent to which Kant's metaphysics of experience is revolutionary' (*ibid.*).[3] And in response to readings such as that of Garve, Kant in the second edition (of his first *Critique*) reiterates his clear *refutation* of what he calls 'psychological idealism' or 'material idealism' (Bxl).[4] To distinguish his position from this, Kant calls his doctrine 'transcendental idealism' or 'formal idealism', which is idealism of a very different form. He writes: 'I have also, elsewhere, sometimes entitled it *formal* idealism, to distinguish it from *material* idealism, that is, from the usual type of idealism which doubts or denies the existence of outer things themselves' (Kant, B519). Kant does not deny the existence of objective reality, but this reality falls *within* experience, within thought, and is not external to it as in traditional epistemology.

Kant is critiquing both rationalism and empiricism; he writes that his 'attempt to alter' the prevailing metaphysics 'by completely revolutionising it' is 'the main purpose of this critique of pure speculative reason' (Bxxii). He writes of empiricist John Locke and the rationalist Gottfried Leibniz:

> In a word, Leibniz *intellectualised* appearances, just as Locke, according to his system of *noogony* (if I may be allowed the use of such expressions), *sensualised* all concepts of the understanding, *i.e.* interpreted them as nothing more than empirical or abstracted concepts of reflection. Instead of seeking in understanding and sensibility two sources of representations which, while quite different, can supply objectively valid judgments of things only in *conjunction* with each other, each of these great men holds to one only of the two, viewing it as in immediate relation to things in themselves. The other faculty is then regarded as serving only to confuse or to order the representations which this selected faculty yields. (B327)

Through his critical work, Kant sees both of these approaches failing, for they each hold to only one of the two sources of representations and assume it is intelligible independently of the other. The difficulty of dislodging traditions with their deeply ingrained presuppositions is reflected in the tendency in educational theory to portray Kant either as a constructivist (*'intellectualising'* appearances) or as a foundationalist (*'sensualising'* all concepts of the understanding).[5]

Like Kant, John McDowell also distinguishes his position from two inherited ways of thinking—traditional empiricism and coherentism. And it is interesting that McDowell, for his *Mind and World*, has been criticised for being too 'empiricist' by some critics and too 'rationalist' by others, and in the second edition he adds an explanatory introduction (1996). In later distinguishing his view from these traditions, McDowell writes: 'I do not picture objects as speaking to us in the world's own language. Objects speak to us ... only because we have learned a human language', but this does not imply that 'objects can only be projections of our thinking' (2009a, p. 43). He continues:

> Objects come into view for us in actualizations of conceptual capacities in *sensory consciousness*, and Kant perfectly naturally connects sensibility with receptivity. If we hold firm to that, we can see that the presence of conceptual capacities in the picture does not imply idealism [in the psychological idealist sense]. (*ibid.*)

McDowell uses Kant to argue that while his view is a move away from traditional empiricism, it should not be read as a subjectivist or idealist position that sees objects as projections of our thinking.

In Anglophone analytic philosophy, while there are many preeminent scholars of Kant, there remains a strong empiricist-naturalist culture, as discussed in Chapter One. Indeed, its deeply ingrained assumptions about mind and an external world are what prompted McDowell's 'diagnostic' account of its 'anxieties'—'an inchoately felt threat that a way of thinking we find ourselves falling into leaves minds simply out of touch with the rest of reality' (1996, xiii). While McDowell and Robert Brandom (Brandom credits Kant with 'revolutionalizing our thinking about what it is to have a mind', 2006, p. 1) certainly initiated a growing interest and engagement with Kant and Hegel, a still dominant naturalist strand means the Copernican way of thinking is not acknowledged by many. Andrea Kern claims that the relevance of the German tradition 'for contemporary epistemology has been seriously underestimated, to say the least' (2017, p. 136). Robert Hanna expresses the point more forcefully, calling the failure of the majority of analytic theorists to learn Kant's lesson: 'the

Copernican Devolution'—a 'retrograde evolution in philosophy that brings us back, full-circle, to naïve, pre-Kantian, pre-critical conceptions of mind, knowledge, and world' (2016a, p. 2). Hanna argues:

> David Lewis, Kit Fine, David Chalmers, John Hawthorne, Theodore Sider, and Timothy Williamson, for all their logico-technical brilliance and their philosophical rigor, and even despite their high-powered contemporary professional philosophical status, are every bit as confused and wrongheaded as Christian Wolff. They make all the same old mistakes, just as if they had never been made before. For example, when Sider asserts, without any doubt, hesitation, or irony whatsoever, just as if the previous 235 years of European philosophy had never happened, that '[t]he world has a distinguished structure, a privileged description,' that '[f]or a representation to be fully successful, truth is not enough; the representation must also use the right concepts, so that its conceptual structure matches reality's structure,' and that 'there is an objectively correct way to "write the book of the world",' it simply takes your Kantian breath away. Amazing. That is the Copernican Devolution. (2016b, p. 9)

It is the spontaneity or power of mind that Kant recognises as significant that is lacking in empiricist-naturalist epistemology.

Sebastian Rödl draws attention to the importance of spontaneity as a source of knowledge, arguing that the concepts of sense experience and perception are not empirical concepts:

> The nature of our faculty of sensory experience is revealed not by empirical inquiry, but by reflection on what we know from spontaneity … Of course it is possible empirically to investigate the physiology and psychology of perception in the human species. But such investigations presuppose, and do not provide, knowledge of what human perception is. (2007, p. 163)

Rödl also reminds us that spontaneity is involved in gaining empirical knowledge (through the senses); for Kant, 'The power of thought transforms human sensibility' (p. 70). This is an important point. It makes for a different conception of our contact with the world when contrasted with both empiricist 'causal' conceptions and constructivist 'imposition' conceptions. As previously noted, understanding this relation is central because, as our contact with the world, it shapes conceptions of experience, cognition and knowledge. Spontaneity and intuition need to be seen not as two separate entities but two aspects of one capacity, a capacity for knowledge. 'That we apprehend substances and their movement through the senses, and forms and their laws through the intellect, are two sides of a coin. In this way the unity of intellect and sensibility,' Rödl argues, 'defines the finite intellect' (2012, p. 207).

Kant's Copernican view can be brought into sharper relief by contrasting it with the British empiricist David Hume. I draw on several theorists whose comparisons are particularly useful for elucidating the spontaneity of mind and its (unifying, synthesising) role in gaining knowledge through the senses.[6] Engstrom explains that Hume's conception of reason 'implicitly relies on a commitment to "the experimental Method of Reasoning" on which Hume founds his science of human nature', but that 'Kant does not subscribe to this experimental program' (2015, p. 20). Engstrom writes:

> Since following this method is a matter of 'deducing general maxims from a comparison of particular instances (*ECPM* 174[7]), Hume must deduce the general propositions that make up his account of reason from a comparison of actual judgments that constitute particular bits of reasoning. It is accordingly not open to him to develop an account in the way that Kant does, from the self-consciousness that figures in reason's activity. (*ibid.*)

That is, Hume attends to impressions from experience only, actual impressions received, which reason compares; this conception of reason 'tracks reality' but it lacks spontaneity as a *source* of knowledge. For Kant, reason, as a power, synthesises our perceptions, ideas and thoughts into a unified worldview. Engstrom clarifies the point by saying that 'both Hume and Kant conceive of human reason as wholly discursive', in contrast to Cartesian epistemology, but the difference is as follows:

> On Hume's conception of it, this discursive capacity lacks any spontaneous power of combination. The basic power of the mind to unite its ideas is vested solely in the imagination, operating in conjunction with the passions. Hume does not investigate the possibility that reason's discursive activity might be originally synthetic in nature. Nor is he alone in leaving this possibility unexplored. Working out the idea

of a synthetically discursive cognitive capacity requires a fundamental rethinking of a standard philosophical conception of human knowledge and how it is related to its object and to its subject. (pp. 21–22)

Rethinking the 'standard conception of human knowledge' of the time led Kant to the idea of reason as a source of knowledge, a power that (blindly) unites or 'holds together' these separate and individual impressions into a single body of knowledge (a worldview I can call 'mine'; self-consciousness). Otherwise, Kant says, 'I should have as many-coloured and diverse a self as I have representations of which I am conscious to myself' (B134). And it is our 'worldview' (the knowledge we have so far acquired in our lives) that is drawn on in our ongoing contact with the world.

Rödl argues that Hume is 'the enemy of reason, who dissipates human experience into sensory impressions, denies any knowledge that extends beyond the moment, and seeks to unmask the semblance of such knowledge as the projections of subjective habits' (2012, p. 2). He contrasts Kant's conception of sensibility with that of Hume:

David Hume held that the senses deliver impressions that in themselves bear no connections among them. If they appear connected, then this reflects subjective habits to associate them in certain ways. In particular, the unity of a substance, which holds together changeable states ... cannot be found in what is given to the senses. It is a construction put on impressions that on their part do not depend on these forms of unity. Kant argues that we must abandon this conception of sensibility. (Rödl, 2007, p. 179)

Again, on Kant's conception of sensibility, our rational capacities (what we know) are drawn into play *in* our contact with, and responses to, the world. Rödl refutes 'the fundamental thesis of any empiricism according to which the knowledge, or at least the perception, of what is here and now and affecting the senses, is self-standing' (2007, p. 11).[8]

Andrea Kern draws attention to different conceptions of experience. Of Hume she writes:

when it comes to explaining how 'experience' can provide us with knowledge of the world, experience itself 'must be entirely silent', for the mind 'cannot possibly reach any experience of [its perceptions'] connexion with objects'—i.e. it cannot possibly acquire through experience an answer to the question of how such experience is hooked up with objects in the world. Thus, Hume concludes that 'the supposition of such a connexion' between experience and objects in the world 'is, therefore, without any foundation in reasoning' (Hume, *Enquiry concerning Human Understanding*, 153f). (Kern, 2017, p. 101)

Kern continues, 'Kant famously takes up this Humean diagnosis and reformulates it' as follows: 'If we start with the thought that "inner [experience] is the only [kind of] immediate experience," then this means that we can "only *infer* [the existence of] external things ... because the cause of our representations that we (perhaps wrongly) ascribe to outer things could lie in us' (p. 102). On Hume's conception, experience does not 'hook up' with objects in the world, we can only infer their existence, and scepticism is unavoidable. Kant's conception of experience has mind 'hooked up' with objects in the world and not disconnected from them; this is in contrast to the vast criticism of Kant in education for a dualism and for holding that the world is unknowable and can only be inferred (examples are given in Part Two).

The spontaneity or power of mind is nicely described by Engstrom as 'the self-consciousness that figures in reason's activity': it 'is present, at least implicitly, in all thinking, and it constitutes the identity of the thinking subject's conscious activity' (2015, p. 22). The self-determining nature of mind is significant for Engstrom who is interested in *practical* knowledge. He writes:

Hume, as we know rejects the possibility of a practical application of reason, famously claiming to have proved that 'reason is perfectly inert' (*T*III.i.1.458). But since Kant's conception of reason derives from reflection on our ordinary understanding of discursive knowledge as a self-conscious synthetic activity, reason as he conceives of it does not lie merely in 'the comparing of ideas', but stands in an active, productive relation to knowledge, as the source of its cognition-constituting unity. His conception is thus open, in a way that Hume's is not, to accommodating the idea that reason has a practical as well as a theoretical use. (Engstrom, 2015, p. 26)

Kant's conception of reason as self-determining means that thought alone can move us to act (our actions are determined from within).

Whereas for Hume, 'the one great impediment to understanding how knowledge can be practical is the assumption that reason, the cognitive capacity itself, is receptive in nature and hence passive in operation', that is 'inert' (Engstrom, 2009, p. 14). For Hume reason is inert, which contrasts with Kant's conception as a self-determining power.

McDowell too contrasts Hume's picture of knowledge with that of Kant, but in respect to conceptions of the world. McDowell argues that for Hume the world is 'disenchanted', there is no meaning or structure in the world; rather meaning is projected onto it by subjects. He writes: '[t]he disenchantment Hume applauds can seem to point to a conception of nature as an ineffable lump, devoid of structure or order. But we cannot entertain such a conception. If we did, we would lose our right to the idea that the world of nature is a world at all' (1998a, p. 178). For Kant, the world is not devoid of meaning, for it is not independent of mind (conceptions of the world are the topic of the next chapter). Pirmin Stekeler-Weithofer also writes of the differences between Kant and Hume, arguing that:

> the reason why Kant departs, and why we all should depart, from Hume's empiricism and scepticism is precisely this: Hume fails, in the end, to give a satisfactory account of the differences between animal behaviour and human action, animal cognition and human knowledge, animal perception and human Intuition. Hence, Hume cannot fulfil the task of philosophical anthropology to make the fundamental differences between the form(s) of leading an animal life and the constitutive form(s) of a human life explicit. (2010b, p. 4)

Stekeler-Weithofer's emphasis on the difference between humans and animals refers to Kant's Copernican insight that human perception and action involve our (distinctively human) 'rational' relation with the world, which implicitly draws on what we know and which is manifested in our responses to it.[9]

Kant's Copernican stance gives a first-person standpoint, which further differentiates it from that of empiricism and which he takes over from Aristotle.[10] Kant is also inspired by Rousseau: 'I am a scientist by inclination', he writes. 'I know the thirst for knowledge and the deep satisfaction of every advance of knowledge ... Rousseau has corrected me. I learned to honor man' (Henrich, 2003, p. 55). Kant was the first to introduce anthropology as a subject at university, and for him we experience the world from our first-person (subjective) stance; we cannot escape this subjectivity. But this is a very different conception of subjectivity, not an in-the-head conception cut off from reality, but one connected with it through the senses, and one we can know through the senses. We cannot know reality *independently* of our perception, or independently of our knowledge of it—the Copernican point. We can talk of a general rational capacity for knowledge and also of specific conceptual capacities, ones that we have acquired (so far) in our lives, and which are drawn into play in experience. While our capacities are fallible (we might be wrong in what we think we see or know), it is nevertheless all we have to go by. This compares with empiricist approaches that, as we have seen, search for certainty or foundations *outside* of mind, in a world conceived of as independent of mind. As exemplified by Boghossian in Chapter One, some feel the need for a solid foundation external to mind. McDowell calls this a 'side-ways on' picture and criticises the desire for foundationalist thinking. This, he says, 'results from the idea that one could not achieve a justified conviction of objective correctness, in thought about anything, from within something as historically contingent as a conceptual scheme; what is required is to break out of a specific cultural inheritance into undistorted contact with the real' (1998a, p. 37). The Copernican point is that we cannot achieve 'undistorted contact', rather our contact involves the (historically contingent but shared) knowledge, concepts and norms that make up our rational capacities. We may put this by saying that from a first-person standpoint the conceptual is 'unbounded'; we are in a perceptual (conceptual) relation with the world and cannot break out of this for a side-ways on view. Mind is not cut off from reality but in touch with things themselves: there is no dualism. '[R]eflection on an inherited scheme of values', McDowell argues, 'takes place at a standpoint within that scheme' (*ibid.*); we might be mistaken, but there is no foundation to appeal to outside of thought.

Again, these different conceptions of the relation between mind and world affect accounts of experience and how we acquire knowledge. McDowell writes:

> According to traditional empiricism, experience yields a foundational level of knowledge, available to us in perception through the operation of capacities that we have at birth or develop in ordinary biological maturation, and are in no way dependent on acculturation or acquired knowledge. In experience, on this picture, objective reality impresses itself on subjects immediately. (2009a, p. 91)

For Kant, concepts are socially learnt and developed through discursive practices and acculturation, or *Bildung*. Rödl similarly argues that empiricist approaches tend to see knowledge as inductively acquired from encounters with particulars, while for Kant there is knowledge of particulars 'through, and only through, knowledge of forms', or concepts (2012, p. 11). Thus, he writes, *'empirical knowledge always already contains general knowledge, which therefore is not inferred inductively from the former'*—rather it depends on it for its possibility (p. 13).[11] This relates back to the discussion between Rorty and Boghossian about the mind-dependence/independence of knowledge. Rorty's point was that we do not know a giraffe just by seeing one, we first need the concept 'giraffe', or at least some idea of what a giraffe is, to know one when we see one. And we develop *general* knowledge through everyday and ongoing experience as well as more formally in schooling. Kant lived before the 'linguistic turn' in philosophy, so does not give an explicit account of the role of language in learning, but it is implicit in his view. McDowell does write of language learning and (in discussing Wittgenstein's idea of 'following a rule') he quotes Stanley Cavell:

> We learn and teach words in certain contexts, and then we are expected, and expect others, to be able to project them into further contexts. Nothing insures that this projection will take place ... just as nothing insures that we will make, and understand, the same projections. That on the whole we do is a matter of our sharing routes of interest and feeling, modes of response, sense of humor and of significance and of fulfilment, of what is outrageous, of what is similar to what else, what a rebuke, what forgiveness, of when an utterance is an assertion, when an appeal, when an explanation—all the whirl of organism Wittgenstein calls 'forms of life.' Human speech and activity, sanity and community, rest upon nothing more, but nothing less, than this. It is a vision as simple as it is difficult, and as difficult as it is (and because it is) terrifying. (Cavell, 1969, p. 52, in McDowell, 1998a, pp. 206–207)

This beautifully captures the way learning is rooted in ordinary social life—Wittgenstein's 'forms of life'. Born into an already up-and-running world (discussed in the next chapter), the particular norms, beliefs and knowledge we acquire will depend on our culture, giving mind a particular socio-historical shape (but the spontaneity of mind means that the norms and knowledge we acquire are subject to change and reflection)—we cannot break free to reflect from the outside. McDowell describes the terror of which Cavell writes as a sort of vertigo 'induced by the thought that there is nothing that keeps our practices in line except the reactions and responses we learn in learning them' (p. 207). 'The cure for the vertigo', McDowell argues, 'is to give up the idea that philosophical thought … should be undertaken at some external standpoint, outside our immersion in our familiar forms of life' (p. 63).[12]

Kant's Copernican standpoint is a first-person stance, with mind embodied and continually developing through immersion in our familiar forms of life. But this first-person standpoint should not be read as an individualist 'mind makes nature' picture or 'imposes meaning' onto it, for these lose the objectivity of Kant's view. Kern argues that beliefs and judgements 'have objective content in the sense that their truth is dependent on how things are in the world' (2017, p. 53); but these constraints are *within* thought and not external to it. The idea of constraints within thought and not external to it, and of how things are in the world, is considered in discussions of naturalism that forms the topic of the next two chapters.

NOTES

1. A reminder that the quotes by Kant used in this book refer to the second edition of his *Critique of Pure Reason* (1787), translated by Norman Kemp Smith (revised second edition 2007).
2. Strawson's reading is considered in Chapter Eleven.
3. Stephen Engstrom similarly argues that, regarding his practical knowledge, Kant's break away from the received view has been underestimated (2009).
4. This form of idealism can be likened to constructivist interpretations of his Copernican insight, discussed in Part Two.
5. Again, portrayals in education are considered in Part Two.
6. In what follows, I do not discuss Hume's rich and complex philosophy, but merely cite some theorists' comparisons as a way of bringing Kant's view into clearer light.
7. This refers to Hume's *Treatise* (1739).
8. This is what Hanna means by the Copernican Devolution (2016a).
9. See also Jesse Mulder for a clear and insightful argument on the limits of Humeanism (2018).
10. Again I note that there are many similarities between the views of Kant and Aristotle that have not been adequately appreciated in educational interpretations.
11. The general here is not absolute or universally unchanging, rather it is culture dependent and subject to change—discussed in Chapter Nine.
12. This is discussed further in Chapter Five.

4

Naturalisms, Materialisms and the Ideal World

SHEILA WEBB

Some alternative ways to interpret Kant's terms and distinctions have been introduced from contemporary work in epistemology and the philosophy of mind for a more positive reading of Kant. This contrasts with the familiar 'Kantian' picture in educational theory that attracts much criticism. Kant's Copernican revolution, it has been suggested, need not be read as a subjectivist position, with mind ordering or structuring what the senses deliver and imposing meaning onto the world. With different understandings of his terms, mind can be read as embodied and his subject immersed in the everyday world in which she lives her life. Attention has so far been focused on conceptions of mind; this chapter focuses on conceptions of world—nature, reality. It may seem odd to discuss conceptions of 'the world', because we habitually think of the world as the way the natural sciences describe it to be, the same with 'nature'. But as with different conceptions of 'experience', 'sensibility' and 'mind', I recommend an unfamiliar conception of 'world'. This is discussed, along with some contrasting versions of naturalism and materialism, to draw attention to different ways of conceiving what is real and natural in the world. The aim is to help with an understanding of Kant's version of idealism, with particular attention on his realist use of the term 'appearance'.

I start by returning to the conceptual problem within traditional epistemology of how to fit a non-material mind into the material world—the long-held 'problem of knowledge' that McDowell

Interpreting Kant for Education: Dissolving Dualisms and Embodying Mind, First Edition. Sheila Webb.
Chapters and editorial organization © 2022 Philosophy of Education Society of Great Britain.
Published 2022 by John Wiley & Sons Ltd.

addresses with his *Mind and World (1996)*. A contemporary response to this problem has been to turn to varieties of naturalism that reduce or completely eliminate the concept of mind from explanations of consciousness. 'Reductionism' and 'Eliminativism' are both naturalist (materialist) positions in the philosophy of mind that involve the idea that mental phenomena such as mind can be 'reduced to' (explained by) physical phenomena. Instead of mind there is the brain, which fits with a physicalist conception of reality and can be investigated by the methods of natural science. The rise of brain-based theories of learning and neuroscientific approaches to educational issues is evidence of this naturalistic trend. While in the philosophy of education much criticism has highlighted the limitations of such approaches, scientific 'values' continue to impact all areas of education, and are dominant in the analytic tradition more widely. The purpose here is to identify familiar scientific understanding of the concepts of nature, world and reality in order, first, to argue that they act as presuppositions through which Kant has typically been interpreted in education, and, second, to contrast these with alternative ways to understand them, to further enable a more valuable reading of Kant to be appreciated.

Naturalism is a contested term; the concept of nature can be understood in different ways. Hilary Putnam gives voice to this:

> Today the most common use of the term 'naturalism' might be described as follows: philosophers—perhaps even a majority of all the philosophers writing about issues in metaphysics, epistemology, philosophy of mind, and philosophy of language—announce in one or another conspicuous place in their essays and books that they are 'naturalists' or that the view or account being defended is a 'naturalist' one; this announcement, in its placing and emphasis, resembles the placing of the announcement in articles written in Stalin's Soviet Union that a view was in agreement with Comrade Stalin's; as in the case of the latter announcement, it is supposed to be clear that any view that is not 'naturalist' (not in agreement with Comrade Stalin's) is anathema, and could not possibly be correct. A further very common feature is that, as a rule, 'naturalism' is not *defined*.

One happy exception to this rule is that in the glossary to Boyd, Gasper, and Trout's *The Philosophy of Science*, naturalism is actually defined, namely as '[t]he view that all phenomena are subject to natural laws, and/or that the methods of the natural sciences are applicable in every area of inquiry. (Putnam, 2004, pp. 59–60)

Putnam continues: 'what is common to most versions of 'naturalism' is that those conceptual resources and conceptual activities that do not fit into the narrowly scientific first-grade system are regarded as something less than *bona fide* rational discourse' (p. 61). Since the rise of this trend, naturalist theories are taken to be more objective, credible and preferable.

What is understood as 'nature' is sometimes further reduced by privileging physics. 'Physicalism' offers a very restrictive ontology, with anything that cannot be subsumed under physics simply eliminated from explanations of reality.[1] However, such 'physicalism' is disputed even from within the scientific camp. J.A. Fodor's 'Special Sciences' argument continues today. 'A typical thesis of positivistic philosophy of science is that all true theories in the special science should reduce to physical theories in the long run', Fodor explains, for they hold the view 'that all events which fall under the laws of any science are physical events and hence fall under the laws of physics' (1974, p. 97). But he famously goes on to argue that the laws of the 'special sciences' are too problematic for reduction to the laws of physics, even in principle.[2] Mario De Caro and David Macarthur similarly point out that 'a scientific naturalist might think there are entities such as acids or predators or phonemes that chemistry or biology or experimental psychology commits him to that are not (reducible to) physical entities, and that, consequently, the explanations of, say, biology are not reducible, even in principle, to the explanations of physics' (2004, p. 5).[3] The debate and literature spawned by Fodor's argument reveal the extent of disagreement in developing ideas about what really counts as 'science' and 'naturalism' in the analytic tradition.

Contemporary German theorists are working with a broader understanding of 'science', as the term *Wissenschaft* refers to enquiry or investigation in general.[4] It captures both philosophical investigation, such as Hegel's *Science of Logic*, and that of the natural sciences; hence, it lays the way for a richer understanding of 'nature' and 'naturalism'. For the purposes of comparison with Kant's epistemology, I will take as a springboard for discussion Boyd, Gasper and Trout's two key commitments of *naturalism* (from the above quote): *that all phenomena are subject to natural laws*, and *that the methods of science are applicable in every area of inquiry.* The first commitment (that 'all phenomena are subject to natural laws') is addressed in this chapter, while the second commitment ('the methods of science are applicable in every area of inquiry') will be discussed in the next.

When Boyd, Gasper and Trout claim that all phenomena are subject to natural laws, they are referring to the laws of nature that are investigated and explained by the natural sciences. The ontological commitment is to a world constituted by the material or physical things described by science; what is real in the world are the things described using the concepts of the natural sciences. Mind, as we have seen, is not considered part of this material world—this is the assumption rooted in traditional empiricist epistemology that sees the objective world as external to mind (discussed in Chapter One). But the question—the philosophical anxiety—of the place of mind in explanations of the world is not a problem for these naturalist theorists because the concept of mind is written out of explanations, which are reduced to scientific concepts of material entities. Mind—and other normative and psychological concepts—are excluded from such a scientific conception of the natural world.

Again, these (empiricist-naturalist) assumptions about a material world and immaterial mind can be seen to have influenced interpretations of Kant. As previously discussed, Kant's use of 'appearances' and 'things-in-themselves' tends to be read dualistically (as ontologically distinct), with 'things-in-themselves' understood as the natural world (objective reality) and 'appearances' as something in the mind. Thus, his view that we cannot know things in-themselves but only as they appear has been interpreted as a subjectivist or traditional idealist view along the lines of 'mind makes nature'. But, as also discussed, it is possible to understand these terms differently: we can think of appearances as objective reality itself. That is, things as they appear and things in-themselves are the very same things but under two descriptions, not two different things. Kant's version of idealism involves thinking of the natural world in a different way. And here McDowell is again pertinent, for he makes explicit and takes issue with the widespread scientific conception, and provides an alternative. McDowell associates what he calls 'modern' or 'bald' naturalism with the rise of science:

> It is commonplace that modern science has given us a disenchanted conception of the natural world. A proper appreciation of science makes it impossible to retain, except perhaps in some symbolic guise, the common mediaeval conception of

nature as filled with meaning, like a book containing messages and lessons for us. The tendency of the scientific outlook is to purge the world of meaning ... reality is exhausted by the natural world, in the sense of the world as the natural sciences are capable of revealing it to us. Part of the truth in the idea that science disenchants nature is that science is committed to a dispassionate and dehumanized stance for investigation; that is taken to be a matter of conforming to a metaphysical insight into the character of reality as such. (1998a, pp. 174–175)

For scientific naturalism the concepts of nature, reality and world are exhausted by natural scientific descriptions, and disenchanted through a 'dehumanised' and 'dispassionate' methodology. But these concepts can be conceived of in a richer sense, one that includes human nature.

This issue is not with science in general, but with the idea that science should be the framework for *all* investigation, as Boyd, Gasper and Trout maintain. De Caro and Macarthur write:

It must be emphasized that what is at issue here is not respect for the results of the natural sciences. This is an attitude every sane philosopher can be expected to have. Scientific naturalism involves the much stronger claim that science is, or ought to be, our *only* genuine or unproblematic guide in matters of method or knowledge or ontology or semantics. (2004, p. 9)

The 'disenchanted' conception of the natural world promoted by the sciences constitutes an impoverished metaphysics, and this contrasts with a richer metaphysics in which mind (thought, our rational capacities) can be seen as part of nature.

As previously noted, Kant's view is similar to that of Aristotle in many ways, but Aristotle's philosophy is not critical, in the way that Kant's is, because 'it did not occur to him that one might conceive the forms of thought he describes as projections onto a reality that in itself is alien to reason' (Rödl, 2012, p. 43). But this was the case with the dualist metaphysics Kant inherited after Descartes and which he addresses with his critical philosophy; yet, as is being argued, Kant has been interpreted by many readers *through* this very dualism, with 'a reality that in itself is alien to reason'. McDowell appeals to Aristotle for a richer conception of nature and reality, claiming that the rise of modern science makes it difficult now to appreciate Greek naturalism. McDowell sheds light on this richer metaphysics.

For Aristotle, the natural world is not disenchanted but full of meaning, a place where objects are seen to have a purpose, a *telos*. Reason, or *logos*, is taken to be part of our nature as human beings, and this can be characterised as a capacity that is actualised through human interaction in a process that moulds our character. McDowell argues that the difficulty of seeing nature as something more than what the natural sciences describe was not a difficulty that the ancient Greeks faced. He writes that pre-modern thinkers:

> did not feel a tension between the idea that knowledge is a normative status and the idea of an exercise of natural powers. Before the modern era, it would not have been intelligible to fear a naturalistic fallacy in epistemology. But the rise of modern science has made available a conception of nature that makes the warning intelligible. (2009b, p. 258)

With this 'new conception of nature, the knowing subject threatens to withdraw from the natural world. That is one way in which it comes to look as if philosophical epistemology needs to reconnect the knowing subject with the rest of reality'—the problem of how to bridge the gap between mind and world (p. 259). A solution is to 'naturalise' the mind by collapsing one side of the dualism to the other in scientific causal explanation, as the trend towards naturalism exemplifies. McDowell illustrates this naturalist picture by referencing Hume, whom he describes as 'the prophet *par excellence*' of the tendency to 'purge the world of meaning' (1998a, p. 174). McDowell writes:

> We have to suppose that the world has an intelligible structure, matching the structure in the space of *logos* possessed by accurate representations of it. The disenchantment Hume applauds can seem to point to a conception of nature as an ineffable lump, devoid of structure or order. But we cannot entertain such a conception. If we did, we would lose our right to the idea that the world of nature is a world at all (something that breaks up into things that are the case), let alone the world (everything that is the case). Hume himself, innocent of the very idea of conceptual articulation, is oblivious of this point; his modern successors lack his excuse. (p. 178)

To help envisage an understanding of Kant's Copernican insight (that the world we know is not independent of mind) without reverting to the subjective 'mind makes nature' interpretation, we can follow McDowell's conception of the world; this is not 'disenchanted' or 'an ineffable lump' but is structured and written through with meaning, as a result of human agency and activity. Before discussing this in more detail however, it is helpful to look at another interpretive issue that stems from the scientific naturalist claim that all phenomena are subject to natural laws.

In the natural sciences, the laws of nature are understood as causal, but Kant has a wider conception of cause and causality, which forms part of his richer metaphysics. In scientific naturalism, a cause is understood as something *external*, where one thing acts on another from outside. A piece of iron or steel will rust if it comes into contact with water and oxygen; water will boil at 100 degrees Celsius at sea level. But as McDowell argues, '[w]e need not see the idea of causal linkages as the exclusive property of natural-scientific thinking' (2009b, p. 258):

> This physicalism about causal relations reflects a scientistic hijacking of the concept of causality, according to which the concept is taken to have its primary role in articulating the partial world view that is characteristic of the physical sciences, so that all other causal thinking needs to be based on causal relations characterizable in physical terms. (p. 139)

Kant recognises the activity of mind as the cause and effect of itself and sees this *self-determining* nature of mind as a distinctively human characteristic. As we saw in earlier chapters, Kant holds that we can understand ourselves in a two-fold sense, as subject to the 'mechanical' causal laws of nature and therefore not free, but also as self-determining agents and therefore free.[5] The activity of thinking can be the cause or causality of judgement and actions, which exemplify rational freedom.[6] Again Kant makes a distinction to capture this, between the laws of heteronomy and autonomy. Rödl explains: '[a] law of heteronomy is one according to which one thing is determined to act by another thing', something other than it 'has solicited its act', while a law of autonomy is one according to which 'nothing other than itself determines the force acting on it' (2007, p. 118). Therefore, '[l]aws of the living are laws of autonomy in this sense, while laws of inanimate nature are laws of heteronomy' (*ibid.*). This relates to Kant's conception of mind as a power—as autonomous and self-legislating. Christine Korsgaard similarly argues that on Kant's view, 'obligation derives from the dictate of the agent's own mind' (1996, p. 31). Thought and reasons can be causes of action. Rödl writes: 'Thought or action in the light of reasons has a cause in virtue of, and only in virtue of, its conceiving that cause as its cause. Thus thought and action resting on reasons are not determined by a cause outside them ... to act in the light of reasons is to be autonomous' (2016, p. 85). In this respect, Kant's wider conception of causality marks a significant difference from scientific naturalism and traditional empiricism; reason itself (as a kind of causality) accounts for human agency and intentionality, and the material world is transformed through such human agency (which we shall come to below). Kant's conception of mind as self-legislating, as autonomous, can be contrasted with the claim that all phenomena are subject only to the laws of nature understood scientifically, the laws of heteronomy; again, the metaphysics are quite distinct.

To be clear, Kant's picture includes science within it; he does not rule out impressions, laws of nature or causal relations in the scientific sense, but has a richer metaphysics in which they are incorporated. Similar is the case with McDowell. McDowell contrasts the realm of law with the space of reasons, but these are not mutually exclusive, rather the former falls within the latter. An exchange with Simon Blackburn helps shed light on McDowell's broader metaphysics. McDowell talks of the unboundedness of the conceptual to get away from the idea of mind as self-contained, as bound within the head and separate from the outside world. (In this picture, as we have seen, the senses—in a 'causal' relation—'impinge' on an inner mind where judgement and meaning take place.) Simon Blackburn questions McDowell's use of the space of reasons, he wants to hold on to cause (in the scientific meaning) in explanations of justification. He gives an everyday example of Mary who believes there is butter in the fridge because she sees it; in asking what justifies her belief he claims the butter *caused* Mary's belief (2006, pp. 203–217). But McDowell's argument, discussed in Chapter One, is that 'we must not confuse *brutely* causal impingements on believers with justifications for belief' (2006, p. 217), for if they are 'caused' in us how do we know if/when we are right or wrong. Nevertheless, he points out that it 'would be quite another matter to suppose *no* causal connections between judgements and their subject matter can be epistemologically significant' (*ibid.*). 'Causal relations between the butter and Mary obviously matter to Mary's acquisition of knowledge that there is butter in the fridge', McDowell writes, and '[o]bservation is possible for us only because we are causally related to the things we observe' (*ibid*.). Blackburn's implication is 'that simply insisting on the relevance of the causal facts about Mary is enough to warrant claiming that a bald scientific metaphysics will accommodate whatever can be said about her in intentionality-involving terms' (p. 219). McDowell continues:

> My skepticism about sideways-on views ... [has] nothing to do with a refusal to acknowledge that, for instance, Mary's possibilities for observational knowledge depend on connections that are suitable for scientific investigation. It is quite wrong to read the skepticism about sideways-on views, in the specific contexts in which I express it, as implying the idiotic idea that once we have decided to place things in the space of reasons, we are precluded from aspiring to understandings that exploit the terms of a restrictive ('bald') naturalism—as if being interested in, say, speech acts as meaningful performances precluded being interested in, say, how certain complex musculature enables us to produce articulate vocal sounds. Naturalistic understandings, in that sense, are just fine. (p. 219)

Sideways-on views are discussed in the next chapter; the point here is that McDowell is not rejecting natural-scientific understandings but setting them within a broader metaphysics. His ideas have been met with resistance; for Blackburn, '[t]he baldest of scientific metaphysics will accommodate Mary, or, if it will not, it will be because of some other way in which intentionality escapes the realm of law, and that other way is not yet on the table' (2006, p. 208). But McDowell responds: 'the way intentionality "escapes the realm of law" is just the way Sellars explains in terms of the image of the space of reasons, and the obvious facts about Mary's causal situation in the world cannot dislodge this thought from the place on the table that I have given it' (2006, p. 219). Intentionality falls outside the realm of law in traditional epistemology, but McDowell is putting on the table a reconceived epistemology with richer metaphysics that includes both intentionality and scientific causes. These ideas continue to be developed and challenged in the growing literature. Regarding intentionality, McDowell writes: 'no one has come closer to showing us how to find intentionality unproblematic than Kant, and there is no better way for us to find intentionality unproblematic than by seeing what Kant was driving at' (2009a, p. 3). Within a richer metaphysics are broader conceptions of nature and naturalism, that contain the restricted sense within them, and which we turn to now.

McDowell has a broad conception of naturalism, which exhibits Kant's insight that rational capacities are part of our human nature. McDowell describes our capacity for knowledge and responsiveness to reasons as our 'second nature', shaped by ordinary upbringing. He explicates this as follows:

> Finding a way to preserve Kant's insight leads, I have claimed, to a conception of reason that is, in one sense, naturalistic: a formed state of practical reason is one's second nature, not something that dictates to one's nature from outside ... [S]econd nature acts in a world in which it finds more than what is open to view from the dehumanized stance that the natural sciences, rightly for their purposes, adopt. And there is nothing against bringing this richer reality under the rubric of nature too. The natural sciences do not have exclusive rights in that notion; and the added richness comes into view, not through the operations of some mysteriously extra-natural power, but because human beings come to possess a second nature. (1998a, p. 192)

McDowell argues that we are born 'mere animals', our first nature, and acquire a second nature, become a person, by developing conceptual capacities through the *Bildungsprozess*. In this way, we become an inhabitant of the space of reasons, learning to respond to what is a reason for what. In this picture, children are born into an already up-and-running world, where learning language is key. McDowell writes: 'the language into which a human being is first initiated stands over against her as a prior embodiment of mindedness, of the possibility of an orientation to the world ... It is a repository of tradition, a store of historically accumulated wisdom about what is a reason for what' (1996, pp. 125–126). In distinguishing between our first and second natures, McDowell refers to Hans-Georg Gadamer's description of the difference between an animal mode of life *in an environment*, one dominated by biological pressures, and a human mode of life *in the world*.

> To acquire the spontaneity of the understanding is to become able, as Gadamer puts it, to 'rise above the pressure of what impinges on us from the world' (Truth and Method, p. 444) ... into a 'free, distanced orientation' (p. 445). And the fact that the orientation is free, that it is above the pressure of

biological need, characterizes it as an orientation to the world.
(pp. 115–116)

McDowell points out that we do not need to 'see ourselves as pecu-
liarly bifurcated, with a foothold in the animal kingdom and a mysterious separate involvement in an extra-natural world of rational
connections' (p. 78). Rather our human life, including our rational
capacities, *is* our natural way of being. 'If the second nature one
has acquired is virtue' then '[t]he dictates of virtue have acquired
an authority that replaces the authority abdicated by first nature with
the onset of reason' (1998a p. 188). Through the *Bildungsprozess* we
acquire a mind, our second nature; this process draws on and continually develops our worldview, our conceptual capacities. What is
important here is that McDowell's concept of second nature over-
comes the problem of normative concepts like mind, thought and
consciousness being seen as something separate and mysterious, for
they are part of our nature.

Sebastian Rödl's conception of nature is slightly different, but it
also draws on Kant and Aristotle and is also richer than scientific
naturalism. It involves the conceptions of cause and causality discussed above. Rödl does not think that McDowell's concept of second nature is needed to dissolve the problem of mind and thought
'looking spooky'—'[t]hat would be troubling only if the natural sciences were the measure of what is spooky and what is not' (2011).
Rödl distinguishes two conceptions of nature. One is the realm of
law as conceived by the natural sciences, a mechanical conception,
explained above, with one event causing—necessitating—change in
something else. Thought and action, like norms and values, lie outside this kind of causality. The second he takes from Kant and is
nature as the *realm of change*: human life is a material life 'that real-
izes itself through change' (*ibid.*). The concept of life, he explains,
is the *form* of the teleological unity of changes, which is the *nature*
of the species of an animal.[7] Kant takes over Aristotle's concepts of
'form' and 'matter'. Life is the *form* of the unity of changes that constitute the nature of a species; change is internal to it. In the case
of a human, this is the path of a normal human life, of which our
intellectual capacities are naturally a part. So too are norms, agency
and morality. This wider sense of nature contains the first restricted
sense within it. That the realm of law exhausts nature is a judgement
or claim, and judgements and claims are not subject to the realm of
law in the scientific sense but are a part of *human* nature.

Rödl points out that McDowell's use of 'first nature' is ambiguous because as well as referring to the realm of law, McDowell also talks of the 'authority abdicated by first nature with the onset of reason' (in the quote above). Rödl explains that '[t]he first nature that abdicates authority is the nature of the species of the animal, and that is not first nature as the realm of law, but the first nature of an animal', and he comments: 'McDowell's ambiguous use of "first nature" is not the cause of, but manifests an idea of, reason as transcending nature. The roots of this idea lie deep; deeper than the modern notion of nature as the realm of law' (2011). So while McDowell talks of leaving our first nature behind with the acquisition of rationality, Rödl sees rationality as part of our first nature, as part of a natural human life. He writes, 'second nature is not something other than first nature; it is its perfection' (2016, p. 96). In other words, *Bildung* cultivates what is part of our first nature, which includes our capacity for knowledge and thought. With Kant's freedom (as a causality), intentional activity springs from capacities that are part of the nature of normal human life that is realised through change. However, the subtle differences between Rödl's and McDowell's conceptions are not important for our purpose here, for what *is* significant is not whether mind and intellectual capacities belong to first or second nature but that they are part of nature at all. This contrasts with scientific conceptions of nature, and the world, that exclude these. The scientific picture is deeply ingrained, but McDowell and Rödl both give voice to Kant's richer metaphysics that captures human characteristics. The importance of education is underscored for its role in the development of intellectual capacities that are part of our nature as humans. 'Education is the child's growth into itself', as Rödl describes it (*ibid.*). These conceptions of nature include us and our human activity within them.

This takes us far from the disenchanted world of scientific naturalism, but are we yet able to see the world as full of meaning? Can we set aside the dualist picture and envisage mind and world as rationally related? McDowell talks of the unboundedness of the conceptual, for which 'we must not picture an outer boundary around the sphere of the conceptual, with a reality outside the boundary impinging inward on the system. Any impingements across such an outer boundary could only be causal, and not rational' (1996, p. 34). He maintains that 'in experience the world exerts a rational influence on our thinking' that is important for objectivity and 'that requires us to delete the outer boundary from the picture' (*ibid.*). To help visualise this—and Kant's Copernican version of idealism—we can think of the world as 'humanised', made 'meaningful', with meanings continuously sustained, changed and developed through our ongoing social and cultural practices. And to help picture this humanised world, I draw on the work of David Bakhurst. In *The Formation of Reason* (2011), Bakhurst defends a socio-historical conception of mind and incorporates this into a view of education. While not a Kantian, Bakhurst's inspiration comes from McDowell, and much of Bakhurst's work, as I read it, is not at odds with the reading of Kant I am urging. However, for a richer conception of the world, it is Bakhurst's other work that I draw on here, his remarkable exposition of the Soviet philosopher Evald Ilyenkov, in his *Consciousness and Revolution in Soviet Philosophy* (1991). Ilyenkov, like Marx and some other Soviet philosophers such as Lev Vygotsky, was influenced (indirectly) by the German idealist tradition. A look at some of Ilyenkov's work helps further distinguish a humanised picture of the world from the scientific 'disenchanted' conception that is implicit in dualist interpretations of Kant's work in educational theory.[8]

Following Ilyenkov (1924–1979), Bakhurst argues that cognition does not start with unprocessed sense experience but with a conception of the world that is inherited 'ready made' from the society one is born into. Ilyenkov criticises empiricism, Bakhurst explains, because empiricist ideas present a picture of 'atomic' minds, self-contained worlds independent from other minds and reality, making for a separation of subject and object.[9] Ilyenkov is also a critic of the idea that we are our brains:

> The psychological definition of man has its reality, its 'being,' not in the system of neurodynamic structures of the brain, but in a broader and more complex system—the system of relations of man to man, mediated by things created by man for man, that is, in the relations of production of the objective-human world and of the capacities that correspond to the organization of this world. (in Bakhurst, 1991, p. 220)[10]

In describing this world, Ilyenkov uses the notion of *ideality*: '"Ideality" is like a peculiar stamp impressed on the substance of nature by social human life activity; it is the form of the functioning of a physical thing in the process of social human life activity' (p. 180). While Ilyenkov uses the term 'nature' in the restricted sense of the natural sciences, he is interested in 'ideality' as the consequence of the 'humanisation' of nature by our human activity. Ilyenkov writes: 'Ideality is a characteristic of things, but not as they are defined by nature, but by labour, the transforming, form-creating activity of social beings, their aim-mediated, sensuously objective activity (p. 182). As Bakhurst explains, objects are made and used for a reason: they have a purpose and come to have symbolic meanings through use in our social practices. In this way, artefacts bear a *form*, which embody the meaning for which they were made and are used, and this is different from their natural properties. For instance, a chair is a chair rather than a piece of wood or sum of atoms. A scientific description of a poppy does not capture its meaning as a symbol of remembrance, or roses as a token of love and beauty, for like currency and kings, these meanings reside in our cultural practices—the *transforming* and *form-creating* activity of social beings. 'In activity', Bakhurst writes, 'human beings create and sustain an environment written through with significance; they nurture a world enriched with ideal properties, with value and meaning. This is the world we know' (p. 217). Thinking of ideality in this way, as a characteristic of objectively existing things, also helps distinguish Kant's version of idealism from traditional (subjective) idealisms. It also further helps distinguish it from the typical 'Kantian' picture in educational theory. To recap the dualist picture, mind is understood as actively structuring or constructing meaning from the data delivered by the senses, and imposing meaning onto the (disenchanted or unknowable) world. Such 'imposing' interpretations can be said to arise from presupposing scientific conceptions of reality, of which mind is not a part. As McDowell notes, '[a]ny candidate feature of reality that science cannot capture is downgraded as a projection, a result of mind's interaction with the rest of nature' (1998a, p. 175). But it is possible to see meaning, not as projected onto, but as already there in the world—'put' there by human activity over time. Kant's use of 'appearances' can be read as ideality. Again, appearances and things in-themselves can be understood as different descriptions of the same things.

Alex Levant also discusses the work of Ilyenkov and explains how 'in the empiricist philosophy of Locke, Berkeley and Hume, the ideal took on a different meaning—as something that does not really exist, or as something that exists only in the mind of an individual', and he shows how 'this meaning was challenged by German classical philosophy, returning it to an objectivity outside the individual mind, albeit idealistically' (2012, pp. 128–129). Kant is idealist as far as *forms* are concerned while acknowledging the independence of reality.[11] Kant distinguishes between form and matter:

These two concepts underlie all other reflection, so inseparably are they bound up with all employment of the understanding ... In every being the constituent elements of it (*essentialia*) are the *matter*, the mode in which they are combined in one thing the essential *form*. (1787, B322, italics added)[12]

Forms are a characteristic of *objectively existing things themselves*. McDowell insists that: 'thought and the world must be understood together. The form of thought is already just as such the form of the world. It is a form that is subjective and objective together' (2009a, p. 143). The ideal takes on this 'formal' but objective existence through human activity, and this culturally and socially shaped activity evolves continuously through history.

Stephen Engstrom, in talking about Kant's practical knowledge of 'the good', also describes this formal but objective existence: 'the goodness itself, being a form that is brought into existence or kept in existence through the concept's efficacy, is in those existing things themselves, as their formal constitution' (2009, pp. 12–13). The formal constitution of things themselves (their ideality) objectively exists, brought into existence and maintained through human minded activity. This can be seen as key to understanding the *unity* of the capacities and Kant's 'transcendental' or 'formal' idealism. Engstrom argues that a proper understanding of the capacities 'must be conceived ... not as interacting parts, but as form and matter' (2006, p. 2). In this way, meanings (ideality, forms, the conceptual) are understood not as in the head but as *objectively existing* in the world, in a richer conception of world. There is no dualism here. Both physical and ideal properties exist as objectively real.

The world can be seen as written through with meaning; and the conceptual can be seen not as 'bound' within the head but as already in the ideal world. That the world can be seen as an objectification of human consciousness is an idea that Ilyenkov holds, and Bakhurst explains:

First, as nature becomes 'humanized,' so it serves humanity as a mirror: Man is able to 'see himself in a world he has created' (Marx 1844: 74). Thus, objectification is construed as the basis of a form of self-consciousness. Second, the humanization of the world is held to transform nature into a different *kind* of environment. Ilyenkov reads humanization as idealization. The natural world after objectification is a different kind of place because it is now laden with ideal properties, with value and significance. It thus confronts human agents no longer as a purely physical environment, but as a *meaningful* one. (1991, p. 187)

That we see consciousness or ideality in the world we have created manifests Kant's Copernican insight that objects conform to our knowledge of them. Kant writes that when we 'approach nature in order to be taught by it', we 'must adopt as [reason's] guide, in so seeking, that which it has itself put into nature':

> Even physics, therefore, owes the beneficent revolution in its point of view entirely to the happy thought, that while reason must seek in nature, not fictitiously ascribe to it, whatever as not being knowable through reason's own resources has to be learnt, if learnt at all, only from nature, it must adopt as its guide, in so seeking, that which it has itself put into nature. (1787, Bxiv)

This suggests a conception of reason capable of learning *from* nature and in doing so being guided by what is already there in ideal form, what has already been 'put into nature'[13]—that is, 'put into nature' by minded beings through historically evolved and ongoing social practices. Robert Stern quotes Kant's successor Hegel: 'To him who looks at the world rationally the world looks rationally back; the two exist in a reciprocal relationship' (2016, p. 161). This echoes Henrich's 'indissoluble' correlation between the unity of mind and the unity of reality (1994) and McDowell's insistence that thought and the world—and subjectivity and objectivity—be understood together.

To recap, we need not interpret Kant's Copernican insight that objects conform to our knowledge in terms of the idea that 'an active reason imposes order on the world' (Fitzsimmons, 2007, p. 561) or as 'Kant's thesis that our mind does not derive laws from nature, but imposes them on it' (von Glasersfeld, 1984, p. 73). Rather it can be put as: we perceive and respond to objects in light of our knowledge of them. Importantly, objectivity is firmly in the picture. With ideal properties existing as objectively real, the meaningful world can be said to act as a 'standard' for correctness, a rational 'constraint' on our judgements and claims. As Andrea Kern says, our judgements have objective content 'in the sense that their truth is dependent on how things are in the world' (2017, p. 53). We can again revisit the difference between Rorty and Boghossian from Chapter One: we cannot know a giraffe merely by seeing one; we first need at least some grasp of the concept *giraffe* to recognise one when we see one;

however, we cannot call any old thing a 'giraffe' (impose our own meaning), for correctness depends on the objectively existing giraffe (already established meaning in the world). It is this *objective material constraint*—the giraffe in the world—that tends to be obscured in typical 'imposition' interpretations of Kant's view in educational theory, as we shall see in Part Two.

Understanding ideality as objectively existing is well illustrated when thinking about the *practical* nature of our engagement with things. In expounding Kant's view of practical knowledge, Engstrom talks of the 'existential relation in which practical knowledge stands to what it knows' (2013, p. 145). He provides a nice example:

An artisan's tool has a specific mode of usefulness, a specific function, present in it as its essential form, and the technical-practical concept, or knowledge, of this form not only governs the tool's initial production but also maintains the form in existence through the care and the skill with which the artisan uses the tool and keeps it in good repair. (2009, p. 13)

Again, there is no dualism here, form and matter exist as one and the concept 'maintains the form in existence' through use and care by us. Knowledge (concept, form) is key: it not only governs the initial production of objects, but we then use objects in light of our knowledge of them, and our actions collectively maintain the form or concept in existence in the already meaningful world. Bakhurst quotes Ilyenkov:

forms of human activity (and the forms of thought which reflect them) are laid down in the course of history independently of the will and consciousness of separate persons, whom they confront as forms of the historically developing system of culture ... a particular process controlled by the laws of development of the material life of society. And these laws not only do not depend on the consciousness and will of particular individuals, but, on the contrary, actively determine consciousness and will. Isolated individuals do not and could not arrive at [*vyrabotat'*] the universal forms of human activity, whatever powers of abstraction they possessed. Rather, they assimilate these forms ready made as they are themselves assimilated into a culture, as they acquire language and the knowledge expressed in it. (in Bakhurst, 1991, p. 200)

The laws mentioned here are not the mechanical laws of nature that are the topic of scientific investigation, but cultural norms, knowledge and standards assimilated through upbringing and education. Kant saw such education as essential to becoming a person in actualising and developing conceptual capacities that are part of our nature as human beings. As a child develops the competence to make conceptual distinctions and respond appropriately to the 'already established' world through interaction with others, so subjectivity and objectivity grow together, and more of the world comes into view.

As with different conceptions of nature, world and causality, 'materialism' too can be understood in different ways. Ilyenkov, following Marx, calls his vision *materialist*, but this is a richer conception than that of scientific materialism. Bakhurst writes of Ilyenkov's conception: 'whereas for Hegel the dialectical structure of reality follows from the dialectical nature of thought, for Marx it is the other way around'; but Marx's materialism 'preserves the idea of reality as a self-developing organism or concrete totality' (Bakhurst, 1991, p. 156). Marx's picture of reality includes the ideal and stands in contrast to scientific materialism, which conceives of reality in merely physicalist terms. Bakhurst quotes from Marx's *Thesis On Feuerbach*: 'The chief defect of all hitherto existing materialism—that of Feuerbach included—is that the thing, reality, sensuousness, is conceived only in the form of the *object or of contemplation*, but not as *sensuous human activity, practice*, not subjectively' (1845, p. 28, in Bakhurst, 1991, p. 215). Marx is criticising 'all hitherto existing materialism' for not conceiving reality subjectively, from a human standpoint. This reflects Kant's Copernican insight.

Rödl also follows Marx in conceiving of his theory of self-consciousness as a *materialist* theory. He writes: 'All hitherto existing materialism is flawed by its empiricism: it conceives of material reality exclusively as an object of intuition, or as to be known receptively' (Rödl, 2007, p. 122). That is, existing materialism holds to a disenchanted conception of the world. For Kant, material reality is to be known through spontaneity, subjectively (in a richer conception of subjectivity that is not cut off from the objective world). Furthermore, Rödl argues that spontaneity *is* a material reality—something to be conceived of in material terms: 'According to Marx, true materialism reveals spontaneity and its knowledge to be of, and thus to be, a material reality' (*ibid.*). Following Marx, Rödl presents his theory of self-consciousness as a true materialism 'which conceives material reality not only as an object of intuition, but as human spontaneity' (p. 131). He argues that '[t]he empiricism that pervades contemporary philosophy produces a flawed materialism, which is unable to think a self-conscious material reality' (p. xi). A significant aspect of Kant's Copernican insight is that *whatever* the context, scientific ones too, it is through subjectivity that the world is 'disclosed' to us and takes the shape it does. As Dieter Henrich writes:

> conceptions of a world arise in particular contexts. It is with regard to a context that we can account for the constitution a world exhibits. Such an account requires reference to operations of the mind, without which the world in question would not be disclosed to us and could not possibly adopt its shape. (1992, p. 3)

It is through subjectivity, spontaneity, that we have any conception of the world, even reductive ones.

Bakhurst tells us that Ilyenkov's picture stems from the classic German tradition and is very Hegelian. Like Kant's other idealist successors, Hegel criticises and changes aspects of Kant's view, but he adopts and works within Kant's Copernican framework (Henrich, 2003). Bakhurst explains that the roots of Ilyenkov's picture of 'absolute' reality or 'organic totality' lie in Kant's description of a living organism 'as a unity of parts', which 'reciprocally *produce* each other' and for meaning depend on their place within the whole. Bakhurst explains:

> Thus understanding the whole is the 'ground of cognition ... of the systematic unity and combination of all the manifold contained in the given material' (219-20). This understanding is teleological: The organism is a 'natural purpose' realized by its parts. Hegel enthusiastically adopted Kant's conception not just for the nature of living things, but as a model for the self-development of reality as a whole, or 'the absolute'. (1991, pp. 154–155)[14]

Hegel's absolute idealism presents a picture of nature as the unity of a living and continually developing system. This offers a conception of nature as essentially rational. Hegelian scholar Stephen Houlgate writes that 'nature is simply *absolute reason itself* existing in a form that is other than that of explicitly self-determining rationality' (2005, p. 109). The idea of nature as absolute reason itself stands in stark contrast to the disenchanted picture of nature held by scientific naturalists that exclude reason entirely.

McDowell argues that the scientific conception of the world is a prejudice, a historically conditioned assumption that needs to be challenged. Bakhurst, though, is pessimistic about the chances of McDowell's attempt to change entrenched assumptions:

> Paramount among them is 'the objectifying mode of conceiving reality' familiar in natural science, which, by representing the constituents of objective reality as bereft of meaning or significance, is unable to find mindedness in bodily movement and is thereby forced to locate mind in an inner realm 'behind' behaviour. The fact is, however, that so deeply entrenched is the assumption, not just in theoretical but in everyday discourse, that diagnosing the philosophical misconceptions that encourage it does not suffice, as McDowell hopes, to 'restore us to a conception of thinking as the exercise of powers possessed, not mysteriously by some part of a thinking being ... but unmysteriously by a thinking being itself, an animal that lives its life in cognitive and practical relations to the world'. (1991, p. 158)

Bakhurst is right to be sceptical about changing an assumption so deeply entrenched in everyday discourse. But it is this assumption—that objective reality is bereft of meaning, which forces us to 'locate mind in an inner realm'—that I see as shaping dualist interpretations of Kant in education. So while 'diagnosing the philosophical misconceptions that encourage it' may not suffice to change the assumption more widely, it can help us be aware of, and set aside, these 'misconceptions' when reading Kant's work. For instance, with an idea of the unboundedness of the conceptual and a richer conception of the world as already meaningful, Kant's 'appearances' can be understood as the very same objective things as things in-themselves. And Kant's conception of mind can be read as embodied and in his subject's minded activity, rather than as located in an inner realm 'behind' behaviour and detached from the world.

In this chapter, attention has been drawn to widespread scientific assumptions about mind and world that act as deep-rooted presuppositions that have influenced readings of Kant in education. Natural-scientific understandings of cause, world and nature were contrasted with broader understandings to show different ways of conceiving what is real and natural in the world. The real can be understood in terms of the ideal, but this is not a projection from a separate mind, rather ideality can be understood as objectively existing in the world, a world made and maintained as ideal by human activity. The aim of these discussions has been to help illustrate the richer metaphysics of Kant's epistemology. In the next chapter, we continue with the topic of naturalism and consider Boyd, Gasper and Trout's other claim: that the methods of science are applicable in all areas of inquiry.

NOTES

1. Under 'eliminativism', human beings are not described as having intentionality and agency but as, say, 'the sum of atoms'. Putnam, among others, challenges this impoverished conception, arguing that our ordinary and familiar objects are missing (Putnam, 2004, pp. 68–69).

2. What counts as a 'special science' is debated; more obviously these would be social sciences, psychology and, say, non-reductive positions in the philosophy of mind, but for some, *any* science other than physics is considered a 'special science', including chemistry, biology and neuroscience (see the Wikipedia entry on 'special sciences').

3. Jesse Mulder also writes of the 'limits of reductionism' (2019). He argues that 'vital categories'—such as life form and life-processes—are irreducible to the concepts used in physical explanations (2016).

4. See the example by Paul Standish (2007, p. 339) that was cited in the Introduction.

5. See, for instance, Kant (Bxxvii).

6. Kant's broader conception of 'causality' is central to his conception of freedom, of autonomy, as reasons can be a 'cause' of our actions. Rödl argues that, in this German tradition, reason and freedom are one and the same (2007, p. 105).

7. Rödl acknowledges the influence here of Michael Thompson (2008).

8. Again examples are given and discussed in Part Two.

9. Empiricism for Ilyenkov is a package of interrelated ideas deriving ultimately from Descartes (p. 17). The criticism of independent minds with a separation of subject and object resembles Kant's critique of traditional empiricism, and critique of Kant in educational theory.

10. This and the following quotes by Ilyenkov are translated by Bakhurst in his *Consciousness and Revolution in Soviet Philosophy* (1991).

11. Kant: 'I have also, elsewhere, sometimes entitled it *formal* idealism, to distinguish it from *material* idealism, that is, from the usual type of idealism which doubts or denies the existence of outer things themselves' (B519n).

12. References to Kant's *Critique of Pure Reason* (1787) are to the B edition, translated by N. Kemp Smith, revised second edition 2007.

13. This particular quote is revisited in Chapter Seven.

14. Hegel is well known, as Robert Stern describes it, for his 'social holism or organicism, namely the view that individual agents musts be seen as essentially tied to the social whole of which they are part' (2016, p. 109).

5

Methodologies and Standpoints

SHEILA WEBB

Alternative ways to understand some of Kant's terms have been suggested for a more friendly reading, one that contrasts with the prevailing 'Kantian' picture in education. A particular set of assumptions about mind and world have been identified for their influence on interpretations that make up the familiar picture, one that receives widespread criticisms for dualisms, intellectualism and a disembodied conception of mind. In the last chapter, Boyd, Gasper and Trout's first commitment of naturalism, *that all phenomena are subject to the laws of nature*, provided a starting point to contrast different ways to understand the concepts cause, nature and world, as well as naturalism and materialism. A conception of the world as full of meaning ('ideality') was contrasted with a 'disenchanted' conception as void of meaning. This chapter continues to give content to a richer reading of Kant, and starts with the second commitment—*that the methods of science are applicable in all areas of inquiry*—again as a springboard for discussion. Scientific methodology is contrasted with Kant's first-person stance for investigation, and attention is drawn to conceptions of subjectivity and objectivity.

An explicit commitment to the view that the methods of science should be applicable in all areas of inquiry is likely to be taken as the scientism it is by many, particularly by philosophers of education. But the *assumption* that the methods of science are the best or most credible way to achieve knowledge is enormously widespread. It influences the managerial and 'standards' culture, where the prioritising of empirical and evidence-based approaches

Interpreting Kant for Education: Dissolving Dualisms and Embodying Mind, First Edition. Sheila Webb.
Chapters and editorial organization © 2022 Philosophy of Education Society of Great Britain.
Published 2022 by John Wiley & Sons Ltd.

is extensive. It also influences funding; the following is a recent entry under Philosophy of Education in the *Stanford Encyclopedia of Philosophy*:

> The most lively debates about education research, however, were set in motion around the turn of the millennium when the US Federal Government moved in the direction of funding only rigorously scientific educational research—the kind that could establish causal factors which could then guide the development of practically effective policies. (It was held that such a causal knowledge base was available for medical decision making.) The definition of 'rigorously scientific', however, was decided by politicians and not by the research community, and it was given in terms of the use of a specific research method—the net effect being that the only research projects to receive Federal funding (until the policy was reversed by the new Obama administration) were those that carried out randomized controlled experiments or field trials (RFTs). It has become common over the last decade to refer to the RFT as the 'gold standard' methodology. (*Stanford Encyclopedia of Philosophy*, 2013)

In the UK too, the push for 'rigorously scientific educational research', such as RCTs, is felt by many. A vast critique comes from a wealth of different perspectives and includes now familiar issues such as the loss of trust in the teacher's judgement (e.g. Cigman and Davis, 2009), the loss of teacher autonomy and professionalism (e.g. Green, 2011), the blurring of information and knowledge (e.g. Derry, 2009), the loss of *understanding* of what is being learnt (e.g. Pring, 2013) and the problems of assessment (e.g. Davis, 1998, 2011, 2013, 2018). To take the latter example, Andrew Davis, who has written widely on the conceptual inadequacies of current assessment practices, argues that they miss much of the real learning that takes place (2009); he draws attention to the high stakes placed on assessment outcomes, for schools as well as teachers with performance tables encouraging teaching to the test, arguing 'the importance of 'real' or 'rich' knowledge in the curriculum is constantly threatened by accountability pressures' (2015, p. 7). As a persistent critic of scientism, Paul Standish argues that 'the prevalence of statistics in our lives alters our sense of the real, and this involves a kind of distortion of experience that is particularly harmful for educational practice' (2010, p. 6). Presented as 'hard' evidence of what is 'real', he points out that statistics and data have become 'part of the way we have learned to see things' and 'what we expect' (p. 7). This scientific 'way we have learned to see things' of course affects the status of philosophical and metaphysical inquiry.

Kant, also, can be considered a critic of scientism; he draws attention to the *limits* of empirical investigation, which is confined to what can be observed, so reducing what can be studied. With his Copernican insight he sees that experience alone is insufficient in providing knowledge, without the contribution of spontaneity. He writes: '[e]xperience teaches us what is, but does not teach us that it could not be other than what it is' (B762). As discussed in earlier chapters, the spontaneity of mind can be conceived as a power, accounting for reflection, new ideas, conceptual change etc. Traditional empiricism discounts the involvement of mind in experience and takes the senses alone as a source of knowledge. Dieter Henrich writes '[t]he empiricism of the allegedly real does not understand what is occurring when history advances ... Kant reproached this kind of practice for having intellectual arrogance and "mole-like vision"' (1993, p. 112). Pirmin Stekeler-Weithofer similarly points out that even empirical perception takes place 'in a domain of conceptually determined possibilities, not only in a realm of present actualities', and argues:

> what I or you perceive is not just a datum for more or less dispositional reactions determined, as we assume, by causal chains mediated by our senses taken as physiologically describable 'mechanism' but stands already in a whole order of possible things (objects) and possible movements (events, states of affairs). These possible things or processes are, as such, not (all) present, for example if they are things or processes in the past or in the future or if they are or happen too far away from the reach of our sense at present. (2010c, p. 4)

Stekeler-Weithofer points out that scientists interpret their empirical, and therefore limited, findings in a speculative way that involves spontaneity. He contrasts Hume's empirical method with that of Kant:

> The cause for Hume's failure lies in his method. His method is 'empirical', 'behavioural', and 'historical', down to his appeal to 'common sense' or 'common opinion'. Kant's method is 'speculative', as Hegel would have called it. It is clear that

empiricist minded readers suspect that it is, as such, no method at all. It appears as dogmatism, arbitrarily brought forward under the misleading title 'critical philosophy'. However, 'speculation' in Hegel's sense means meta-level conceptual analysis. It aims at a logical topography which should help us, and hopefully can help us, to find our way around (Wittgenstein) in the messy realms of particular 'experience'. Kant's crucial words 'a priori' and 'transcendental' are just sign-posts for the insight that we always have to be aware that logical and methodological presuppositions and generic pre-judgments belong to the conditions of possibility of 'empirical' judgements with concrete and particular content. (2010b, p. 4)

Being a speculative, or philosophical, method, Kant's standpoint is human and first-personal, which contrasts with the perceived impartiality of science, but objectivity is not lost in his version of idealism (despite the subjective characterisations of his view in educational theory, addressed in Part Two of this book).

Speculative or philosophical investigation can be contrasted with what McDowell calls the 'sideways-on' stance of scientific investigation—paradigmatically observation. This is not to criticise the methods of science themselves, but to draw attention to the limitations of empirical investigation for *all* areas of reflection. Implicit in different methodologies are conceptions of the object to be studied. When it comes to mind, for instance, Kant's conception of mind as a power contrasts with those who think of it as an object—a blank slate, mirror, brain. Jerry Fodor draws attention to the blank slate conception of mind in cognitive science, and talks of the deeply ingrained nature of this presupposition in this influential paradigm:

Most cognitive scientists still work in a tradition of empiricism and associationism whose main tenets haven't changed much since Locke and Hume. The human mind is a blank slate at birth. Experience writes on the slate, and association extracts and extrapolates whatever trends there are in the record that experience leaves. The structure of the mind is thus an image, made a posteriori, of the statistical regularities in the world in which it finds itself. I would guess that quite a substantial majority of cognitive scientists believe something of this sort; so deeply, indeed, that many hardly notice that they do. (1998, pp. 11–13)

In referring to the 'new movement' of analytic philosophy (that draws on German Idealist ideas), Robert Brandom writes: 'we have failed to communicate some of the most basic of those ideas' to 'those working in allied disciplines who are also professionally concerned to understand the nature of thought, minds, and reason' (2008, pp. 2, 3).

McDowell provides an example of a side-ways on standpoint and points to a conceptual confusion. Famously pushing the reductive programme (explaining mental phenomena in terms of physical phenomena), Daniel Dennett investigates mind, or consciousness, which he takes to be brain processes. He argues, 'there is only one sort of stuff, namely matter—the physical stuff of physics, chemistry and physiology—and the mind is somehow nothing but a physical phenomenon' (1991, p. 33). McDowell argues that '[o]f course there is an organ, the brain, whose proper functioning is necessary to mental life. But that is not to say that the proper functioning of that organ is what mental life, in itself, is' (1998b, p. 281). He criticises Dennett's 'sub-personal, cognitive-scientific account of the operations of our internal machinery' for presenting it as 'consciousness'. McDowell explains the concern:

> Dennett alludes to a famous paper called 'What the Frog's Eye Tells the Frog's Brain', but he commends a suggestion, by Michael Arbib, that one might prefer the formula 'What the frog's eye tells the frog'. His point is that 'sub-personal' content-ascription in the theory of frog perception is controlled by the requirements of a biological account whose topic is the life of *frogs* rather than the doings of their parts. (1998b, p. 347)

McDowell questions this by asking how the frog gets in on the act.

> In accounts of the inner workings, one sub-froggy part of a frog transmits information to another: the frog's eye talks to the frog's brain, not to the frog. In the sense in which the frog's eye tells the frog's brain things, nothing tells the frog anything ... The 'sub-personal' account of a sensory system, which treats it as an information-processing device that transmits its informational results to something else inside an animal, cannot adequately characterize what its sensory systems are for the animal 'itself'. (p. 349)

The heteronomous conception of cause is at play here: a sub-personal information system is a physical mechanism responding to impacts from outside of itself. McDowell argues this is a *syntactic* engine and not a *semantic* one. Thus, 'the attempt to see a constitutive relation between the lower and the upper levels undermines our hold on the fact that animals are semantic engines' (p. 355). There is a conceptual jump from the sub-personal to the animal level. McDowell concludes:

> the real lesson of Dennett's paper is this: a dualism of intuitions and concepts cannot be made safe by simply removing it from the sphere of the transcendental—by assigning the task of fitting intuitions and concepts together to something empirical. (p. 358)[1]

This way of thinking about what consciousness is loses the conceptual resources to talk about psychological, social and normative aspects. As McDowell argues, 'there is nothing wrong with having the internal machinery that controls behaviour as one's subject matter', the problem lies 'in thinking that truth about it is truth about the mental' (2004, pp. 99–100).

Similarly in education there is a literature that explains learning in terms of the brain, with titles such as *How Brains Think: The Evolution of Intelligence* (Calvin, 1997) and *How Brains Make Up Their Minds* (Freeman, 1999). *The Art of Changing the Brain* offers a brain-based model for learning (Zull, 2002), as does *Brain-based Learning: The New Paradigm of Teaching* (Jensen, 2008). David Sousa's *How the Brain Learns* (2011) is the latest of his series of books on educational neuroscience (2005, 2007, 2008). Other examples include John Geake and Paul Cooper, who present future scenarios of using brain scans in parents' evenings to show that a child has a weak short-term memory circuit for number solutions, in order to explain his inadequate maths (2003). And Usha Goswami has long written of the benefits to education of neuroscience, which 'investigates the process by which the brain learns and remembers, from the molecular and cellular levels right through to brain systems' (2004, p. 175, and 2008). While Goswami's work, and that of the Centre for Neuroscience in Education, is important to science and education,[2] such approaches are conceptually problematic. For one thing, *interpreting* brain scans, *thinking* what this means, *designing* appropriate curricula and *explaining* this to others become conceptually difficult to account for.[3] Bennett and Hacker make this point in their book *Philosophical Foundations of Neuroscience* (2003), in which they write: '[t]alk of the brain's perceiving, thinking, guessing or believing, or of one hemisphere of the brain's knowing things of which the other hemisphere is ignorant, is widespread among contemporary neuroscientists' (p. 3).[4] Like McDowell, they criticise the idea of ascribing concepts such as learning and remembering to a part of the body rather than to the person. The fact that their claims have attracted so much controversy within mainstream philosophy highlights the entrenched nature of presuppositions from empiricist epistemology. But the debate cannot be settled empirically because it is a conceptual matter. As Bennett and Hacker rightly argue, conceptual questions are not amenable to scientific investigation because the concepts and conceptual relationships in question are presupposed by any such investigations and cannot be verified by the methods of science.[5]

Subjectivity and other first-person human aspects are written out of scientific methodology in order to be seen to provide objective and mind-independent knowledge; 'science is committed to a dispassionate and dehumanized stance for investigation' as McDowell puts it (1998a, p. 175). Objectivity is understood as independent of subjectivity, which is to be avoided for its prejudice and unreliability; the search is for certainty and foundations *outside* of mind, in an external world. Kant's Copernican view is quite radically different for, as has been discussed, we cannot escape our subjective standpoint—but subjectivity is conceived of in a much richer sense. For one thing, rather than cut off from reality, it can be perceptually connected with things in the ('ideal') meaningful world. Günter Zöller writes of McDowell that he pursues Kant's project 'of integrating the Kantian mind into the Kantian world, of embedding the subject of cognition into the world it cognizes and thus of integrating our vantage point on the world into our picture of the world' (2010, p. 68).[6] Our standpoint is one embedded in the already meaningful (humanised, ideal) world with its already up-and-running system of norms and concepts, and investigation takes place from here. McDowell argues that we need to give up the idea of an external standpoint. In understanding another person, we are 'coming to share with her a standpoint *within* a system of concepts, a standpoint from which we can join her in directing a shared attention at the world, without needing to break out through a boundary that encloses the system of concepts', he writes (1996, p. 36).

For Kant, we are always within a human frame of reference. Concepts and norms come up for reflection to be challenged, altered, replaced or revised, but always from within a shared normative space—a web of presupposed conceptual relations and a network of joint human practices that maintain them. The search for knowledge 'must always be pursued', Kant states, but 'can never be completely achieved' (B593). 'There must be a standing willingness to refashion concepts and conceptions if that is what reflection recommends', McDowell argues (1996, pp. 12–13); '[N]o putative conceptual grasp is ever sacrosanct, fit to be placed once and for all in an archive of achieved wisdom' (2009a, p. 182). Kant was particularly innovative himself in redefining and reinventing many philosophical concepts and introducing new ones; for him concepts are 'the discursive outcome of an open-ended process of reflection upon philosophical problems', as Howard Caygill tells us (1995, p. 2). This is in contrast to the Kant in educational theory who is associated with a view of concepts as fixed and unchanging. Caygill writes of Kant:

> He was famous for bringing to his lectures interesting examples drawn from a wide range of diverse sources. In this respect, the lectures reveal the process by which Kant was able, while working within the philosophical tradition, to adapt the tradition to the new concerns of modernity, whether those of natural science, politics, art and literature, or medicine. His lectures fused the traditional concerns and language of the philosophical *compendia* with new material drawn from the newspapers, journals and books satisfying the demands of a new reading public. (1995, p. 21)

The 'marginalia Kant brought to his texts emerged from his wider reading and thinking, and point to the way in which he transformed and extended the philosophical tradition' (*ibid.*). However, some deeply rooted concepts are very difficult to even recognise. Wittgenstein makes this point:

> The aspects of things that are most important for us are hidden because of their simplicity and familiarity. (One is unable to notice something—because it is always before one's eyes.) The real foundations of his inquiry do not strike a man at all. Unless that fact has at some time struck him.—And this means: we fail to be struck by what, once seen, is most striking and most powerful. (1958, §129)

It can be difficult to recognise what is hidden because of its familiarity. Albert Einstein also writes of this difficulty:

> Concepts that have proven useful in ordering things easily achieve such an authority over us that we forget their earthly origins and accept them as unalterable givens ... The path of scientific advance is often made impassable for a long time through such errors. For that reason, it is by no means an idle game if we become practiced in analysing the long commonplace concepts and exhibiting those circumstances upon which their justification and usefulness depend, how they have grown up individually, out of the givens of experience. By this means, their all-too-great authority will be broken. They will be removed if they cannot be properly legitimated, corrected if their correlation with given things be far too superfluous, replaced by others if a new system can be established that we prefer for whatever reason. (1916, p. 129)

Concepts can easily achieve an authority over us. This is particularly pertinent when reading historical works from a different tradition but also when meeting new ideas within one. In Kant's case, he complained he was being read by his critics through the very (Cartesian) metaphysics he was rejecting, and it is this dualist metaphysics that continue implicitly to have influence today. The enormous variety of readings of Kant reflects the changing conditions within which he has been understood and interpreted, and which continues here.

While our rational capacities are fallible (we might be wrong in what we think we see or know), they are nevertheless all we have to go by. Through the process of *Bildung*, we acquire, assimilate and develop concepts, knowledge, ideas etc. from our inherited culture, from the already meaningful world in which we live, and language plays a big part in this. McDowell writes:

> In being initiated into a language, a human being is introduced into something that already embodies putatively rational linkages between concepts, putatively constitutive of the layout of the space of reasons, before she comes on the scene. This is a picture of initiation into the space of reasons as an already going concern ... [T]he language into which a human being is first initiated stands over against her as a prior embodiment of mindedness, of the possibility of an orientation to the world. (1996, p. 125)

Similarly Kant writes, as previously noted, that even physics 'must adopt as its guide' when investigating nature, 'that which [reason] has itself put into nature' (Bxiv),[7] because this ideality constitutes, to switch to McDowell's terms, the layout of the space of reasons as an already going concern before a human being comes on the scene. It is worth repeating Stanley Cavell here, from Chapter Three, on learning language:

> We learn and teach words in certain contexts, and then we are expected, and expect others, to be able to project them into further contexts. Nothing insures ... that we will make, and understand, the same projections. That on the whole we do is a matter of our sharing routes of interest and feeling, modes of response, sense of humor and of significance and of fulfilment, of what is outrageous, of what is similar to what else, what a rebuke, what forgiveness, of when an utterance is an assertion, when an appeal, when an explanation—all the whirl of organism Wittgenstein calls 'forms of life'. (Cavell, 1969, p. 52, in McDowell, 1998a, pp. 206–207)

McDowell argues that we should 'give up the idea that philosophical thought' should take place 'outside our immersion in our familiar forms of life' (p. 63).

However, there is a long-standing reluctance to give up the idea that investigation should be undertaken from an external standpoint, because this is seen to lead to relativism and the loss of objectivity, as discussed in Chapter One. The idea of an Archimedean point of view—a view from nowhere—has been much discussed in philosophy. Thinking about the world from nowhere, for complete objectivity, has been theorised for instance by Bernard Williams[8] (1985, 2002, 2005), and by Kantian scholar Adrian Moore (1997). Thomas Nagel too reflects on subjectivity and objectivity in his influential book *The View from Nowhere*. On the one hand, Nagel recognises the importance of a first-person perspective:

> For many philosophers the exemplary case of reality is the world described by physics, the science in which we have achieved our greatest detachment from a specifically human perspective on the world. But for precisely that reason physics is bound to leave undescribed the irreducibly subjective character of conscious mental processes, whatever may be their intimate relation to the physical operation of the brain.

The subjectivity of consciousness is an irreducible feature of reality—without which we couldn't do physics or anything else—and it must occupy as fundamental a place in any credible world view as matter, energy, space, time, and numbers. (1986, pp. 7–8)

Nagel's argument that the subjectivity of consciousness is an irreducible feature of reality, without which we could not do physics or anything else, is in line with Kant's Copernican view. At the same time, however, Nagel recommends that we work towards a universal conception of the world, *away from* a subjective—a *'parochial'*—one. The idea of even wanting to achieve this is questioned by Rödl:

The human intellect is situational, and it relates to intuition. That is its essence, according to Kant, its deficiency, according to Nagel ... Nagel believes that we will never be able completely to cleanse ourselves of intuition-dependent and situational thoughts, for which reason we will never know the thing in itself: 'we can't free it entirely of infection with a particular human view' (*The View From Nowhere*, p. 63). Nevertheless, the thing in itself is the measure of our thought, and as long as we have not reached it, our thought is deficient. According to Kant, by contrast, our thoughts are not empty because and to the extent that they are situational or connected to situational thought. It is therefore not the case that we, qua intellect, aspire to free ourselves of situational thoughts, for that would mean that we, qua intellect, strive after empty thoughts. (Rödl, 2012, p. 73)

For Kant, the thing in itself is not the measure of human knowledge (*ibid.*); human thought only has content, Rödl argues, 'because human thought and intuition form an essential unity', and this makes it 'situational', representing its objects in space and time (p. 79). Always rooted in a particular place and time, intuition gives content to our thoughts, concepts, knowledge etc.; without any content our thoughts would be empty, so the idea of freeing ourselves from situational thought means striving after empty thoughts. We cannot free ourselves from our subjective connection with objects, and Rödl questions the desire to do so.

Harvey Siegel also discusses objectivity and the possibility of an external standpoint. Like Williams and Nagel, Siegel on the one hand questions the possibility of a neutral view from nowhere; he criticises the prioritising of scientific values and methods, and affirms epistemological diversity in educational research (2006). However, at the same time, like Moore's argument in *Points of View* (1997), Siegel defends the need for 'a local neutrality' for evaluating different epistemologies; that is, he hangs on to the idea of an external viewpoint and talks of 'criteria being the property not of any given epistemology but rather of an overarching epistemological and philosophical perspective (or metaperspective) that is *neutral* with respect to them all' (p. 7). Elsewhere Siegel defends the neutrality of empiricist knowledge from feminist and postmodern criticisms (2010). The perceived need to be free from a subjective standpoint, and search for objectivity in a reality that is separate from subjectivity, is referred to by McDowell as 'over-objectification', and he argues 'the idea of a view from nowhere is incoherent' (1998a, p. 118).

On Kant's view objectivity is understood as something *within* thought and not something external to it, and this includes the validation of scientific investigation. McDowell says, 'science has presented itself as the very exemplar of access to objective truth' but he takes issue with the idea that scientific findings 'can be validated on the basis of the facts of nature, conceived in the disenchanted way that is encouraged by modern science' (1998a, p. 175). He argues that validation is subject to 'coming up to scratch by standards internal to the formed second nature that is practical *logos*' (p. 193). He reminds us of Neurath's image: the mariner repairing his ship while afloat—it can be altered piecemeal, but not rebuilt in its entirety at any one time. Writing on ethics, McDowell refers to different conceptions of causation:

> the role of causation, in scientific thought's well-grounded conception of itself, does not rescue scientific thought from Neurath's boat. Empiricistic naturalism misses the significance of the fact that the Neurathian 'predicament' is quite general. If one protests that science is in the same boat, that tends to be misconceived as expressing a relativistic refusal to accept that science is objectively special … [I]t is a mistake to think we cannot show proper respect for science unless we suppose that truth about disenchanted nature is the sole context in which the material good standing of an exercise of intellect can be directly apparent, so that any good standing that is not that must be either merely formal or indirectly grounded on such truth. Good standing is, everywhere, for *logos* to pronounce on, using whatever

standards it can lay hands on; nothing but bad metaphysics suggests that the standards in ethics must be somehow constructed out of facts of disenchanted nature. (1998a, p. 187)

Correctness is a matter of coming up to scratch by standards internal to second nature. And the process by which these 'standards' or norms come up to scratch—are validated or changed—is through our up-and-running discursive and social practices, embedded in human activity.

The active process of altering standards and what are accepted as norms (from within Neurath's boat) is illustrated in the following example. It involves competing ideas about what 'science' should be, and the direction it should take. In his autobiography, the biologist Edward Wilson (1994) describes his feelings when molecular biologist James Watson arrived at Harvard after his hugely significant discovery of DNA with Francis Crick. Kenan Malik describes this meeting in his book *Man, Beast and Zombie*, and paraphrases Wilson:

> [Watson] arrived with a conviction that biology must be transformed into a science directed at molecules and cells and rewritten in the language of physics and chemistry. What had gone before 'traditional biology'—*my* biology—was infested by stamp collectors who lacked the wit to transform their subject into a modern science … [I]t is impossible to imagine the impact that the discovery of DNA had on our perception of how the world works. (2000, p. 165)

Physics was becoming the universal standard for judging all scientific approaches to understanding and describing the world, including the human. The concepts of biology were being reduced to the concepts of physics. 'There is only one science, physics: everything else is social work', Watson later said (*ibid.*). However, Wilson responded to this reductive agenda not by defending the 'traditional biology' that had been his life's work, but by jumping on the reductive bandwagon and introducing 'sociobiology'—a new approach that reduces social behaviour and even human nature to evolutionary and genetic concepts (1975). Malik describes the effort to turn traditional biology into a 'proper' science by making it quantifiable:

> Human sociobiology was the attempt to carry through the reductive approach to the study of Man … [I]t allowed

sociobiologists to adopt a 'more reductive than thou' attitude towards social scientists: if reductionism was the measure of a true science, then human sociobiology, by demonstrating how reductionism could explain human affairs, measured up. (p. 168)

Reductionism was becoming the new standard for measuring a true science. Sociobiology is now an established field. We can say that this most reductive of reductive sciences resulted from ideas that spring from spontaneity and the power of mind. We can picture Watson and Wilson arguing for their positions, challenging, defending, persuading—exercising the very agency and rational freedom denied in such theories. Moreover, rooted in social activity—debates, conferences, articles, books, peer reviewed papers etc.—ideas about what 'biology' and 'science' ought to be are worked through and continually developed through participation in social practices. This exhibits the movement of thought, the life of a discipline in motion, conceptual change—change that is never complete. Intentionality and the normative forces that drive change are not captured and cannot be expressed by the conceptual resources of the reductive sciences, or of traditional empiricist epistemology; Kant recognised this with his criticism of 'mole-like vision'.

Expanding on Kant's concept of intuition can help illustrate the objectivity within his view and begin to show how subjectivity and objectivity can be seen as interdependent. As has been emphasised through the chapters, intuition is not to be conceived of as empiricism's sense data, but as a capacity or ability that explains a source of knowledge, one which provides the worldly content of *what* we perceive when we perceive something. Stekeler-Weithofer talks of intuition as a competence, a human capacity for joint conduct, and argues that if it is misinterpreted as opinion or subjective feeling then we miss its objective and factive aspects. Kant uses the word *Anschauung* (intuition), Stekeler-Weithofer explains, as 'objective perception', that is object-directed perception that is necessary for any shared reference to the world. He writes:

[T]he word 'intuition' is as perfective and factive as the word 'murder' is: One cannot murder anybody without him being dead afterwards. In the same vein, we cannot have an intuition of x without x being there. The factive feature of Kant's notion of intuition is regularly overlooked. But it is absolutely clear that intuition is perfective observation and, as such, guarantees the existence of the observed process or things in just the same way as knowledge of p guarantees that p is true. Moreover, Kant's whole analysis is misread if we do not keep this in mind. (2010c, p. 5)

The factive dimension of intuition has, as Stekeler-Weithofer argues, been regularly overlooked, and is missing from the widespread 'Kantian' picture in educational theory. 'This objectivity has to be understood as a certain situation-invariance of *deictical reference to present objects and object-related processes* like movements, but also changes of qualities', he explains (2010b, p. 10). This ability to intuit, to identify objects and movements in experience, presupposes mutual recognition. We can think of it as interpersonal activity, a joint practice that involves joint attention to real objects in the world—a practice in which normative commitments and concepts are learnt and developed along with empirical ones. Such 'objective perception' cannot be understood *apart* from subjectivity, as objects are perceived through and only through a first-person stance. Perception is subjective and objective at the same time. This is not a 'detached' conception of mind, as Kant's critics say of him.

Stekeler-Weithofer draws attention to the cooperative and social norms involved. He points out that Kant uses the generic 'I', but in an important sense this is also a 'we' and a 'you'; 'correct Intuition is determined by the common ground, or rather common goal or success conditions, of joint reference to the present world around us, not only by the "thing and me", so to speak' (2010a). That is, intuition presupposes mutual recognition as it allows for deictic reference to things through *joint consciousness*: shared knowledge and shared normative commitments. Kant says that 'I think' must be able to accompany all my representations (B132), this is the self-consciousness of thought. But again this 'I think' is also a 'you think' or 'we think', because becoming minded means being initiated into a shared culture and developing the competence to take part in the everyday social practices that maintain it, including joint reference.[9] Joint consciousness—shared knowledge and understanding—allows successful reference to be made. Stekeler-Weithofer writes:

something is an object of *my Anschauung* only if it can (or could) be an object of *your* and hence *our Anschauung* as well. I.e. an object of my intuition already lies in the realm of possible access by present *Anschauung*, which is something like *our present perceptual space*. (2010c, p. 6)

Stekeler-Weithofer credits 'Kant's deep insights' here, explaining that time and space are forms of intuition:

> The comprehensive form of *Anschauung* is a form of *our practical attitude* with respect to objects *in our perceptual field*. It presupposes that you and I and he, i.e. *we together*, can refer to the *same object* from our different positions of perspectives—if we take these differences of perspectives properly into account. This 'proper account' defines the forms and norms of *one common spatial order*. This order is *space*. (p. 7)

Time and space are forms of intuition (2010b, p. 19).[10] The point here is that objectivity comes from such joint perceptual access to objects in the world—through subjectivity.

In contrast to the causal role of sense data in empiricist epistemology, this competence to intuit is socially learnt, which underscores the relevance of education and the participation of others. Children acquire and develop the ability to change perspectives from one point of view to another: 'practical mastery of perspectival change, including the control of jointness in reference, is part of a normatively constituted social practice. It is a form of cooperation', Stekeler-Weithofer explains (2010a, p. 19). This does not come simply from biological maturity or genetic endowment but is a competence that is acquired and developed early in life, in order to successfully participate in jointly referring to things in the world. Even young children together gain the competence to refer to the same object from their different positions and perspectives; objectivity cannot be separated from the subjective stance of subjects. Subjectivity and objectivity are both internal to perception.

Kant's insights involve the idea that the conceptual unity of an object is not simply 'Given' (as a collection of sense data), but is learnt, gradually learnt, through discursive activity with others. And once learnt it is exercised in encountering particular instances of it. In this sense, objects conform to our knowledge of them. Conceptual unity is grasped along with other conceptual connections and distinctions as children develop the practical competence to identify an object and refer to the same object over time. Pointing plays an important role early in life, after which language allows reference to (jointly perceived) objects; as Rödl writes, 'a substance and its form enter thought together' (2012, p. 205). This is to argue that subjectivity and objectivity emerge together. Intuition provides the content (how an object looks, smells, feels, its weight, texture etc.), and language (concepts and forms of thought) is learnt to be able to refer to these objects, and this knowledge is then manifested in our responses to them. As Stekeler-Weithofer puts it, 'our social conceptual distinctions and our (joint) perceptual access to the object are 'grown together', and embedded in our practices' (2010a, p. 15). In this way, experience 'as Kant uses the word is already conceptually formed' and 'must always already be seen as taking part in complex and joint practice' (p. 19). Similarly, McDowell writes on acquiring new concepts:

> If a subject does not already have a discursive capacity associated with some aspect of the content of an intuition of hers, all she needs to do, to acquire such a discursive capacity, is to isolate that aspect by equipping herself with a means to make that content—that very content—explicit in speech or judgment. (2009a, p. 264)

Through shared experience and joint intuition, our rational capacities are continuously developed, becoming more refined, discriminating and discerning.[11] Again, this is not a subjectivity, or conception of mind, that is detached from the world but is connected with it through the senses; intuition 'situates' us, providing the worldly content of our thought. As Engstrom (2006) insists, a proper understanding of Kant's capacities shows no dualism between them. Mental life is an aspect of *our* lives, to repeat McDowell: '[w]here mental life takes place need not be pinpointed any more precisely than by saying that it takes place where our lives take place. And then its states and occurrences can be no less intrinsically related to our environment than our lives are' (1998b, p. 281). Read in a different light, Kant's conception of mind need not be read as detached but rather embodied and his subject embedded in the life she leads.

This chapter has sought to bring more of a contemporary reading of Kant into view through a discussion of the naturalist commitment: that the methods of science be applicable in all areas of inquiry. Speculative or philosophical inquiry was contrasted with scientific approaches to give content to Kant's first-person stance and begin to bring out the objectivity of his view, which continues to be developed through the chapters. So far Kant's view has been differentiated from empiricist and naturalist (mind-independent) epistemologies; in the next chapter, it is contrasted with Rorty's mind-dependent view of knowledge, for further elucidation.

NOTES

1. Kant's use of *transcendental* is another term that is often mischaracterised, for it is something quite distinct from the English word. Kant writes that '*transcendental* and *transcendent* are not interchangeable terms'; transcendent refers to principles 'which profess to pass beyond' the limits of experience, whereas Kant is concerned with immanent principles which operate 'entirely within the limits' of experience (B352).
2. Established in 2005 at Cambridge University, this centre aims to 'apply the substantial advances in understanding the brain to education. http://www.cne.psychol.cam.ac.uk
3. See for instance Andrew Davis (2004) and David Bakhurst (2009) as two of the very many who critique such naturalist theories in education.
4. For their follow-up discussion, see Bennett and Hacker (2007).
5. This is a compelling reason against the idea that scientific methods be used in all areas of inquiry.
6. Having recognised this, Zöller criticises McDowell's Kant in *Mind and World* for remnants of a dualist interpretation of Kant, discussed in Chapter Eleven.
7. 'Put into nature' as ideality—meaning put there by collective social consciousness, through layers of historically evolved social practices—as discussed in the previous chapter.
8. Williams is another theorist with a 'two worlds' reading of Kant; he appreciates Kant's systematic approach to ethical thinking but does not agree with the abstract and detached conception of person that he reads Kant's ethical agent to be (1985).
9. This, of course, does not mean we have to agree, but we have to share enough background knowledge and social practices to voice our disagreement (such disagreements and argumentation are worked out through shared cultural practices, illustrated above by Wilson and Watson).
10. This is discussed further in Part Two of the book, and the concept of intuition is developed as we proceed.
11. This is discussed further in Chapter Nine.

6

Mind-Dependent Views of Knowledge

SHEILA WEBB

Kant's Copernican view has so far been contrasted with empiricist and naturalist epistemology in order to gradually develop a contemporary reading that is profoundly different to the predominant 'Kantian' picture in the philosophy of education. Alternative and unfamiliar understandings of some key concepts have been presented to show that Kant's distinctions can be understood in less oppositional ways, showing a conception of mind as embodied and his subject embedded in the world. This chapter looks at Richard Rorty's mind-dependent view, again with the help of McDowell, to differentiate and further elaborate Kant's mind-dependent view.

Rorty famously rejects traditional empiricism completely for being 'a whole set of terms and assumptions which center around the image of mind as mirroring nature' (1979, p. 97). In contrast, Rorty has, as has Kant, a mind-dependent view of knowledge. However, Rorty defines his pragmatist position *in opposition* to Kant, because he reads Kant (and Enlightenment thought generally) as sharing with empiricism and representationalism the same idea of mind as mirror of a mind-external nature. Kant's rejection of the traditional (Cartesian) metaphysics that had long been dominant in his own time has been documented through the chapters, but, as argued, Kant continues to be read by many through presuppositions from this traditional picture—Rorty included. In this chapter, Rorty's key commitments are identified and discussed, through exchanges with McDowell, to show that (despite his explicit rejection of empiricism) Rorty understands epistemological concepts in the 'scientific' way of traditional empiricism. This reveals the deep

Interpreting Kant for Education: Dissolving Dualisms and Embodying Mind, First Edition. Sheila Webb.
Chapters and editorial organization © 2022 Philosophy of Education Society of Great Britain.
Published 2022 by John Wiley & Sons Ltd.

reach of these empiricist presuppositions, which I argue have influenced interpretations of Kant. Again, the discussion is not to engage with or critique Rorty's view, but to get to the issues that allow articulation of the differences between contemporary readings of Kant and the widespread 'Kantian' picture in education.

Rorty is highly critical of the widespread privilege accorded to science, seeing science as one social practice among others. He denies that the natural sciences are in touch with what he calls 'The Intrinsic Nature of Reality', insisting 'no area of culture, and no period of history, gets Reality more right than any other' (2000, p. 375). This is because, he believes:

> There is no such thing as Reality to be gotten right—only snow, fog, Olympian deities, relative aesthetic worth, the elementary particles, human rights, the divine right of kings, the Trinity, and the like. (Can you get right something that does not exist? Sure. Thanks to advances in archaeology and epigraphy, for example, we know a lot more about Zeus than was known in the Renaissance.) (*Ibid.*)

As far as Rorty is concerned, the fundamental empiricist idea that something is Given by the world, and that our knowledge claims are answerable to this, is as immature an idea as religious ideas held by defenders of religious belief. A closer look serves to bring into view his presuppositions and commitments, and thus help differentiate Rorty's mind-dependent view with that of Kant. McDowell explains Rorty's thinking:

> What Rorty takes to parallel authoritarian religion is the very idea that in everyday and scientific investigation we submit to standards constituted by the things themselves, the reality that is supposed to be the topic of the investigation. Accepting that idea, Rorty suggests, is casting the world in the role of the non-human Other before which we are to humble ourselves. Full human maturity would require us to acknowledge authority only if the acknowledgement does not involve abasing ourselves before something non-human. The only authority that meets this requirement is that of human consensus. (2000, pp. 109–110)

Opposed to empiricist ideas of knowledge and justification as stemming directly from the external world, Rorty argues that these arise from social agreement; knowledge is solidarity, agreement with our fellow peers (1989). Instead of looking at reality, he insists that we should concentrate on consensus.

Rorty famously rejects the concept of objectivity—replacing it with solidarity.[1] He dismisses objectivity because in empiricist epistemology, objectivity derives from the external world, and is a non-human authority; for Rorty justification comes from agreement with one's peers and *not* from the world. Rorty also discards the concept of truth, on the grounds that 'there is little to be said about truth' (1999, p. 37). He writes:

> It may seem strange to say that there is no connection between justification and truth. This is because we are inclined to say that truth is the aim of inquiry. But I think we pragmatists must grasp the nettle and say that this claim is either empty or false. (*Ibid.*)

Instead, Rorty argues, 'philosophers should explicitly and self-consciously confine themselves to justification' through as much agreement as possible (p. 32). Epistemology and metaphysics are put in the same empiricist boat as truth and objectivity, along with foundationalism—and rejected. In this picture of knowledge, central epistemological concepts are simply eliminated.

Rorty closely follows the philosophy of Donald Davidson; a brief résumé of this will help identify commitments and assumptions in this approach to understanding knowledge, and make it possible to differentiate Kant from these below. Invoking an argument similar to that of Sellars's Myth of the Given in his *Empiricism and the Philosophy of Mind* (1956), Davidson rejects the very idea of a dualism of conceptual scheme and empirical content. Instead he advocates a coherentist theory of knowledge and truth, which highlights language and the *social* nature of knowledge (2001). It is through interpersonal communication within our social practices that we learn to speak a language and acquire concepts of knowledge, objectivity and truth at all, despite the hesitant and ungrammatical character of much of our discourse (1986). According to Davidson, we learn standards of correctness by using a public language in our interactions with other people, and it is the shared reactions to common stimuli that provide content and meaning to our concepts. That is, he sees our relation with the world as *causal*, an impact on sensibility, but the language and concepts that we use in communicating and justifying what we say are *normative*. Davidson famously argues that 'nothing can count as a reason for holding a belief except another belief' (2001), conceiving justification as stemming from our conceptual system of beliefs and not directly from the empirical world.[2] The emphasis on the social nature of knowledge, through interpersonal communication with others, contrasts starkly with empiricism, and it is Davidson's picture that Rorty largely adopts.[3]

Rorty urges us to use Davidson's notion of *triangulation*: a three-way interdependence of speaker, fellow speaker (or interpreter) and the shared world (1991). This compares with empiricism's two-way picture between individual subject and object. Rorty believes it is better to think of knowledge as this triangulation than as 'zeroing in on the way things really are' (2000, p. 374). Of the empiricist view he remarks:

> You think you can escape the inescapable, cut off one corner of Davidson's triangle, and just ask about a relation called 'correspondence' or 'representation' between your beliefs and the world ... [N]one of the three corners of his process of triangulation can be what they are in independence of the other two. (*Ibid.*)

Returning to Rorty's point about the giraffe in the debate with Boghossian, we do not see a giraffe and know what it is without first learning how to name it, through interaction with others, and the norms for using the concept giraffe in future contexts. Rorty insists on the *inescapability* of triangulation:

> Whereas you can, in the course of triangulation, criticize any given claim about anything you talk about, you cannot ask for agreement that others shall take part in a process of triangulation, for the attempt to reach such an agreement would just be more triangulation. The inescapability of norms is the inescapability, for both describers and agents, of triangulating. (pp. 373–374)

For Rorty it is this process of triangulation that provides us with the world of Human Rights and kings, as well as snow and giraffes, and particles and atoms.

Rorty's position stimulated what has come to be called the naturalist-normative debate; in contrast to those who look to the objective world for knowledge and justification, Rorty argues that these are *ours* and are not provided by the world, there simply is no 'alien authority'.[4] Vocabulary gets its content through *use*, he argues, and is not constrained by an external world. He insists that a 'normative vocabulary is presupposed by any descriptive vocabulary ... We could not deploy the descriptive vocabulary unless we could also deploy the normative one, just as we could not employ a screwdriver if we did not have hands' (2000, p. 372). Not only are norms inescapable, but according to Rorty they ought to be the *focus* of any account of knowledge. The emphasis on normativity contrasts altogether with empiricist/naturalist views that exclude normative notions in their explanations. Rorty recommends that we conceive knowledge as a 'conversation', for it is through social consensus that knowledge and norms come to be accepted, not from reality.

While Rorty rejects empiricism entirely, setting up his view in opposition to it, he can be seen to adhere to the empiricist understandings and assumptions about key concepts that have been identified in previous chapters. Consider his conception of reality for instance; in denying that anything is given by the world (no alien authority) and holding that we know objects (cabbages as well as kings) only in virtue of social agreement, reality itself, he insists, is 'normless' and disenchanted. '"Reality" and "Our knowledge of Reality" are alternative names for the normless. That is why metaphysics and epistemology go together like ham and eggs', he writes (2000, p. 376). Rorty commits to a conception of reality as bereft of meaning; meaning lies in language, in the social and conceptual sphere, and he insists there are no constraints from the world (1998).

Rorty's conception of mind is also naturalist in the reductive sense—for he eliminates it. He holds that mental vocabulary allows us to describe people but does not reveal anything about the nature of mind, for there is no such thing, no such nature. Believing *nothing* to be 'written on the face of the world', Rorty writes about the nature of anything:

> You know about the nature of X when you know the inferential relationships which are generally agreed to hold between the sentences using the word 'X' and the other sentences of the language. On this view, you may always learn more about the nature of X, because new scientific developments (for example) may bring about agreement upon new such relationships. But there is nothing beyond such relationships to be discovered. (1982, p. 340)

Meaning is not discovered in the world but is constituted by agreement about inferential relationships between sentences of a language. Rorty conceives meaning as stemming from language, because reality is presupposed as disenchanted.

Along with empiricists and naturalists, Rorty commits to (science's mechanical) 'causal' relation between thought and reality, denying a 'rational' relation. This commitment is reflected in his likening humans to computers, with mind/brain as a kind of information processor. In dismissing the idea that in experience our perceptual relation with the world is rational, Rorty criticises McDowell's argument that perceptual experience (in the Kantian sense, in which experience comes already conceptually structured) can be justificatory or warrant a particular belief. In contrast, he describes experience in the following way:

> human beings' only 'confrontation' with the world is the sort that computers also have. Computers are programmed to respond to certain causal transactions with input devices by entering certain program states. We humans program ourselves to respond to causal transaction between the higher brain centers and the sense organs with dispositions to make assertions. There is no epistemologically interesting difference between a machine's program state and our dispositions, and both may equally well be called 'beliefs' or 'judgments'. There is no more or less intentionality, world-directedness, or rationality in the one case than in the other. (Rorty, 1998, pp. 141–142)

Rorty's conception, with its 'causal transactions' with the world, is mechanistic. He rejects Kant's notion of freedom (with autonomy as a kind of 'cause').[5] Rorty talks of knowledge as a human phenomenon, but with knowledge as 'aspiring to vocalise in step with one another' and no concept of anything like spontaneity or self-determination, Rorty's view can be said to be behaviouristic—we are determined by the attitudes and judgments of others, with no rational freedom in the Kantian sense.[6]

McDowell takes issue with Rorty over his denial of rational freedom; he argues of a similar position: 'How can it be rational to commit oneself if it is up to others to determine what one has committed oneself to?' (2011, p. 10).[7] But Rorty insists that he has no use for vocabulary such as rational freedom. Mind is a concept he associates with empiricism (as the mirror of nature) and that he rejects. Interestingly, Rorty elsewhere writes:

We cannot, no matter how hard we try, continue to hold a belief which we have tried, and conspicuously failed, to weave together with other beliefs into a justificatory web. No matter how much I want to believe an unjustifiable belief, I cannot will myself into doing so. (1999, p. 37)

This wonderfully exemplifies Kant's rational freedom (the power of mind, spontaneity, self-consciousness)—which Rorty rejects. In other words, Rorty *presupposes* rational freedom, but rejects the vocabulary used to express it.

From the above we can see the extent to which empiricist understandings of central epistemological concepts (including epistemology itself) are at play in Rorty's view. His overall position is acutely and radically different from empiricism, yet he remains committed to empiricist conceptions of key concepts, many of which he altogether rejects. It is these understandings that likely shaped his negative reading of Kant. For instance, Rorty sees epistemology as centring around 'the Kantian picture of concepts and intuitions getting together to produce knowledge, and both as sharing "representationalism": the idea of mind as mirror of a mind-external nature' (1979, p. 168).[8] Heavily influenced by Peter Strawson's critical reading of Kant in *The Bounds of Sense* (1966), Rorty's interpretation is exemplary of a 'two-worlds' reading, with concepts and intuitions 'getting together' to produce knowledge. This dualist interpretation is typical of those, to repeat Engstrom, 'who see these stems as distinct parts, each able on its own to produce representations, which must somehow interact, determining or constraining one another, in order to secure the fit, requisite for cognition, between concept and intuition' (2006, p. 2). But this reading 'cannot be squared', Engstrom argues, 'with what Kant actually says about theoretical cognition and the way understanding and sensibility cooperate in it' (*ibid.*). Andrea Kern similarly argues that spontaneity and intuition are not two separate realms but two aspects of a single capacity (2006). Also, Rödl argues 'that we apprehend substances and their movement through the senses, and forms and their laws through the intellect, are two sides of a coin', and the unity of these sources 'defines the finite intellect' (2012, p. 207). As has been emphasised through the chapters, the capacities can be understood not as interacting parts getting together but as two sources of one single capacity for knowledge, the (conceptual not ontological) distinction describes their different functions.

Rorty's dualist interpretation leads him to disagree with McDowell's reading of Kant. Rorty declines to conceive of the world as already meaningful, which can act as a constraint on our thinking, he rejects objectivity and explicitly denies a 'rational' relation between mind and world. Unable to see meaning in the world—because for Rorty this would be admitting to an alien authority, or the Given—Rorty sees all meaning and content residing in the normative sphere of social agreement. This means that meaning, knowledge, norms, values etc. all lie within the conceptual realm—which amounts to recognising only one side of the mind–world dualism. In Kant's terms, this is a case of 'intellectualising appearances'. A conceptual realm that is responsive only to itself makes it, McDowell argues, free floating and out of touch with reality.

A significant aspect of Kant's view that is lost in the typical 'Kantian' picture of him in education is the objectivity of his mind-dependent view. This objectivity also differentiates Kant from Rorty's mind-dependent view. The idea of objectivity that is provided by intuition has already been introduced and is further illustrated by McDowell. McDowell's arguments against traditional empiricism have been discussed, but in *Mind and World* he has *two* epistemological targets: traditional empiricism and (the other 'horn of the dilemma') coherentism, associated with Davidson and Rorty. McDowell acknowledges that Rorty was an influence on his thinking, and Davidson even more so, but despite the 'massive agreement' McDowell alerts us to what he sees as the dangers of coherentism.[9] He describes a coherentism that does not acknowledge a role for worldly constraint on our thinking; it leaves us out of touch with reality:

> It can seem that we are retaining a role for spontaneity but refusing to acknowledge any role for receptivity and that is intolerable. If our activity in empirical thought and judgement is to be recognizable at all, there must be external constraint. There must be a role for receptivity as well as spontaneity, for sensibility as well as understanding. (1996, p. 9)

With no constraint from the world, McDowell colourfully describes coherentism as 'a frictionless spinning in a void' (p. 11). For Davidson a belief can only be justified by another belief, whereas McDowell wants belief to be 'answerable' to the world, with the (meaningful) world providing 'friction'. It might appear that if we give up coherentism we have to resort to traditional empiricism and its incoherent Myth of the Given. McDowell says we are 'prone to fall into an intolerable oscillation' recoiling from one way of thinking into the other (p. 23), with both positions exhibiting a disconnect between mind and world—traditional (dualist) metaphysics.

Kant faced a similar dilemma, as previously discussed, with the two prevailing traditions of his time—empiricism and rationalism. His deep engagement with these in his critical work, over time, shifted the direction of thought. He moved from a long-term concern about the source and success of justification, to thinking about what makes our thoughts objective *at all*, how is it they have objective purport. His question became something like, how does thought connect with or 'hook onto' objects in the world to make thought 'objective' and not just a free-floating realm of concepts and representations? 'Objective meaning', Kant writes, 'cannot consist in the relation to another representation (of that which we desire to entitle object), for in that case the question again arises, how this latter representation goes out beyond itself, acquiring objective meaning in addition to the subjective meaning which belongs to it as determination of the mental state' (B242). Graham Bird describes this:

> Plainly, for Kant, some way out of the network of mental states is recognized if we are to understand the term 'object' properly. It cannot signify merely relations to other representations, other mental states, as in phenomenalism but equally it cannot signify some thing in itself wholly divorced from perception and its successive mode of accessing any objects. To reject both of these alternatives is to reject a dualist assumption which appeals only to subjective mental state or transcendent things in themselves, and to confirm Kant's revolutionary rejection of traditional dualism. (2006, p. 467)

This confirmation of Kant's revolutionary rejection of traditional dualism is what I am emphasising here, for a reading of Kant that contrasts with the typical 'Kantian' picture in education. McDowell writes, 'when we reject the dualism of scheme and world, we cannot take meaning to constitute the stuff of schemes on the dualistic conception of schemes. But that does not deprive us of the very idea of meaning' (1996, p. 157). 'We can dismount from the seesaw if we can achieve a firm grip on this thought: receptivity does not make an even notionally separable contribution to the co-operation' with spontaneity (p. 9)—it is intuition and spontaneity *together*, not spontaneity on its own through which the world comes into view. Bird writes, Kant 'distinguishes the *mode* of representing from the *content* of representation', and holds that the 'categories are responsible for the determination or articulation of what is presented indeterminately to the senses', which 'underlines the ineliminable reference to our cognitive powers in Kant's nontraditional account of mind-dependence' (2006, p. 467).

Kant's non-traditional mind-dependence account is metaphysically different from other mind-dependence accounts (such as 'mind makes nature' and coherentist versions) in terms of its objectivity. This difference is manifested, and can be illustrated, in conceptions of justification. For Rorty justification comes from social agreement, as we have seen. In responding to this, McDowell argues that instead of justification consisting 'in one's being able to get away with it among certain conversational partners', it comes from the question 'in the light of what?' (2009b, p. 218). McDowell argues that:

> There is a norm for making claims with the words 'Cold fusion has not occurred' that is constituted by whether or not cold fusion has occurred; and whether or not cold fusion has occurred is not the same as whether or not saying it has occurred will pass muster in the current practice. (2000, p. 118)

If cold fusion is jointly intuited (Kant's 'objective perception'), then it is in the light of joint intuition (of cold fusion being jointly perceived and experienced) that answers the question whether or not cold fusion has occurred. Intuition provides worldly content—shared content for all who are there, with the relevant knowledge—rooting observers in that place at that time. What they jointly experience, jointly witness, can be said to act as a constraint or 'friction' to which thought and claims are 'answerable'. We cannot decide what to perceive; these observers cannot undo the actuality of seeing cold fusion occur even if they decide (for some reason) to deny it to others. Objectivity is also entailed in Kant's conception of 'appearance', for as he points out, there cannot be an appearance of something 'without anything that appears' (Bxxvi); appearance guarantees the existence of objects, there for all to see. In this way, the humanised (idealised) world acts as a constraint on our thinking and justification. McDowell writes 'a belief or judgment whose content (as we say) is that things are thus and so—must be a posture or stance that is *correctly* or *incorrectly* adopted according to whether or not things are indeed thus and so' (1996, pp. xi, xii); coherentism, he argues, does not provide this. Kant's non-traditional mind-dependent view does, but the objectivity of his view has been largely obscured in educational characterisations.[10]

Rorty rejects both Kant and traditional epistemology because he rejects the idea of an extra-conceptual constraint on our thinking, an alien authority. However, as I am attempting to articulate, this constraint is not extra-conceptual but a conceptual one, because the world is not outside a conceptual boundary. Objects that are perceived not only provide justification but make thought possible in the first place (as the object of thought). Rödl writes of this:

> She who expresses a thought with 'This pepper is red' asserts something as opposed to nothing because and insofar as she perceives the pepper of which she speaks. It is not just that, in asserting this thought, she relates directly to something she perceives; rather, this is what makes her thought possible. (2012, p. 56)

Objects make thought possible. 'The human intellect depends on the independent existence of the object of its thought' (p. 8). This is a mind that is finite and embodied, connected with objects, with the subject able to 'think' the objects she perceives. McDowell also makes this point: 'Objects come into view for us in actualizations of conceptual capacities in *sensory consciousness*, and Kant perfectly naturally connects sensibility with receptivity' (2009a, p. 43). Objects exist independently but their ideality—their objectively-existing appearance—falls within the conceptual realm, making for conceptual (rational) constraint.

Rorty, Kant and McDowell all want to acknowledge human finitude and see knowledge as a human phenomenon, but Rorty rejects the idea that the world plays an objective and rationally constraining role. Rorty does concede a little on this point; he admits:

> McDowell would be right to point out that I should not speak of 'norms set by our peers'. It was a mistake to locate the norms at one corner of the triangle—where my peers are—rather than seeing them as, so to speak, hovering over the whole process of triangulation ... It is not that my peers have more to do with my obligation to say that snow is white than the snow does, or than I do. (2000, p. 376)

However, Rorty holds fast to replacing objectivity with solidarity, seeing anything else as alien authority. A consequence of this view has been that without objectivity and worldly constraint, this way of thinking about knowledge can give credibility to some radically relativist positions, and Rorty has been charged with this, as we saw in Chapter One. But in typical response, Rorty dismisses this as well. In defending pragmatism against charges of relativism, Rorty writes 'relativistic' is what the realist calls pragmatists, but:

> the pragmatist does not have a theory of truth, much less a relativistic one. As a partisan of solidarity, his account of the value of cooperative human inquiry has only an ethical base, not an epistemological or metaphysical one. Not having *any* epistemology, a fortiori he does not have a relativistic one. (1990, p. 24)

Social solidarity, for Rorty, captures all that is needed to talk about knowledge. He is equally disparaging of Kant's conception of rational freedom:

> Just because the notion of 'rational freedom' is, as McDowell uses it, so interlocked with other notions I have no use for—notions like answerability and content—I have no use for it. So I construe 'rational freedom' as 'that funny thing McDowell thinks we would not have if Davidson were right that there is "a merely causal, not rational, linkage between thinking and independent reality"'. (1998, pp. 149–150)

Rorty agrees with Davidson's 'merely causal' account. He admits, 'Sometimes McDowell almost persuades me that I should back off from my highly unpopular attempt to replace objectivity with solidarity', and 'Sometimes I think that I really must have the blind spot he diagnoses' (2000, pp. 124–125). But, Rorty continues, 'I still cannot see the difference between "expressing a world view" and "merely aspiring to vocalize in step with one another"' (*ibid.*). Rorty confesses, 'my problem is that practically everybody agrees with McDowell that I have a blind spot' (p. 127). Nevertheless, Rorty holds on to his causal conception and rejection of objectivity, claiming his normative view is 'as natural as the beaver's teeth, and equally in touch (causal touch, rather than any sort of "answerability" touch) with the world' (p. 123). Furthermore, 'as Davidson teaches us, you and your peers and the world are always bouncing off each other in causal ways. That causal interaction—that perpetual triangulation—is as intimate as a connection with either world or peers can get' (p. 127).

Discussion of Rorty's view has shown that his conceptions of the key concepts of knowledge—objectivity, truth, epistemology, metaphysics, as well as mind, reality and their causal relation—are the empiricist/scientific conceptions still dominant in Anglo-American philosophy. Correctly recognising the problematic nature of the empiricist way of thinking about knowledge, Rorty rejects the whole vocabulary along with empiricism itself, and turns to pragmatism with a new vocabulary, such as solidarity. However, this leaves in place empiricist presuppositions and understanding of key concepts, which I have been attempting to 'set aside' to make way for other understandings of them in order to better appreciate Kant. The important point here is that Rorty rejects epistemological concepts rather than reconceive them in a different way. As Einstein says, concepts can easily achieve 'an authority over us' and we 'accept them as unalterable givens' (1916, p. 147); but, as McDowell often argues, we have a standing obligation to reflect on the concepts and conceptions that we inherit. In simply eliminating these central concepts of knowledge, Rorty is eliminating the very possibility of being able to express and discuss the ideas that these concepts represent. It blocks the way to reconceive these same concepts in a different way—a way that provides for appreciating Kant's non-traditional mind-dependent view.

Of Rorty's rejection of empiricism and its vocabulary, McDowell argues '[i]t is true that Rorty resists the blandishment of traditional philosophy, but the effect of the framework he assumes is that he can do that only by plugging his ears, like Odysseus sailing past the Sirens' (1996, *p.* 147). In contrast, as we have seen, McDowell takes the time to diagnose and elucidate the dualism that causes anxiety in traditional empiricism in order to show that it is an illusion, and that the dualism problem is 'dissolved' by thinking differently about mind and world. In holding on to a 'minimal empiricism', McDowell is suggesting a 'reconceived empiricism',[11] with the world exerting a *rational* constraint on our thinking.[12] However, with his empiricist presuppositions, Rorty reads McDowell as he reads Kant, with a dualism between intuition and spontaneity (through the dualist metaphysics Kant rejects). So Rorty charges McDowell with *prolonging* the dualism between mind and world, and prolonging traditional empiricism. Indeed Rorty, who sees 'nothing worth saving in empiricism', reads McDowell as successfully *rehabilitating* empiricism (1998, p. 150).[13] Rorty responds to McDowell: 'I, of course, think that McDowell has been seduced by an empiricist siren song and that my deafness to that song is an example of hard won intellectual virtue rather than the result of a perverse act of will' (1998, p. 151). Rorty concludes: 'I simply cannot read Kant as McDowell does' (2000, p. 124).

I finish with another exchange between Rorty and McDowell that illustrates the continuing legacy of Cartesianism and entrenched nature of empiricist presuppositions that I am attempting to 'dislodge' for a more valuable reading of Kant. This is how Rorty describes himself vis-à-vis McDowell:

> Like me, McDowell regards himself as a therapeutic philosopher. He hopes, as I do, to create a 'frame of mind in which we would no longer seem to be faced with problems that call on philosophy to bring subject and object back together again'. We both want to 'achieve an intellectual right to shrug our shoulders at skeptical questions' and to 'disown an obligation to try to answer the characteristic questions of modern philosophy'.
>
> But McDowell believes, as I do not, that 'a real insight is operative in seeming to be faced with that obligation'. So he thinks that empiricism, expelled with a pitchfork, will return again through the window … 'So long as the attractions of empiricism are not explained away', he says, the incoherence of the Myth of the Given will be 'a source of continuing philosophical discomfort.' (Rorty, 1998, p. 142)

So while they both see the errors of traditional empiricism, Rorty rejects it and moves on. McDowell, on the other hand, recognises the truly ingrained nature of the assumptions involved, and sees that ignoring them will not be enough to dislodge them as the 'source of continuing philosophical discomfort'. I have been uncovering and drawing attention to these empiricist assumptions and understandings because they influence interpretations of Kant in education, but they also continue to influence and permeate much educational thought in general. So I believe McDowell is right, despite empiricism being expelled with a pitchfork, it returns through the window (such is its implicit influence). And thus McDowell's work in 'explaining away' its attractions is important to educationalists—to properly understand the problematic inherent in empiricist epistemology and allow easier movement beyond this Cartesian influence.

Looking at Rorty's view of knowledge has shown that despite being a fervent critic of empiricism, he remains party to what McDowell describes as 'the deformations to which the vocabulary of objectivity [truth, etc.] has historically been prone' (2000, p. 121). That is, instead of reflecting on the understanding or conceptions of the concepts, he rejects the concepts themselves. This is how McDowell sees himself vis-à-vis Rorty:

> I applaud Rorty's hostility to the sort of philosophy that sets itself up as providing necessary foundations for intellectual activity in general. But I think he is wrong in supposing that the way to cure people of the impulse towards that sort of philosophy is to proscribe, or at least try to persuade people to drop, the vocabulary of objectivity ... The way to cure ourselves of unwarranted expectations for philosophy is not to drop the vocabulary of objectivity, but to work at understanding the sources of the deformations to which the vocabulary of objectivity has historically been prone. If we could do that, it would enable us to undo the deformations, and see our way clear of the seemingly compulsory philosophical problematic that Rorty wants us to get out from under. This would be an epistemological achievement, in a perfectly intelligible sense of 'epistemological' that does not restrict epistemology to accepting the traditional problematic. It is the deformations, to which Rorty's discussions of truth reveal him to be a party, and not the vocabulary itself, that lead to philosophical trouble. (McDowell, 2000, pp. 120–121)

McDowell's aim in 'undoing the deformations' is to 'see our way clear of the seemingly compulsory philosophical problematic'. The purpose of using McDowell's work in this book is to help 'undo the deformations' of epistemological concepts in order to allow a more friendly reading of Kant's non-traditional view to be appreciated.

Discussion of Rorty's view in this chapter has demonstrated the reach and influence of empiricist presuppositions beyond this tradition, revealing the implicit extent of the Cartesian legacy. Associating Kant with this traditional epistemology, Rorty does not see Kant as an *alternative to* it. Kant's mind-dependent view has been distinguished from Rorty's mind-dependent view by drawing particular attention to objectivity and the idea of worldly content and constraint, for these constitute important areas that are obscured in the typical 'Kantian' picture in education. In Part One, Kant's view has been contrasted with other predominant epistemological approaches in mainstream philosophy. In making explicit traditional empiricist presuppositions and suggesting different ways to think about some familiar concepts, I have aimed at a gradual shift in the way Kant's philosophy can be understood. In Part Two, the reading that has been developed so far is used to respond to interpretations and characterisations of Kant in educational theory. This includes discussing widespread charges of intellectualism, dualism and a detached conception of mind, which allows further elaboration of the more friendly reading being developed.

NOTES

1. This is a substantial difference with Kant, for whom objectivity is in the picture.
2. Davidson does not agree with Rorty's rejection of objectivity and truth. He argues that '[s]entences are understood on condition that one has the concept of objective truth' and '[w]ithout a grasp of the concept of truth, not only language, but thought itself, is impossible'. Rorty disagrees with this (2000, p. 72). (See Davidson's 'Truth Rehabilitated' (2000) and Rorty's response in *Rorty and His Critics* (2000)
3. Both Davidson's and Rorty's views are obviously more philosophically sophisticated than presented here, and there are differences, but they share a coherentist approach to understanding knowledge, which is of relevance below.
4. Wittgenstein contemplates the philosophical question: 'We have a colour system as we have a number system. Do the systems reside in our nature or in the nature of things? How are we to put it?—*Not* in the nature of numbers or colours' (1967, *Zettel*, §357).
5. As previously discussed, mind (thought, intentionality, rational freedom) can be a 'cause' of our actions, for cause can be conceived as autonomous as well as heteronomous.
6. I think the significance of Rorty's behaviourism has been lost in the influence of his philosophy, making his presuppositions explicit reveals this surprising naturalistic thread of his thinking.
7. McDowell is referring to Robert Brandom's 'deontic scorekeeping' approach to meaning in his theory of inferentialism (2011). Rorty largely adopts Brandom's ideas for his arguments against McDowell.
8. The theorists I draw on, including Robert Brandom, read Kant as *opposing* this conception of representationalism, and critique this traditional representationalist way of understanding knowledge and mind.
9. McDowell says that he singles Davidson's work out as a mark of respect (1996).
10. This is particularly relevant to chapters in Part Two where it is discussed further.
11. McDowell suggests 'Sellars might be aiming to rescue a non-traditional empiricism from the wreckage of traditional empiricism, so that he can show us how to be good empiricists.' McDowell's paper is entitled 'Why Sellars's Essay is called "Empiricism and the Philosophy of Mind"' (2012).
12. How far McDowell succeeds in reconceiving empiricism, given its entrenched assumptions, and whether it is worth it, is a topic of debate.

13. Certain readings of McDowell might suggest this. For example, Marie McGinn explains McDowell's 'minimal empiricism' as: '[t]he idea that our thoughts have an empirical content is, he claims, the idea that we take our thoughts to be answerable to something *outside* thought' and '[t]his leads, he claims, to the idea of a *tribunal* that is independent of thought' (2009). This suggests an internalist conception of thought, and reality as independent of it. I do not take this to be McDowell's position, and it illustrates the entrenched nature of the assumptions McDowell is endeavouring to dislodge.

7

A Disappearing World

SHEILA WEBB

Kant attracts a great deal of criticism in the philosophy of education, mainly for dualisms, intellectualism and disembedded conceptions of mind and knowledge—as was illustrated in the Introduction. In Part One I identified a set of presuppositions about mind and world rooted in empiricist epistemology that, I argue, have influenced interpretations that make up the familiar 'Kantian' picture. Alternative understandings of Kant's key terms have been developed through the chapters that suggest a very different picture, one in which Kant's conception of mind, as a capacity for knowledge, is embodied and his subject immersed in the world in which she lives her life. Part Two continues to develop this reading by looking at what theorists of education have said about Kant and the way his view has been interpreted and portrayed. Challenging and discussing various aspects of this allow further articulation of the reading being presented.

In educational theory, Kant tends to be associated either with the foundationalism and representationalism of traditional empiricism[1] or, more frequently, Kant is portrayed as a constructivist.[2] Constructivism, being immensely influential, comes in a wide variety of versions, from psychological and linguistic to social and hermeneutic, the enormous range of constructivist theories and practices in education are evidence of its predominance. Kant's mind-dependent view has been seen as an influence on a central idea of constructivist epistemology: that knowledge is constructed rather than discovered. But there are many ways to understand this, and Kant's influence on constructivist thinking when it comes to theories of knowledge ranges from Jean Piaget's genetic epistemology to some radical

Interpreting Kant for Education: Dissolving Dualisms and Embodying Mind, First Edition. Sheila Webb.
Chapters and editorial organization © 2022 Philosophy of Education Society of Great Britain.
Published 2022 by John Wiley & Sons Ltd.

constructivist and relativist theories. What is significant is that the dualist presuppositions about mind and world discussed in Part One are implicit in characterisations of Kant in educational theory that form the (frequently criticised) 'Kantian' picture. I have argued that Kant's philosophy takes on a very different shape if we do not ascribe these assumptions to him, but that the tendency has been to read Kant through this implicit (Cartesian) dualism. Looking at what educational theorists actually say about Kant shows this tendency and allows a contrast to be made with readings from exegesis and contemporary Kantian commentary.

Many educationalists who refer to Kant do so as a negative contrast to their own theory or position, some merely tap into the familiar picture, and many make merely cursory comments; but even of those who appropriate Kant in defence of their position, discussion is often on a surface level. This makes it hard to engage with them, particularly at the metaphysical level necessary for comparison of readings. Nevertheless, I attempt to make explicit what is implicit in depictions of Kant, identifying presuppositions and discussing their effect on interpretation. While many references to Kant in educational theory are critical, this chapter starts with some theorists who see Kant in a more friendly light and draw on his philosophy for their constructivist positions. As with other theorists in Part Two, I do not engage with their theories or take a position on their arguments, rather I am interested in the way they understand Kant and present his view. In this chapter, attention is drawn to just what is mind-dependent on Kant's view, with a focus on conceptions of experience and the objectivity that becomes obscured.

I start with Jean Piaget's enormously influential cognitive approach to knowledge development. Piaget draws on Kant for his theory of cognitive development in various ways. In contrast to the behaviourist and empiricist approaches of his time, Piaget adopts Kant's Copernican insight that knowledge does not emerge from sensory experience alone, but relies on what Piaget calls a schema or mental model of the world. He famously describes a process of assimilation and accommodation, in which concepts are not innate but constructed by the subject in an active process of qualitative development in stages, over time (1928, 1936). Piaget takes from Kant the idea that concepts and categories are a source of apprehension of the world, as opposed to a passive mind that simply receives impressions. Piaget writes of empiricism that it: 'tends to consider experience as imposing itself without the subject's having to organize it, that is to say, as impressing itself directly on the organism without activity of the subject being necessary to constitute it' (Piaget, 1955, p. 362). Piaget's influence on educational thinking has been vast, and it includes the take-up of his ideas in Lawrence Kohlberg's also influential stage theory of moral development (1973, 1981).

But Piaget's mind-dependent theory differs from Kant in significant respects.[3] For instance, in conceptions of experience, as the above quote suggests, the 'activity of the subject' is necessary for 'organising' experience—which forms part of the typical 'Kantian' picture. However, as I will argue, an overemphasis on the activity of mind conceals the way concepts can be understood as passively and unreflectively exercised in experience.[4] Moreover, Piaget has a genetic epistemology (1971). He sees the process of the child constructing a mental model of the world through experience as occurring due to biological maturation. His stages of cognitive development are the same for all; children construct a view of reality for each stage, with one stage having to be accomplished before the next can occur. This biological conception of the adaption of knowledge—his genetic epistemology—does not account for individual differences or cultural and social affects. His critics, including Vygotsky (1934, 1987, 1998), Bruner (1973, 1986, 1990, 1996) and Donaldson (1978), famously point to this lack of appreciation of the effects of social and cultural backgrounds, and also critique his stage theory, arguing instead that development is a continuous process. A universal or ahistorical rationality is similarly something Kant is often charged with. I argue that in the sense that a capacity for self-conscious rationality is part of our nature as humans, then it can be said to be universal, but what provides the *content* of rationality depends on the particular social and cultural life the subject leads. As previously discussed, Kant is interested in what it is for representations to have objective content; to repeat Brandom, 'Kant wants to know what it is for mental states to *be*, or to *appear to us* to be, to function for us as, *representings* of represented objects' (2006, p. 2). In this respect, the rationality—the self-consciousness—that is the focus of Kant's investigation is common to humans; it is a general account. However, the particular content (the particular knowledge, concepts, beliefs, memories, feelings etc.) that constitutes our individual rationality will depend on where and when we live our lives, and, that is to say, rationality is culturally and historically shaped, and subject to continuous change. And education (*Bildung*) is integral to this. Andrea Kern writes:

> In the case of a self-conscious form of life its concept is not that of an individual whose capacities have reached the stage of biological maturity, but the concept of an individual whose self-consciousness has acquired a conceptual character, partly by being formed by another individual's self-consciousness made manifest to her. (2020, p. 286)

For Kant, a child's rationality, at any stage, will reflect the social and cultural norms of her community and times—for it depends on her particular experience—and this is different to Piaget's 'ahistorical' conception of cognitive development.

Furthermore, while Piaget has a mind-dependent theory, his genetic epistemology is cased within biological and scientific-naturalist terms that do not adequately capture self-consciousness in Kant's sense. The *spontaneity* of mind (rational freedom) is lacking in the sort of explanations Piaget makes, for instance he writes:

> Accommodation of mental structures to reality implies the existence of assimilatory schemata apart from which any structure would be impossible. Inversely, the formation of schemata through assimilation entails the utilization of external realities to which the former must accommodate, however crudely. Assimilation and accommodation are therefore the two poles of an interaction between the organism and the environment, which is the condition for all biological and intellectual operation. (1955, pp. 352–353)

These scientific-naturalist resources do not allow us to think *beyond* what is given in experience (to account for autonomy, judgement, creativity, imagination—or self-consciousness). In many respects, Piaget's view of cognitive development is quite far from Kant's philosophy.

Jerome Bruner's constructivist approach to knowledge and cognitive development has also been extremely influential (1973, 1983, 1986, 1990, 1996). It is much closer to Kant in many ways, and includes utilising the idea of *a priori* knowledge. However, *a priori* knowledge has come to have a contemporary conventional meaning, as knowledge that is known independently of any kind of experience; it is logically deduced rather than derived from observation or experience—for instance, 'bachelors are unmarried men'. But as with Kant's other terms, we can understand *a priori* in different ways, including the more direct Latin translation 'from earlier' or 'from before'. In this more straightforward way, we can understand a subject's *a priori* knowledge simply as the knowledge she has already acquired, knowledge she has so far learnt about the world (through interacting with others). It is this *a priori* knowledge (which is constantly changing) that is passively drawn into play in our ongoing contact with the world—in experience. Bruner takes this Copernican insight into his theory of cognitive development, emphasising the importance of the child's prior knowledge in new learning situations. He sees learning as an active process through interaction with others ('scaffolding'), in which children acquire new concepts based on their current knowledge, which continuously develops. While Bruner's view has much in common with the reading of Kant that I am developing,[5] rather than engaging with this to pick out implicit Kantian ideas, it is more helpful to turn to other constructivist theorists who explicitly refer to Kant in their appropriations of him, in order to more clearly contrast interpretations.

Ernst von Glasersfeld is a constructivist theorist, prominent in mathematics education, who draws on Kant for his influential 'radical constructivist' view of knowledge. He puts forward a view similar to that of Rorty, for like Rorty he also rejects traditional epistemology entirely, and sets up his own constructivist theory in opposition to it. The following is illustrative of his position:

> For constructivists, the word knowledge refers to a commodity that is radically different from the objective representation of an observer-independent world which the mainstream of the Western philosophical tradition has been looking for. Instead, knowledge refers to conceptual structures which, given the range of present experience within their tradition of thought and language, epistemic agents consider viable. This constitutes a drastic modification of the relation between the cognitive structures we build up and that 'real' world which we are inclined to assume as 'existing' beyond our perceptual interface. Instead of the illusory relation of 'representation', one has to find a way of relating knowledge to reality that does not imply anything like a match or correspondence. (Von Glasersfeld, 1989, p. 124)

Von Glasersfeld rejects empiricism but (leaves a dualism in place as he) continues to find a way of relating knowledge to a reality that we can only 'assume as existing'. Elsewhere he wonders, 'how cognitive structures or knowledge might be related to an ontological world beyond our experience' (1984, p. 24). (As McDowell warns, empiricism is expelled with a pitchfork but creeps in through the window.) Von Glasersfeld also rejects the concept of truth:

> To claim that one's theory of knowing is true, in the traditional sense of representing a state or feature of an experiencer-independent world, would be perjury for a radical constructivist. One of the central points of the theory is precisely that this kind of "truth" can never be claimed for the knowledge (or any piece of it) that human reason produces. (Von Glasersfeld, 1990, p. 127)

In dismissing traditional empiricism, von Glasersfeld rejects its key vocabulary. He comes to radical constructivism, he says, through the realisation 'that knowledge, i.e., what is "known," cannot be the result of a passive receiving but originates as the product of an active subject's activity' (1984, p. 25, see also 1995b). He argues that constructivism 'does not purport to describe characteristics of the world but proposes a way of thinking that may be useful in dealing with a good many problems that face us today' (2001, p. 31). He uses 'viability' in place of truth. We cannot *know* reality, von Glasersfeld claims: 'Given that there is nothing but a hypothetical connection between our experience and what philosophers call ontological reality, that reality has for us the status of a black box' (1995a, p. 157). The world is inaccessible, a black box. And following many postmodernists, von Glasersfeld considers his view to be *post*-epistemological.

We can see from this that for von Glasersfeld, like Rorty, central concepts of knowledge—objectivity, truth, reality, epistemology—are understood with empiricist meanings and rejected. That is to say, these concepts are understood with meanings restricted to those within empiricism and—recognising the problematic inherent in this way of thinking about knowledge—are dropped from explanations. But there are alternatives to dropping this vocabulary. For instance, we could agree with McDowell, in his response to Rorty in the previous chapter, in holding that the 'cure' to this problematic philosophy is not to drop the vocabulary, but 'to work at understanding the sources of the deformations to which the vocabulary' has 'historically been prone' (2000, p. 121). If we can 'undo the deformations', to repeat McDowell, '[t]his would be an epistemological achievement, in a perfectly intelligible sense of "epistemological" that does not restrict epistemology to accepting the traditional problematic. It is the deformations, to which Rorty's discussions of truth reveal him to be a party, and not the vocabulary itself, that lead to philosophical trouble' (*ibid.*). And as shown in Part One, McDowell uses Kant's resources to 'exorcise' the dualism anxiety and show a way of thinking that does not give rise to the traditional problematic.

This is not to challenge von Glasersfeld's radical constructivism, but to question the appropriation of Kant for his view. For he reads Kant as saying, 'no truths about a "real" world could be derived from experience', and unknown to Kant, 'Giambattesta Vico had come to a very similar conclusion in 1710. The human mind can know only what the human mind has made' (1990, p. 3). Von Glasersfeld also writes of 'Kant's thesis that our mind does not derive laws from nature, but imposes them on it' (1984, p. 73). This raises several interpretive points (considered as we proceed). That mind 'imposes' laws or meaning onto nature fits with and reinforces the widespread 'Kantian' picture. This can be contrasted with the reading being presented, on which meaning is not 'imposed' by individual minds but is already there in the world (the 'humanised' or 'ideal' world), there to be encountered *in* experience (by those with the relevant capacities). As our concepts and knowledge become continuously more fine-tuned—developed through participating in the everyday activities of our community—so more of the world comes into view. This is to say we become better at discerning what is already there in the world, which contrasts with 'imposing' or 'mind making nature' pictures.

Von Glasersfeld rejects the idea that a true picture of the objective world is possible. He writes of Kant, that by 'considering space and time aspects of our way of experiencing, he shifted them out of reality into the realm of the phenomenal', and this means 'we can no longer be sure that there actually exists an object such as we experience it', which, he continues, 'undermines any representation of objective structure in the real world' (1984, pp. 6–7). The 'phenomenal' and 'appearances' are understood as something mental and not part of the 'real' world. Von Glasersfeld argues 'one can no longer maintain that the cognizing activity should or could produce a true representation of an objective world' (1990, p. 3). He again refers to Kant's space and time:

> The final demolition of realism was brought about when Kant suggested that the concepts of space and time were the necessary forms of human experience, rather than characteristics of the universe. This meant that we cannot even imagine what the structure of the real world might be like, because whatever we call structure is necessarily an arrangement in space, time, or both. (p. 2)

Space and time are understood as forms 'imposed' by reason (1995a, p. 40); we come to this below but first continue with von Glasersfeld's claim that we cannot imagine what the structure of the real world might be like, for, as he says above, the world is a 'black box' and unknowable (p. 175). That the world is unknowable contrasts with established readings of Kant on which the structure of the real world *is* knowable. Von Glasersfeld is ascribing to Kant a wild or 'unconstrained' subjectivism, which, as we will see in the next chapters, is frequently the case in educational interpretations. This subjectivist reading also stems from understandings of Kant's things in themselves; of this, von Glasersfeld writes:

> Realists may be tempted to read it as indicating that Kant's theory requires the existence of 'real things' in the sense of actual 'things-in-themselves'. I think, this would be the wrong reading. Rather, Kant speaks here of a need that arises in 'practical life', especially when we want to coordinate our actions with those of others. The thing-in-itself, Kant reiterates in many places (e.g., 1787; pp. 591, 610), is intended as a 'product of thought' (*Gedankending*) that serves as a 'heuristic fiction' (1787, p. 799). To my mind, this covers any conception of an ontic reality that is structured in space and time. The fiction of such a reality, however, becomes necessary for the purpose of social interaction. (1995a, p. 40)

Reality is read here as a 'thing-in-itself', and thus a product of thought, a fiction. This exemplifies the tendency discussed in Part One to interpret things in themselves as ordinary empirical objects, and with things in themselves being unknowable, the ordinary empirical world is interpreted to be unknowable.

On such a reading, an implicit dualism can be detected, for everything is located on one side of a mind–world divide—that is, it is all on the mind side, as discussed in the previous chapter with coherentism. A consequence here is that the familiar empirical world disappears from interpretation and accounts of knowledge. Von Glasersfeld writes:

> From my perspective, those who merely speak of the construction of knowledge, but do not explicitly give up the notion that our conceptual constructions can or should in some way represent an independent, 'objective' reality, are still caught up in the traditional theory of knowledge that is defenceless against the sceptics' arguments. (1991, p. 5)

It seems that in giving up traditional empiricism (for some right reasons), the obvious alternative is a conception of knowledge as constructed by the mind. Talbot J. Taylor encapsulates the choice in asking '[d]o people call certain things "boulders" and others "pebbles" because of some natural, immutable connection between those words and their *nominata*? If so, the laws of logic originate in nature itself and are universal. Or does the source of their appellations lie in human convention?' (2001, p. 86). Talbot's question presupposes two choices: the source of knowledge is either 'in nature itself' or 'in human convention' (and he advocates the latter), reflecting the prevalence of empiricist and constructivist metaphysics. In McDowell's terms, this is a choice between an unacceptable 'Myth of the Given' and a free-floating coherentism out of touch with reality, and illustrates his claim that we are 'prone to fall into an intolerable oscillation' recoiling from one way of thinking into the other (1996, p. 23). But as has been discussed, these alternatives do not exhaust the possibilities, and Kant and his German Idealist successors provide some. McDowell says '[t]he idea of a structure that must be found in any intelligible conceptual scheme need not involve picturing the scheme as one side of a scheme-world dualism' (p. 158); what we need is to acknowledge that in experience 'receptivity does not make an even notionally separable contribution to the co-operation' with spontaneity (p. 9). An appreciation of receptivity (and sensibility and intuition) not as empiricist sense data but as providing content makes for conceptions of perception and experience that are objective.

Differences in interpretation are revealed by taking a closer look at the way experience, as our contact with the world, is conceived. Experience for von Glasersfeld 'is what the thinking subject coordinates (constructs) out of elements of the manifold' (1995a, p. 41) and the manifold 'is the raw material, the stuff on which constructive perception and reason can operate. William James called it, "one big blooming buzzing confusion"' (p. 40). This is similar to David Carr's interpretation mentioned in Chapter One: the 'active imposition of meaning-constitutive rules and principles on the brute data of sensory perception' (2003, p. 100).[6] With the world unknowable, mind does all the work, actively organising, structuring and imposing rules or meaning. In contrast, on the reading being presented the world is already meaningful, and this meaning is 'disclosed' in experience, as our *a priori* knowledge (what we have so far learnt) is passively exercised. McDowell writes of this:

> our relation to the world, including our perceptual relation to it, is pervasively shaped by our conceptual mindedness ... If an experience is world-disclosing, any aspect of its content hangs together with other aspects of its content in a unity of the sort Kant identifies as categorial. And Kant connects the categorial unity that provides for world-disclosingness with the transcendental unity of apperception. Experiences in which the world is disclosed are apperceptive. Perception discloses the world only to a subject capable of the 'I think' that expresses apperception. (2009b, p. 318)

This is to say that once we have acquired concepts (categorial unity), even rudimentary ones (enough of a grasp to recognise something), then the world is disclosed in apperception, usually referred to simply as perception.[7] As a child develops the ability to intuit and jointly refer to things with others, so she acquires and expands her conceptual repertoire—through which the world is disclosed. This does not mean that disclosure is clear and precise, or the world is ever fully in view—perception and experience are mostly unreflective and at any time our concepts are partial, opaque and underdetermined, and subject to error. Nevertheless, that the shared and meaningful world is disclosed in perception can be contrasted with interpretation of mind actively ordering, constructing and imposing meaning onto an 'unknowable' and 'merely assumed' world. These are quite different conceptions of experience—and mind and world.

With the world unknowable, it disappears from explanation and mind becomes all there is, making for a subjective idealism along the lines of 'mind makes nature'—a picture 'of what in Kantian terms, would be concepts without intuition, concepts without responsiveness to anything other than themselves in a self-contained dance of inferences' as Simon Blackburn puts it (2010, p. 265).[8] Conceiving the world as unknowable prompts von Glasersfeld to write that 'no truths about a "real" world could be derived from experience' (1990, p. 3). But this does not sit well with what Kant actually says, for instance his first sentence (in his first Critique) is: 'There can be no doubt that all our knowledge begins with experience ... [W]ith experience all our knowledge begins' (B1). While Kant has no doubt that knowledge of the world is derived from experience, his insight is that this is not the *only* source, and that some elements of our experience have to be understood in another way. But in holding that spontaneity is also a source of knowledge, he does not mean knowledge is derived from spontaneity alone, as suggested by 'mind making nature' interpretations. These are one-sided characterisations of Kant's view. As Kant himself insists '[t]o neither of these powers may a preference be given over the other. Without sensibility no object would be given to us' and 'thoughts without content are empty' (B75). Understanding sensibility, intuition and receptivity as blind sense data loses the worldly content of thought. 'Kant asserts that thought depends on intuition. We must receive the object about which we think, if we are to think something as opposed to nothing', Rödl writes (2005, p. 91). Appreciating the *unity* of the capacities *in* experience (apperception), we can say that experience comes already structured, already meaningful, and this is immanent and mostly passive—which again is different to experience interpreted as an active process of 'reason operating on a buzzing confusion'.[9]

These different readings also involve distinct understandings of space and time. Von Glasersfeld writes that 'space and time are the fundamental forms which human reason imposes on all experience' (1995a, p. 40), and that 'the processing of the raw material in Kant's system is governed *automatically* by space and time' (1984, p. 24). Furthermore, (to repeat) 'Kant suggested that the concepts of space and time were the necessary forms of human experience, rather than characteristics of the universe. This meant that we cannot even imagine what the structure of the real world might be like' (1990, p. 2). Space and time are located on the subjective side of a divide with reality, the side that 'governs the processing of raw material' and which imposes them on all experience. Again, the roles of intuition and receptivity are neglected, losing the objective world. It is right to say that Kant holds that we cannot perceive time itself, 'Time is not an empirical concept that has been derived from any experience' (B46).

However, while we do not perceive time itself, we learn to refer to things (temporally and spatially) that *are* in the world and that we do (or did) perceive. That is, we learn deictic reference through joint intuiting, which develops our practical capacity to refer to changes of aspect and time—for instance using 'was doing/is doing' and 'here or there', 'now or then'. We might say, 'Maya is reading' and later 'Maya was reading', which captures a time difference. Similarly with Kant's concept of space: '[s]pace is not an empirical concept' (B38). Rather space and time are forms of intuition; but in contrast to something internal and 'imposed' by reason, intuition can be read as objective and factive (as argued in Part One). Like receptivity and sensibility, intuition 'situates' us—roots us in the world that we jointly perceive with others.

Pirmin Stekeler-Weithofer explains that Kant's *Transcendental Aesthetic* and *Transcendental Analytic* together provide an account of the temporal and spatial order of things. Intuition acts as a reference point for joint attention and joint perception, and space and time are, he explains, 'names for this joint perspective on things, such that the *unity of space* and the *unity of time* mirror the *jointness of reference*' (2010a, p. 7). As we learn to refer to jointly perceived objects, we learn the language to talk about where they are and when we saw them, and how 'the chronological and spatial order of things starting with our present perceptual field, relate to logical forms in statements about objective things' (p. 20). There is an objectivity and situational specificity inherent in this. An appreciation of being in the world, the humanised world, helps explain Kant's space and time as forms of intuition, for intuition presents things 'as they appear in the world in such a way that we can *jointly* refer to them, by mediation of our senses' (Stekeler-Weithofer, 2010c). As young children learn from others how to refer to what they jointly intuit, they grasp what is captured by a word or concept, what normally falls under it and what does not—its categorial unity—and over time become better at discerning what there is, and using the language in different contexts. And this process is continuous; from everyday chat to formal learning, our understanding of the world is continuously developed (changed, reinforced, radically altered) through talking about things we jointly perceive. This is to argue that intuition roots us in the particular and connects us with objects and others, and that this objectivity is missing in 'imposition' interpretations that make up the typical 'Kantian' picture.

Subjectivist readings are right in acknowledging that 'the world in which we live, move, and have our being (by which I mean the phenomenal natural and social world of our ordinary human existence) is fundamentally dependent on *our* minded nature, and not the converse', as Robert Hanna puts it (2016b, p. 3). However, it matters how this mind-dependence is understood. As previously argued, Kant's Copernican insight is typically read as a subjectivist 'mind-makes-nature' view—but then the world disappears from explanation. That things in themselves are unknowable is interpreted to mean that the ordinary empirical world is unknowable. But as argued in Part One, things 'in themselves' and things 'as they appear' can be understood as the same things, the same things but under different descriptions. Kant makes a *logical*, a conceptual, distinction between things in themselves and appearances (for the purposes of explanation) and not an *ontological* distinction positing two separate domains. For instance, in saying that we cannot know things in themselves, Kant critiques mind-independent accounts of knowledge, for he is sceptical of the idea that knowledge of reality is possible *independently* of thought or experience. This is not the same as being sceptical about knowledge of reality, or its existence—which he is not. 'Since Kant thinks the world of things in themselves is totally outside our cognitive range he is a skeptic about those transcendent claims', Graham Bird writes, but he is not a sceptic about 'the immanent world of our ordinary experience' (2006, p. 252). For Kant, what is mind-dependent is the *formal* constitution of things—the humanised or ideal world—not the *existence* of the world. Bird's response to Barry Stroud brings out the difference and reflects some of the discussion in Part One of this book about the search for an 'absolute' conception of reality, 'untainted' by subjectivity. 'The absolute conception is of a reality pruned of the peculiarities of any observer, and identifies what is independently "there anyway"' (*ibid.*). For Stroud, Kant's human standpoint in a world that we do not know independently of thought and experience makes it relativist. In his *The Quest for Reality*, Stroud writes of Kant:

> Accepting his theory presumably means believing that the sun and planets and mountains on earth and everything else that has been here so much longer than we have, are nonetheless in some way or other dependent on the possibility of our human thought and experience. (2000, p. 196)

Bird points out that Stroud fails to notice 'that the dependence is claimed to be not material but purely formal' (2006, p. 353)—not referring to the existence of planets and mountains, but their ideality (as we can say). Bird explains:

> What depends on our thought and experience is not the presence of planets or mountains but the recognition of them as things of a certain kind embedded in a formal spatiotemporal-causal system. Their material existence is patently neither formal nor a priori, but their conception as "substances" in that spatiotemporal-causal system *is* for Kant dependent on formal a priori aspects of our thought and intuition. The distinction between *natura materialiter* and *natura formaliter* at B163-65 is designed to make this clear. (*ibid.*)

Kant distinguishes between form and matter; what is mind-dependent is the meaningful world not in respect of its existence but its objectively-existing ideal properties that make up our familiar empirical world—its 'formal' constitution. This also relates back to discussion in Part One about conceptions of the world. Widespread interpretations in educational theory tend to, like Stroud, read into Kant an 'unconstrained' subjectivism or idealism that takes the material existence of things to be dependent on mind; hence von Glasersfeld's 'real' world that we can never know but have to 'assume as existing'.

With a subjectivism 'unconstrained' by the world, it is an easy step to relativist positions. David Elkind writes of Kant's influence on Piaget's work:

> [T]he categories change with age. This idea adds a developmental dimension to the Kantian version of the construction of knowledge. As their mental operations develop, children are required to reconstruct the realities they constructed at the previous developmental level. In effect, a child creates and re-creates reality out of his or her experiences with the environment. (1989, p. 115)

It depends, of course, on how this is understood, but the idea of children creating different realities and different knowledge, and sometimes truth, can be found in other theories,[10] and radical relativism can follow from this way of thinking. It is a worry expressed over the years by many writing about education, including Ian Hacking (1999), Mary Warnock (2006), Derek Meyer (2008) and Michael Young (2008). Citing Kant in support of relativist positions would be a mistake, for as previously argued, Kant insists that he does not intend his work to be read in this way. Under his *Refutation of Idealism*, Kant writes: 'Idealism—meaning thereby material idealism—is the theory which declares the existence of objects in space outside us either to be merely doubtful and indemonstrable or to be false and impossible' (B274). The former, he says, is the 'problematic' idealism of Descartes, and the latter the 'dogmatic' idealism of Berkeley (*ibid.*). Kant continues his point:

> Idealism assumed that the only immediate experience is inner experience, and that from it we can only *infer* outer things—and this, moreover, only in an untrustworthy manner, … the cause of the representations, which we ascribe, perhaps falsely, to outer things, may lie in ourselves. (Kant, B276)

This reflects views such as von Glasersfeld's, according to which we cannot imagine what the structure of the real world might be like. For Kant, this falls under the 'problematic' idealism of Descartes (with its inherent dualism). Kant refutes such views because they do not allow us 'any properly demonstrable distinction between truth and dreams' (B519). To stress this, Kant reaffirms his refutation again in the preface to the second edition of his first *Critique*:

> it still remains a scandal to philosophy and to human reason in general that the existence of things outside us (from which we derive the whole material of knowledge, even for our inner sense) must be accepted merely on *faith*, and that if anyone thinks good to doubt their existence, we are unable to counter his doubts by any satisfactory proof. (Bxl, footnote)

Kant holds that thought is only possible through its relation with real things; as Rödl says, 'thought is nothing at all unless it refers back to the sensory and temporal reality of human life' (2012, p. 1). Objectivity differentiates Kant's version of idealism, on which we can know the real world, from 'problematic' and 'dogmatic' versions.

David Jardine is another educationalist who reads Kant as a constructivist, more precisely as a major influence on contemporary constructivism, and while he is cautionary about constructivism, it is his interpretation of Kant that is of interest here. Jardine writes:

> The first telling theme for educators in Immanuel Kant's epoch-making *Critique of Pure Reason* is the conceiving of

knowledge as an active, constructive, orderly and ordering, demand made upon things. 'To know', henceforth, is no longer understood as merely and simply and passively receiving information from an object (think of all those old 'filling an empty vessel' images of education, or ones of 'writing on a blank tablet', a *tabula rasa*)... Rather, 'to know' is to demand that the world suffer our acts of knowing: to know is 'to impose structure', 'to (give) order(s)', 'to demand', 'to determine', 'to make', 'to produce', 'to create'— in popular contemporary educational parlance, 'to construct'. (2005, p. 40)

Jardine exemplifies the tendency to overplay the activity of mind, which becomes reified as it orders, determines, makes and imposes. This is not idiosyncratic interpretation, as will be seen in the chapters that follow, it forms (and reinforces) the 'Kantian' picture that can be widely found (hence criticisms of intellectualism). Jardine also writes:

According to Kant, human reason, by its very nature, puts things together in clearly definable ways. It is an actively organizing, ordering, constructive human faculty, not a passive one. It is, as Kant defined it, a synthesizing faculty that, in the act of knowing something in the world, actively constructs orderliness out of the chaos of experience in accordance with human reason's own structure, forms and categories. (2006, p. 23)

The active nature of reason is overemphasised when contrasted to more mainstream interpretations, losing sight of (indeed misunderstanding) intuition and receptivity—and thus losing objectivity. Talk of a synthesising faculty that 'actively constructs orderliness out of the chaos of experience' implies that this is a conscious act. However, for Kant synthesis is an *unconscious* act. 'Synthesis in general', Kant writes, is 'a blind but indispensable function of the soul, without which we should have no knowledge whatsoever, but of which we are scarcely ever conscious' (B103). Like many, Jardine conceives of experience as chaotic, something that requires active ordering and synthesising,[11] but on the readings I draw on, experience for Kant comes already structured and is mostly passive. As McDowell argues, 'it does not take cognitive work for objects to come into view for us. "Mere synthesis" just happens; it is not our doing, unlike making judgments, deciding what to think about something' (2009a, p. 35). Interpretations in educational theory do not make the distinction between the passive aspects of experience (and synthesis), which accounts for much of our ongoing unreflective responses to the world, and the active nature of, say, discursive activity and making judgements (something we return to in the next chapter).

Dualist presuppositions about mind and world can be identified with a closer look at Jardine's interpretation. In the following passage, he quotes Kant twice, and he comments in between:

"The order and regularity in [what] we call *nature*, we ourselves introduce. We could never find [such orderliness and regularity] ... had not we ourselves, or the nature of our mind, originally set them there. (Kant, 1964, p. 147)"

This is starting to sound rather bizarre – the orderliness of the world is our construction? Again:

"[H]uman understanding is itself the lawgiver of nature. Save through it, nature, that is, synthetic unity of the manifold of [perceptual] appearances according to rules [imposed by reason itself], should not exist at all. (Kant, 1964, p. 148)" (Jardine, 2006, p. 13)

Note the *addition* to Kant's second text referring to rules: '[imposed by reason itself]'". This 'imposition' of rules by reason suggests an internalist conception of reason that is doing the 'imposing', and imposed onto a presupposed disenchanted/unknowable nature. Again, objectivity is lost in such subjectivist interpretations. Kant's Copernican insight that objects conform to our knowledge takes on a different shape if we conceive of the world as already meaningful. A translation by Norman Kemp Smith of the same Kantian text that Jardine quotes above provides a different picture:[12]

Even physics therefore, owes the beneficent revolution in its point of view entirely to the happy thought, that while reason must seek in nature, not fictitiously ascribe to it, whatever as not being knowable through reason's own resources has to be learnt, if learnt at all, only from nature, it must adopt as its guide, in so seeking, that which it has itself put into nature. (Bxiv)

This implies that reason is capable of learning *from* nature, *not* fictitiously ascribing something to it (or imposing on it), rather being guided by what is already there: the world as a prior embodiment of mindedness. As discussed in Chapter Four, meaning is 'put into nature' and maintained through participation in our (historically evolved) cultural and social activities and practices. 'Objects are *given* to us by means of sensibility', Kant writes, 'because in no other way can an object be given to us' (B33). Objects being given is different to being imposed.

This difference matters. It matters that meaning is already objectively there in the world and not imposed by individuals because a world written through with meaning is something against which individual judgements can be true or false. Our judgements are 'answerable' to the world not as an alien authority or as foundations external to thought, but answerable to the meaning that we have already 'put into' the world, and which provide objectivity. Kern explains that the task 'Kant sets himself in the course of his inquiry' is 'to give an account of what a receptive capacity for knowledge is by showing us how we have to conceive of it' in order to understand the objectivity of thought and perception (2017, p. 240). Objectivity is lost in interpretations that put all the emphasis on the activity of mind—we are reminded of a free-floating coherentism without 'constraint'. For example, Jardine writes of a pine tree he sees from his window:

> The patterns 'of' that pine-tree (I now parenthesize 'of' since the precise nature of this ascription to the tree is now in limbo) are, somehow or other, 'human constructs'. In knowing the pine tree, we don't know the pine tree and its patterns, but only the outcomes of what we make of it. (2005, p. 41)

I argue that on Kant's view we can and do know the pine tree and its patterns. Of interpretations such as Jardine's, I quote McDowell again:

> It can seem that we are retaining a role for spontaneity but refusing to acknowledge any role for receptivity and that is intolerable. If our activity in empirical thought and judgement is to be recognizable at all, there must be external constraint. There must be a role for receptivity as well as spontaneity, for sensibility as well as understanding. (1996, p. 9)

Not recognising the 'constraining' role of sensibility and receptivity makes for one-sided 'mind-makes-nature' interpretations that lack objectivity, typical of the widespread 'Kantian' picture in education.

To expand on external 'constraint' and why it matters, I return again to what is mind-dependent on Kant's mind-dependent view. Attributing to Kant an unconstrained subjectivism leads Jardine, for instance, to say: 'We become like little gods, the world (as far as we know) becomes our creation and we become its orderwielding centre' (2005, p. 41). This puts too much weight on the minds of individuals, creating the world, and although he adds 'as far as we know', this does nothing to capture the objectivity and 'rational' constraint of the (already meaningful) world, as discussed in Part One. Kant carefully distinguishes his account of human *finite* knowledge from the idea of *infinite* knowledge precisely to emphasise the dependence of our (empirical) knowledge on objects in the world. Kern writes of the difference:

> As Kant characterizes it, infinite knowledge, if there is such a thing, would be infinite in the sense that the knowing subject would not be answerable to the objects of knowledge but instead would bring them into being through having knowledge of them. Infinite knowledge would not be bound by the object of its knowledge but would be the source of what it knows. For this reason, Kant refers to infinite knowledge as 'originary' in order to indicate that it is 'not dependent on the existence of the object' but instead brings about 'even the existence of the object'. (2017, p. 16)

With human finite knowledge of empirical objects,[13] the knowing subject is 'bound' by, or 'answerable' to, these objects for correctness. Jardine's interpretation misses the 'worldly constraints', the objectivity, inherent in Kant's conceptions of intuition and receptivity. This is a significant difference in interpretations.

While judgement is central to Kant's view, we need the idea of an already humanised world that acts as a constraint, which, as discussed, arises from the multitude of cultural norms and practices that are part and parcel of the socialised world we live in. Judgements, Kern writes, 'are precisely those acts of the intellect whose defining feature it is that they can be true or false' (2017, p. 17), and these have objective content 'in the sense that their truth is dependent on how things are in the world' (p. 55). Human knowledge, she argues, belongs to intellects that are 'as Kant puts it, "discursive" in character', for only 'a discursive intellect can perform acts that one can rightly say are guided by the world as the standard of their truth—i.e., acts of judgment. Creatures that lack the capacity for making judgments about the world lack the capacity to relate to the world as the standard of truth of their acts' (p. 22). This refers back to McDowell's argument against Rorty's social agreement view of knowledge: the claim 'cold fusion has not occurred' is justified, McDowell argues, not by our peers agreeing it, but by whether or not it has occurred. A judgement is a 'stance that is *correctly* or *incorrectly* adopted according to whether or not things are indeed thus and so' (1996, p. xii). The fallibility of our capacity for knowledge means we can be mistaken (we take responsibility), but it is objects themselves that act as a 'norm' or 'standard' for correctness. As Graham Bird says, 'appearances themselves provide the required objectivity' (2006, p. 2). Subjectivist readings of Kant overlook the objective role played by the world as a 'standard' that determines the correctness or truth of judgments. With the world as unknowable, it disappears from explanations and interpretations of Kant.

Again, Kant's conceptions of receptivity and sensibility need not be seen as empiricism's sense data but as providing meaningful content, that a subject can endorse as true. And the world need not be seen as an alien authority (or disenchanted or unknowable) for while there is no mind-independent reality that acts as 'a warrant' on our thinking, the humanised world *can* be seen as something against which our individual claims, judgements and actions are assessed. To capture this, McDowell talks of 'the space of reasons' that he aligns with Kant's 'realm of freedom', and Rödl talks of a 'normative background', in which individual actions and claims take place and are judged. As Kern points out, however, judgement can be misunderstood, and is sometimes interpreted:

> as though it meant to claim that judgment is at our command, that it is within the sphere of our will … [W]e are by no means saying that one can judge and believe whatever one wants. Quite the contrary. We are instead saying that judgments and beliefs are acts that intrinsically fall within the space of truth and falsity, because they consist in an answer to the question of truth. The concept of decision here is meant to explain what we mean when we say that judging is 'answering' or 'taking a stance on' the question of truth. (2017, p. 21, footnote)

The 'answering' to the question of truth, with the meaningful world being a normative background against which our judgements are assessed, lacks visibility in (and stands in stark contrast to) subjectivist interpretations such as those above, that characterise mind as organising, constructing and imposing rules and meaning onto an unknowable reality.

That this 'normative background' is something 'put there' by *us* (evolved over time and continuously changing through ongoing practices) should not undermine our confidence 'that we have reality more or less within our cognitive grasp', as McDowell says (1998a, p. 128). At any one time it acts as a standard or norm of correctness for empirical thought and judgement. This worldly constraint—the worldly content provided by intuition (and receptivity and sensibility)—is missing in portrayals of Kant in education. With an overemphasis on the activity of mind, the world disappears. This chapter has drawn attention to this objectivity in Kant's version of idealism as found in contemporary readings, in order to distinguish it from subjective readings such as those considered above. Kant has also been distinguished from Piaget's genetic epistemology with its more naturalist explanations. In the next chapter, attention continues to be given to conceptions of experience, in order to further differentiate Kant from the 'Kantian' Kant, and to address criticisms of intellectualism.

NOTES

1. For instance, Wilfred Carr (1995, 2006), as well as many feminist and postmodern theorists in more mainstream philosophy, such as Rorty.
2. For instance, by von Glasersfeld (1984, 1990), David Carr (2003, 2007), David Jardine (2006) and Wolff-Michael Roth (2011a, 2011b), whose interpretations are discussed in the chapters that follow.
3. A proper engagement with Piaget's complex theories lies outside the scope of this chapter, but drawing on the way Piaget is usually read, several aspects stand out as telling differences.
4. This is discussed in more detail in the following chapter.
5. Bruner was much influenced by the work of Vygotsky, who was himself indirectly influenced by the German tradition, which may explain the source of many of Bruner's ideas about cognition and development—particularly the social and interpersonal aspects such as mother–child interaction, and the role of culture in shaping the mind. There are differences though, such as the very language of construction.
6. These are examples of the 'layer-cake' conception of human mindedness (taken from Conant 2016, 2017), which is contrasted with Kant's 'transformative' conception in the next chapter.
7. Another way to say this is that we encounter 'general' knowledge (or concepts) in the 'particular', and the particular in the general (Rödl 2012); this is unpacked in Chapter Nine.
8. Blackburn is describing McDowell's attempt to 'stop the exercise of judgement from being entirely self-contained, disengaged from a reality outside the mind' with his unboundedness of the conceptual (2010, p. 265); but he is critical of McDowell, particularly of the use of the metaphor the space of reasons.
9. The unity of the capacities *in* experience is further discussed in the next chapter, because obscuring the role of intuition (and thus objectivity) is a characteristic of the widespread 'Kantian' picture in education.

10. See, for instance, James Wertsch (1997) and André Kukla (2000).
11. This is another example of the layer-cake conception of human mindedness (James Conant, 2016, 2017), which is discussed in the next chapter.
12. Normal Kemp Smith's translation is widely accepted in Kantian scholarship.
13. This discussion refers to *empirical* knowledge—derived through the senses. There is also knowledge derived from spontaneity such as the content of pure mathematics, or the many concepts like mind and value, that do not depend directly on objects.

8

The 'Layer-Cake' versus 'Transformative' Conceptions of Human Mindedness

SHEILA WEBB

The previous chapter gave examples of the tendency in the philosophy of education for theorists to ascribe to Kant a conception of mind as actively organising the 'raw data' it receives from the senses, and imposing rules or structure onto reality. Such 'imposition' readings form and reinforce the widespread 'Kantian' picture that has long drawn criticism for its intellectualism, dualisms and detached conception of mind. It was argued that an over-emphasis on the activity of mind obscures important aspects of Kant's view, and this distorts the overall picture. In this chapter the focus remains on differing conceptions of mind by drawing on contemporary Kant commentary, particularly that of James Conant. A careful look at contrasting understandings of the capacities helps show the way passed dualism, for it further exposes the assumptions that give rise to it (a running theme through the chapters) and provides a way to think of Kant's subject as immersed in the here and now of lived experience. I see the contrast as also significant because the metaphysics inherent in different pictures of mind shape differing ideas about the nature of concepts, their use, and the learning process, in turn shaping wider ideas about what education can or should be.

This chapter continues with conceptions of experience in order to make explicit the different pictures of mind that are involved. Attention is drawn to interpretations of sensibility and intuition

Interpreting Kant for Education: Dissolving Dualisms and Embodying Mind, First Edition. Sheila Webb.
Chapters and editorial organization © 2022 Philosophy of Education Society of Great Britain.
Published 2022 by John Wiley & Sons Ltd.

to help address criticisms of intellectualism. I draw from James Conant (2016, 2017) and use his contrast between the 'layer-cake' conception of human mindedness and Kant's 'transformative' conception. On the 'transformative' conception, both the objective and passive aspects of experience are discussed, to show how mind can be understood as exercised unreflectively in perception and activity, rather than as actively organising and constructing meaning. Of the many critical references to Kant in educational theory, this chapter considers some of those made by Wolff-Michael Roth. Again, I do not comment on Roth's influential work but use his characterisations of Kant as a springboard for discussion.

Roth is prominent in mathematics and science education (2005, 2006, 2009, 2011, 2013, 2017), and he presents his theory as a contrast to Kant, of whom he is very critical. Roth also critiques Cartesian dualism (2017), but instead of reading Kant as an alternative to this, Roth reads him as the 'founder' of 'ultimate intellectualism' (2011a, p. 6). Contrasted with his own 'non-intellectualist' and 'non-intentional' view, he holds that intellectualist theories like Kant's emerged: 'during the Greek antiquity, and characterizes a form of thought generally known as metaphysics (idealism). Thus, thought is thought as something above and beyond the physical, that is, ultimately, above and beyond real, living/lived life' (p. 4). Roth reads Kant in particular as having a detached conception of mind and providing 'an epistemological subject that has no hold in and on this actual world that we inhabit' (p. 23). Like the interpretations discussed in the previous chapter, Kant is attributed a radical subjectivism with an exaggerated emphasis on the activity of mind. But before continuing, a reminder that Kant *critiques* the kind of intellectualist view that Roth is charging him with, describing such a view as 'a completely isolated speculative science of reason, which soars far above the teachings of experience, and in which reason is indeed meant to be its own pupil' (Bxiv). In contrast, Kant has (and is read by many as having) a down-to-earth and anthropological standpoint. For instance, Béatrice Longuesse writes '"[t]he human standpoint" expounded in his first *Critique* is that standpoint on the world which, according to Kant, is proper to human beings' (2005, p. 3). And in distinguishing Kant's 'real' metaphysics from the isolated version that 'soars above experience', Robert Hanna writes:

> according to Kant, real metaphysics must be evidentially grounded on human experience. Or otherwise put, real metaphysics reverse-engineers its basic metaphysical (including

ontological) theses and explanations in order to conform strictly to all and only what is *phenomenologically self-evident* in human experience. (2016a, p. 5)

Kant's metaphysics is grounded in human experience.[1] It is possible to understand Kant's subject as 'a conscious being that actively orients in the (social, material) world it perceives'—which is what Roth tells us he is after in his non-cognitive *phronesis* view that emphasises the 'living/lived life' (Roth, 2013, p. 399).

Roth interprets Kant's conception of mind as actively taking charge of synthesis in experience. For instance, he writes 'Kant has prepared this constructivist approach to the question of learning by placing an enormous emphasis on the mind to bring about the mental structures' when connecting with sense-based intuition (2011a, p. 45). He continues:

The unity of the mind and the manifold of sensual experiences are of different order ... The mind has to make this connection. And it is for this reason that Kant requires the faculty of *synthesis*: it is precisely because Kant has produced a difference between mental concept and sense-based intuition that he requires a powerful mind to hold it all together (Rorty 1979). The mind takes the entire charge of the integration. (*Ibid.*)

This is similar to David Jardine (2006) in the previous chapter, who sees synthesis as an active act. Read through a dualist lens, mental concept and sense-based intuition are understood as separate entities that have to be actively integrated. I repeat Stephen Engstrom here, who argues that such readings see the senses and understanding as 'each able on its own to produce representations, which must somehow interact' in order 'to secure the fit, requisite for cognition, between concept and intuition. This reading cannot be squared, however, with what Kant actually says about theoretical cognition and the way understanding and sensibility cooperate in it' (2006, p. 2). Andrea Kern similarly argues against such 'two-world' readings of the capacities, 'according to which knowledge is the product of two capacities whose exercises can be conceived to be logically independent of one another. Although this is a widespread reading of Kant, it fails to do justice to what Kant actually achieves', because 'such a reading of Kant fails to appreciate the fundamental thought at which Kant arrives by the end of the Deduction' (2017, p. 256).[2] As discussed in Part One, the capacities tend to be understood as exercised independently and the result somehow connected, reflected in Roth's criticism above that 'the unity of the mind and the manifold of sensual experiences are of different order' and need to be connected by the mind.

What is significant for a non-dualist understanding of the capacities and a more valuable reading of Kant is that these are understood as the *same* order. The unity of mind and manifold of sensual experiences have the same order because they are provided by the same function. Another way to put this is that intuited content has the *same* conceptual unity as in judgements, and Kant writes of this:

> The same function which gives unity to the various representations in a judgment also gives unity to the mere synthesis of various representations in an intuition; and this unity in its most general expression, we entitle the pure concept of the understanding. (B104-105)

McDowell often quotes Kant on this and argues: 'That is why it is right to say the content unified in intuitions is of the same kind as the content unified in judgments: that is, conceptual content' (2009a, p. 264). Also, 'The right point is just that the unity of intuitions is the same as the unity of possible judgments' (p. 72, footnote 7). Pirmin Stekeler-Weithofer similarly argues: 'if we use the word experience as Kant does, for conceptually determined object-related empirical knowledge it is clear that experience is to be taken as the empirical content of possible empirically meaningful statements or propositions. In other words, objective experience is always already of a form that can be expressed by words and sentences' (2010c, p. 26). Sebastian Rödl argues more forcefully that intuitions *necessarily* exhibit the forms of unity described by concepts (2007, pp. 179–180), and Dieter Henrich argues that Kant reveals 'the indissoluble mutual correlation between the unity of self-consciousness and the unity of the world' (2003, p. 22). The unity of self-consciousness[3] functions as *a priori* knowledge through which we apprehend objects as the objects they are; importantly, however, while perceived empirical content is of a form that *can* be expressed, in the thick of experience it rarely is. That synthesis is unconscious and that in experience *a priori* knowledge is mostly exercised unreflectively is in contrast to Roth's interpretation of two different orders that a powerful mind has to 'hold together' and 'actively integrate'.[4]

The content unified in intuition (being the same content as possible judgements) brings us back to the different conceptions of experience previously discussed, which, as our contact with the world. affects how we understand perception and cognition. With the dualist assumptions about mind and world that shape the typical 'Kantian' picture, experience (and cognition) is a two-step process. On this picture something like raw data is delivered to the mind, which takes charge of the integration, organising and constructing meaning. James Conant, in his paper entitled 'Why Kant Is Not a Kantian', claims that 'Kant is not a proponent of (what often goes by the name of) 'Kantianism'; on the contrary, he is its first great critic' (2016, p. 76). Conant refers to Kantianism as the layer-cake conception of human mindedness (2016, 2017). To 'understand human cognitive functioning in this way is to picture it as a layer cake: the bottom level of the cake is the layer of our merely animal capacities for interacting with the world' (interpreted as raw data given through the senses), and the 'layer that sits on top of that is the upper layer of human cognitive functioning' (mind that goes to work on this, ordering and structuring it) (Conant, 2016, p. 77). What is crucial to this deep-seated assumption, Conant continues, is the idea:

> that the internal character of the manifold constituting the bottom layer remains unaffected by the introduction of the upper layer. Just as in a layer cake with a lower layer of chocolate and an upper layer of vanilla: the fact that there is a layer of vanilla sitting on top of the chocolate does not affect the internal character of what it is to be chocolate. So, too, according to the deep-seated assumption: just because, in the human case, there happens to be a layer of cognitive functioning, which involves 'additional' capacities (say, the capacities to employ concepts and make judgments) sitting on top of our merely animal nature, does not alter or otherwise affect the internal character of the capacities which make up the lower level—the human animal's capacities to be sensibly affected by and desire objects in the world. (*Ibid.*)

In contrast to this layer-cake conception, which is a compound picture, Conant calls Kant's conception the 'transformative conception of human mindedness', for on this conception rational capacities *transform* human sensibility. Human sensibility is different in *form*. That is, 'something's being given to the sensory consciousness' of human beings, as rational animals, 'requires that *that* capacity for sensory affection is radically different *in its internal character'* (p. 79, emphasis added). Human sensibility is not empiricism's raw sense data, but is transformed by rational capacities, making cognition immediate, immanent, rather than a two-step process. The metaphysics are quite distinct.

A reminder that Kant is critiquing both empiricism (for prioritising the senses) and rationalism (for prioritising mind). For 'a proper understanding of the structure of the B Deduction' (which requires accepting its *conclusion*, rather than taking the Aesthetic to stand alone), Conant explains Kant's argument:

> For the front of the argument that is directed against the empiricist, this means coming to see how a reading of the text that is informed by the layer-cake conception (and which therefore takes the Transcendental Aesthetic to furnish us with the full story about the nature of our faculty for sensory apprehension) is mistaken. For the front of the argument which is directed against the rationalist, this requires coming to see how a mere *inversion* of the central claim of such a reading would be equally wrong. It would require seeing how a discursive faculty of understanding able to traffic in nothing more than empty concepts would no more amount to a genuinely cognitive power than would a faculty of intuition able to traffic in nothing more than blind intuitions. That is, it requires seeing how each of these faculties depends on its relation to the other to be the sort of faculty that it is in a finite rational being. (pp. 75, 76)

Henry Allison similarly points out that 'The difference between rationalism and empiricism on this score concerns only the identification of the faculty that is viewed as the ultimate cognitive power to which the other is reducible' (2015, p. 47). So, on the one hand, as Allison describes it, Kant critiques 'sensationalist epistemology, i.e., the view that cognition is built up entirely from sensations or sense data which provide the unfiltered raw material of cognition' (p. 55). But, on the other hand, as Conant makes clear, in recognising problems with this empiricist way of thinking, there is a tendency to 'inverse' the capacities and prioritise mind—as we have seen in constructivist interpretations of Kant that constitute the widespread 'Kantian' picture in education. However, inversing the capacities is, for Conant, trafficking in nothing more than empty concepts, and in McDowellian terms it is a free-floating conceptual sphere out of touch with reality—and Kant clearly rejects such rationalism. Kant's 'transformative' conception of human mindedness is fundamentally different for it changes the way sensibility and experience (and therefore cognition) are conceived. To repeat Rödl here, 'that we apprehend substances and their movement through the senses, and forms and their laws through the intellect, are two sides of a coin', and the unity of these sources 'defines the finite intellect' (2012, p. 207). As previously argued, properly appreciating the *unity* of the capacities in experience gives a conception of experience as *already conceptually formed*—meaningful and objective.

Stekeler-Weithofer similarly writes that experience, 'as Kant uses the word is already conceptually formed' and 'must always already be seen as taking part in complex and joint practices' (2010a, p. 19). He warns about interpretations of 'experience': 'It is fairly crucial to realize the difference between Kant's word *'Erfahrung'* and the common use of "experience" with its empiricist connotations', which is merely subjective knowledge; 'Kant's *Erfahrung* is already conceptually articulated, objective (or object related) Knowledge' (2010c). On this 'transformative' conception of human mindedness, experience directly provides objective knowledge. This can be contrasted with the 'layer-cake' conception, on which mind actively makes sense of the data it receives in a two-step process. Examples of this were given in the previous chapter: experience for von Glasersfeld 'is what the thinking subject coordinates (constructs) out of elements of the manifold' (1995a, p. 41), and the manifold 'is the raw material, the stuff on which constructive perception and reason can operate' (p. 40). Also, Jardine writes that for Kant, mind 'actively constructs orderliness out of the chaos of experience' (2006, p. 23), and David Carr (mentioned in Chapter One) writes of the 'active imposition of meaning-constitutive rules and principles on the brute data of sensory perception' (2003, p. 100). Inherent in the 'layer-cake' and 'transformative' pictures are considerably different conceptions of experience, cognition, knowledge and mind.

These different interpretations also affect how the learning process is understood. Roth's 'layer-cake' interpretation leads him to argue that for Kant the concept has to exist before perception of an object, giving rise to the problem of how a concept arises in the first place. Roth gives an example of a child, Chris, acquiring the concept of a cube, and writes: 'For Kant, the category (idea) of a triangle exists before (a priori) the apperception of a triangle, even when it is the first time that an individual subject perceives an entity such as a cube. For Kant, Chris cannot perceive the cube or rectangular prism prior to knowing one' (2011b, p. 37). And because, Roth claims, 'Kant discards any possibility that the concept of an object, such as cube, could arise from experience', he wants to ask Kant this: 'A few years earlier, how did Chris know that he was looking at a cube when he gazed at a dice for the first time? How did Chris achieve a synthesis of the manifold experiences that he has had with a dice so that he comes to know it as a cube?' (*ibid.*). Roth continues, 'Kant's response to my question is clear: Chris cannot have constituted the conception of a cube from experience' (*ibid.*). This is similar to von Glasersfeld's claim in the previous chapter: 'no truths about a "real" world could be derived from experience' (1990, p. 3). In contrast to these readings, and as previously discussed, Kant has no doubt that knowledge arises from experience: 'There can be no doubt that all our knowledge begins with experience' (B1).[5] To be clear, Kant does not reject the senses, but rejects the *prioritising* of the senses; his insight is, as Graham Bird puts it, that some elements of our experience 'are not already "there" to be detected or tracked in experience and must be understood in some other way' (2006, p. 355), and that other way is through spontaneity, our capacity for concepts. But as I have been emphasising, in rejecting empiricist epistemology we need to resist the tendency to inverse the capacities and prioritise spontaneity, as in the 'Kantian' picture of an all-powerful mind that constructs meaning out of sense data it receives. As McDowell argues, the question 'how the non-conceptual given is converted into a given with conceptual content' should 'be rejected, not answered' (2009b, p. 321). The capacities need to be understood as working *together* in experience; to reiterate, on the 'transformative' conception of mindedness our senses are transformed by our conceptual capacities. As Bird argues, 'our immanent reality *is* the integral mix of those a posteriori and a priori given elements' and there is no way 'of notionally separating' these—except for metaphysical explanatory purposes (2006, p. 356).

With the 'transformative' conception, we can revisit Roth's questions to Kant. 'A few years earlier, how did Chris know that he was looking at a cube when he gazed at a dice for the first time?' An answer is that Chris did not know he was looking at a cube when he gazed at a dice for the first time, for he didn't know what a cube was; but he would know—if he'd grasped the relevant concepts—that he was looking at something small and hard, with dots on, called a dice and used to play a game. To the question how did Chris learn this, 'how did Chris achieve a synthesis of the manifold experiences that he has had with a dice so that he comes to know it as a cube?', an answer is: he learnt it from another person, through experience (through joint practices, maybe playing dice with someone or maybe in a maths class). Experience provides joint perceptual access and joint attention to objects in the already conceptually articulated world. Through intuiting with someone about an aspect of this (perhaps when playing a game with dice), a child learns how to refer to it in more and more fine-tuned ways, thus acquiring and developing conceptual capacities. Importantly, for example with a dice, the way it feels, looks, its size, weight, the way it rolls, its function in a game, all make up the *sensory content* of the concept. Sensory content is given by intuition, but the role of intuition is obscured in intellectualist interpretations. McDowell argues:

> What we need is an idea of content that is not propositional but intuitional, in what I take to be a Kantian sense. 'Intuition' is the standard English translation of Kant's *'Anschauung'*. The etymology of 'intuition' fits Kant's notion, and Kant uses a cognate expression when he writes in Latin. But we need to forget much of the philosophical resonance of the English word. An *Anschauung* is a having in view. (As is usual in philosophy, Kant treats visual experiences as exemplary.) (2009a, p. 260)

Intuition is a 'having in view' and 'not something I know by bringing a conceptual capacity to bear on what I anyway see' (*ibid.*), such as imposing concepts on experience.

McDowell also talks of 'knowledge that experience makes available by bringing something into view for someone who has a suitable recognitional capacity' (p. 259). We develop recognitional capacities before we have sufficient grasp of certain concepts to successfully use them. Chris, for instance, might hear the word 'dice' when watching or playing a game with others and (isolating the content of an intuition) grasp what it refers to. Acquiring the capacity to recognise one first, he'll gradually be able to successfully refer to one. Someone might point out that the shape of a dice is a cube, or maybe it will be in formal schooling that Chris will learn about shapes such as cubes (where teachers focus attention on jointly perceived content). While '[o]ne can make use of contents being given in an intuition to acquire a new discursive capacity', McDowell argues, 'with much of the content of an ordinary intuition, one never does that. (Think of the finely discriminable shapes and shades of colour that visual experience present to one.)' (p. 265). That is, 'even though all of our epistemic life can be accompanied by the "I think", in much of it we unreflectively go with the flow' (p. 271). The *passive* element of experience (in perception and cognition) is obscured in the widespread 'layer-cake' interpretations in educational theory that characterise mind as *actively* making sense of, or constructing knowledge from, sense data.

Appreciating the way conceptual capacities are *unconsciously* called into play in perceptual experience is significant for addressing charges of intellectualism. We cannot decide what to perceive. 'We cannot produce intuition as such and at will' (Stekeler-Weithofer, 2010b, p. 25), and as McDowell similarly says, in experience 'the conceptual capacities we currently have are drawn into operation in a way that is not up to us' (2009a, p. 97). Again, synthesis for Kant is 'a blind' function, 'of which we are scarcely ever conscious' (B103). McDowell argues that 'capacities belong to spontaneity in that they *can* be used in responsible cognitive activity, paradigmatically judging. But in experience they come into operation outside our control' (2006, p. 218). Intuition provides the content we *can* think, or judge, even if we do not. 'The unity of intuitional content is *given*, not a result of our putting significances together' as in discursive activity, McDowell says (2009a, p. 263), and explains the difference:

> every aspect of the content of an intuition is present in a form in which it is already suitable to be the content associated with a discursive capacity, if it is not—at least not yet—actually so associated. That is part of the force of saying, with Kant, that what gives unity to intuitions is the same function that gives unity to judgments. If a subject does not already have a discursive capacity associated with some aspect of the content of an intuition of hers, all she needs to do, to acquire such a discursive capacity, is to isolate that aspect by equipping herself with a means to make that content—that very content—explicit in speech or judgment ... Whether by way of introducing new discursive capacities or not, the subject of an intuition is in a position to put aspects of its content, the very content that is already there in the intuition, together in discursive performances. (p. 264)

Related to the discussion above, the point is that the unity of intuitions is the same as the unity of (possible) speech, judgements or thought about something, for it is provided by the same function, which Kant calls the understanding (B104). But the distinction between unreflective perception and *actually* judging, talking about things or deciding what to do, is lost in the widespread 'Kantian' picture that (over)emphasises the activity of mind.

With criticisms of intellectualism, Roth alleges that Kant 'reduced all knowing to the mind' (2011b, p. 49) and has 'nothing to say about the relation of the body and thought' (p. 53). Such a charge presupposes dualist interpretation and the 'layer-cake' conception of mindedness on which the senses provide only blind data. On the 'transformative' conception, senses provide thinkable content; body and thought are integrally related as we 'think' what we perceive. On this conception, sensibility (also intuition and receptivity) reveals both the embodiment of mind and the embeddedness or situatedness of Kant's subject in the real world, for we perceive objective content from our situated position in the here and now of experience. Kant 'recovers the internal connection between thought and sensory perception without, like Hume, declaring though to be an illusion', Rödl argues (2012, p. 2), and also:

It is straightforward that intuition-dependent thought is fundamentally situational. In the simplest case, in which I directly relate to *intuition*, I think something as opposed to nothing in virtue of perceiving what I think. A thought that I think in this way is situational. For, if it is essential for thinking what I think that I perceive what I think, then it is essential that I think it when I do. For what I perceive depends on the time: at one time, I perceive this, at another time, that. (p. 63)

Thought depends on intuition, on our senses, at a particular time and place and this makes it, in Rödl's terms, situational, and thus objective. This is to argue that a proper appreciation of intuition (and receptivity and sensibility) shows Kant's conception of mind as embodied and his subject situated in the real world.[6]

Roth heads his chapter concerning Chris above: 'From Intellectualist Metaphysics to Embodiment Epistemologies'. In educational characterisations, Kant is repeatedly ascribed an intellectualist metaphysics, and then criticised for it, but he can be read as providing an embodiment epistemology. 'What is given through the senses' on the *empiricist* picture, Rödl argues, 'is, as such, formless, a matter external to thought upon which thought may impose its form. This is the position of empiricism … which everywhere impedes analytic philosophy' (2012, p. 11). This picture can be said to impede readings of Kant, for it is prevalent in educational interpretations: mind is seen to impose its form on a formless matter external to it. Karl Ameriks, in his many works on Kant since his *Kant's Theory of Mind* in 1982, frequently refers to misreadings of Kant by his critics, particularly for 'alleged subjectivism'. To defend Kant, 'a series of interpretative clarifications needs to be made to counter the subjectivist presumptions present from the start in many understandings of the meaning of Kant's idealism', he writes (2019, p. 143). For instance, concerning Kant's doctrine of transcendental idealism:

> To even begin properly to evaluate Kant's own doctrine one has to carefully distinguish and order the main steps of the *Critique of Pure Reason's* overall argument. All too often it is falsely assumed—in part because of ambiguous terms in the B Preface, of his approach as involving a 'Copernican thought' (B xvi)—that the *starting* point of the *Critique* is its idealism, as if the book's trajectory is to take, from the very start, a general subjectivist turn toward the self rather than to objects, and then simply to proceed from there. This broadly 'Cartesian' type of interpretative approach misses the crucial fact that in the text proper Kant presents his highly original form of idealism only as a *consequence* of a *long* sequence of arguments, that it, as a last step in a complex four-step series of considerations, and with crucial and often overlooked non-subjectivist premises that are absolutely essential to understanding his reasoning and the precise nature of his ultimate idealist conclusion. (p. 140)

As other Kantians also argue, including Kern and Conant above, it is the conclusion Kant arrives at, after a long series of arguments, that needs to be appreciated in understanding his 'highly original form' of idealism. Stekeler-Weithofer also talks of widespread misreadings of Kant's philosophy, especially in Anglophone traditions, explaining that 'We would miss [his] point if we read Kant along the lines of Berkeley's empiricist idealism and "constructivism"—as if Kant had thought that real things were constructions out of sense data, bundles of appearances, as Hume had suggested, or mere objects of imagination' (2010b, p. 4). In the Anglophone tradition, Stekeler-Weithofer writes, Kant's and Hegel's philosophy are 'not understood as such until today, perhaps because the basic form of philosophical thinking in Anglophone philosophy is still Humean not yet Kantian' (2010c). If we can set aside the dualist presuppositions—and the 'layer-cake' conception of mindedness that sees real things as constructions out of sense data—we can (begin to) appreciate Kant's version of idealism as an embodiment epistemology.

To further respond to charges of intellectualism, I want to finish by drawing attention to the unreflective nature of much of our perception and experience that is obscured in the widespread 'Kantian' picture in education. In contrast to this picture, our rational capacities are operative in experience but this is mostly passively, as we 'go with the flow' and unconsciously respond to things. McDowell has, like Kant, faced accusations of intellectualism, for instance by Hubert Dreyfus (2005), who argues that our situated and embodied engagement with the world is *non-conceptual*.[7] I draw on McDowell's arguments in as far as they can be seen as a response to intellectualist criticisms of Kant. McDowell argues that our rational capacities are operative in *all* our activities—including perceptual experience and skilful embodied comportment, whether or not we are aware of exercising them. The charge of intellectualism can be understood as a phenomenological one, which Andrea Kern articulates as follows: 'we can sensibly distinguish far more colors than we can express through our repertoire of color concepts. The fineness of grain of these color differentiations, which our sensory experience enable us to make, cannot be captured by our color concepts' (2017, p. 188). This leads to a view of sensory experience as non-conceptual.[8] Kern responds to this objection:

> As McDowell, among others, has argued, we can easily do justice to the fine-grained character of our sensory experience of colors if we disentangle the idea that our sensory experience of color has conceptual content from the idea that 'we must have ready, in advance of the course our colour experience actually takes, as many colour concepts as there are shades of colour that we can sensibly discriminate'. (p. 189)

This reflects Roth's criticism above, that for Kant the concept must be known before perception of something. But in *Mind and World*, drawing on the work of Gareth Evans (1982), McDowell talks of recognitional capacities that in experience 'can be made explicit with the help of a concept' such as a 'shade of colour' (1996, p. 57). That is, 'if we have the concept of a shade, our conceptual powers are fully adequate to capture our colour experience in all its determinate detail' (p. 58). He explains:

> A capacity to embrace a shade within one's thinking (as *that* shade, we can say in favourable circumstances) is initiated by the figuring of an instance of the shade in one's experience.

> There is no saying which capacity it is in abstraction from the activating experience itself. That is how these capacities permit the fine-grained sensuous detail that figures in the actual course of visual life to be taken up into the conceptual content of visual experience. (p. 59)

A subject's conceptual repertoire will always be partial, with concepts underdetermined, vague and unclear, but all we need is the concept 'a shade' to say 'that shade' to refer to something jointly intuited. As McDowell argues, we do not need as many colour concepts are there are shades of colour to recognise the fineness of grain of sensible experience.

Again, sensibility, our senses, are transformed by our rational capacities, in a rational relation with the world; but the *passive* nature of this in much of our sensible experience—the way we unreflectingly respond to things—has been underestimated. I think it is best illustrated when thinking of a subject immersed in ongoing activity, and McDowell gives an example—of a signpost. 'Consider someone following a marked trail', he says, 'who at a crossing of paths goes to the right in response to a signpost pointing that way' (2009a, p. 129). A scientific description of a signpost would be in physical terms, stripped of its ideal properties, and therefore normatively inert (any action could be described in sub-personal terms). A subjectivist interpretation of Kant might describe mind as ordering or structuring what is given in sense data—an inert signpost with mind making sense or interpreting it. However, McDowell writes: 'it is disastrous to conclude that what points the way, to someone to whom a sign-post does point the way, is such a thing—a board on a post—under an interpretation. On the contrary, what points the way is a sign-post, something that is what it is by virtue of its involvement in the relevant practice' (2009b. p. 105). We 'fall into a bind' he continues 'if we abstract sign-posts (for instance) from their place in the lives of those who use them. For someone who is party to the relevant practice, a sign-post is something that points the way. And that is what a sign-post as such is' (*ibid.*). Our knowledge (of a sign-post) is manifested in our unreflective responses and actions in ordinary experience. We act in the light of our knowledge.

Another way to put this is that the meaningful world prompts normative responses. It can move us to act in a particular way; however vague our knowledge of a signpost might be it is operative in our response. What makes going to the right a *rational* response to the signpost and not a random action is, as McDowell argues, because the signpost points to the right; without knowing what a signpost is—without being party to the practice—turning right or left would be arbitrary or accidental. Experience for Kant is not mind actively making sense of a world void of meaning, or imposing meaning; rather in everyday experience, as McDowell puts it, 'a subject is passively saddled with conceptual contents, drawing into operation capacities seamlessly integrated into a conceptual repertoire that she employs in the continuing activity of adjusting her world-view' (1996, p. 31). Again, while this is mostly unconscious, any aspect of experience *can* be made the object of discussion or judgement if drawn attention to, or explicitly referred to. The passive aspects of perception and experience in which we unreflectingly go with the flow are contrasted with actively talking, reasoning, reflecting etc., and this distinction is not apparent in the typical 'Kantian' picture, or in interpretations of Kant that overemphasise the activity of mind.

This chapter has again exemplified the tendency in educational theory to attribute to Kant a radical subjectivism, an all-powerful mind, that obscures valuable aspects of his view and leads to accusations of intellectualism. I hold that Kant can be read in a way that accommodates Roth's desire for an embodied epistemology, with a subject 'in the world' and who 'lives life'. The 'layer-cake' conception of mind, that is inherent in the typical 'Kantian' picture, was contrasted with Kant's 'transformative' conception, on which our senses are transformed by what we know; but while rational capacities are operative, it was argued that this happens unreflectingly in most of our ongoing sense experience. Kant provides for bodily experience with his concepts of intuition, sensibility and receptivity, which provide the sensory content of thought and situate us in the world as embodied perceivers. The next chapter continues to challenge familiar criticisms of Kant in educational theory for the purpose of expanding on the reading being presented.

NOTES

1. Richard Velkley also talks of Kant's anthropological standpoint, writing that (even) when characterising the philosophy of religion, Kant 'proposes a kind of antimystical Platonism in which human reason, starting from an "earthly" standpoint, never loses sight of itself "as its own final end" ..., instead of pursuing an "alchemical" *inspiratio* from higher realities' (1994, footnote 12, p. 213).
2. Kern adds that this 'is one of the crucial points of McDowell's *Mind and World* as well as of his criticism of Sellars's reading of Kant' (*ibid.*). We return to this below.

3. James Conant writes of Kant's 'unity of the understanding', that it 'exhibits the structural feature which became so important to Hegel: any determination of it is one in which the unity of the whole remains prior to the unity of the parts' (2016, p. 114).

4. As discussed in the previous chapter, synthesis in general is 'a blind but indispensable function', Kant writes, 'without which we should have no knowledge whatsoever, but of which we are scarcely ever conscious' (B103).

5. Roth argues that 'Kant studies the human mind in the abstract, separated from the subject in which this mind [is] embodied and that gives rise to this mind in and through its participation with others in the world' (2011b, p. 37). Again, this is in contrast to the reading being presented, on which the (embodied) human mind develops precisely through the subject's participation with others in the world.

6. This is discussed further in the next chapter.

7. There is a literature on this debate. For some useful reading, see Koichiro Misawa (2013, 2017), Erik Rietveld (2010), and Joseph Schear (2013).

8. Christopher Peacocke (1992) and Tim Crane (1992), for instance, argue for the non-conceptual content of experience.

9

On Concepts: The General and the Particular

SHEILA WEBB

The preceding chapter further illustrated the tendency by philosophers of education to read Kant as a constructivist with an overemphasis on the activity of mind, reinforcing the widespread picture that attracts much criticism. It has been maintained that these interpretations mischaracterise Kant's view by obscuring important aspects, including its significance for removing conceptual barriers to non-dualist thinking. A quite distinct reading has been developed; rather than picturing mind as making and *imposing* meaning, it is pictured as embodied and his subject *encountering* meaning in experience. Attention has been drawn to the more human features of Kant's view, such as the unreflective nature of much of our perception and experience, and the dependence on others to become minded at all. This chapter continues to respond to criticisms by educational theorists in order to further delineate the Kant who is not a 'Kantian'.

As previously noted, in the philosophy of education references to Kant are often cursory or fleeting disparagements, and this makes it difficult to engage with them in a meaningful way. Most of these however are directed at the dualisms seen to be at the heart of Kant's philosophy, which lead to accusations of a detached conception of mind, as we have seen. Unable to respond to one-line or short references adequately, in what follows I first identify some of these familiar criticisms and then attempt to challenge them by drawing further attention to the *intuition dependent* nature of perception which

Interpreting Kant for Education: Dissolving Dualisms and Embodying Mind, First Edition. Sheila Webb.
Chapters and editorial organization © 2022 Philosophy of Education Society of Great Britain.
Published 2022 by John Wiley & Sons Ltd.

shows the embeddedness of Kant's subject in the here and now of experience. Through a discussion of concepts and concept use, the *unity* of the capacities in perception and experience is stressed anew, and for this I draw on Sebastian Rödl's fascinating work on the general and particular.

Wilfred Carr, like Rorty and other postmodernists, reads Kant not as a constructivist but as a foundationalist. He points to 'Immanuel Kant's attempt to provide the philosophical foundations for universal principles of rational justification that are independent of particular historical, social or cultural circumstances and that are grounded in the capacity of enlightened human reason to achieve objectivity and truth' (2006, p. 143). Carr has long argued for the 'need to give up the abstract Enlightenment idea of an ahistorical reason common to all people' (1995, p. 126), and he rejects the idea of a 'disembodied rational autonomous subject' associated with Kant (p. 124). Daniel Royer also sees Kant as a foundationalist: 'Certainly much of Kant's foundationalist epistemology has been refuted or corrected in the last century' (2006, p. 61). I respond by drawing on previous arguments. Kant 'revolutionalised' our thinking about what it is to have a mind, and thus this new conception of ourselves—as self-determining or autonomous—figures prominently during the Enlightenment period. But it is far from a foundationalist position. Reason for Kant is 'common to all people' only insofar as it is a distinctively human capacity, but the determinate shape of any individual's capacity depends exactly on the 'particular historical, social and cultural circumstances' of her life, and is not independent of this.

The perceived dualism is widely criticised. Roland Reichenbach, for instance, writes: 'Postmodernists often refer to the aesthetic mode of judgement ... but, of course, they wouldn't accept Kant's strict dualism of an empirical world and a world of reason' (1999, p. 241). Jan Derry writes of 'The dualist separation of mind and world, central to Kant's investigation of the possibility of reason and knowledge', and also of his 'stark separation of receptivity and spontaneity' (2013, p. 112).[1] According to Sally Sedgwick, 'the empirical self is not only split off from its noumenal counterpart, but also clearly subordinated to it' (1997, p. 80). Wilfred Carr similarly refers to the dualism 'implicit in Kant's idea of a transcendental, noumenal "self" stipulating absolute standards to which the earth-bound, phenomenal self should conform' (1995, p. 38). And John White writes: 'Kant's rationale for his view depends on his "two-world" view of man as consisting of a noumenal self and a phenomenal self'; and, '[d]etached from desire, the concept of reason in both Kant and Peters becomes obscure, the transcendental arguments of *Ethics and Education* leaving the reader as unenlightened as Kant's delineation of the noumenal self' (2005, p. 34).[2]

Each reference reinforces the negative 'Kantian' picture and centres on dualist understandings of Kant's key terms. This affects how his overall view is grasped. But to repeat James Conant, 'Kant is not a proponent of (what often goes by the name of) "Kantianism"; on the contrary, he is its first great critic' (2017, p. 76). Like others, Conant warns against dualist interpretations of sensibility and understanding (and other distinctions) that are each understood as distinct realms, and this has been a running argument through the chapters. To further bring into view the Kant who is a critic of Kantianism, I turn to the distinction between noumena and phenomena.

This distinction, as previously discussed, can be read as different ways of knowing the same things. As a thing in itself we can *know ourselves* as self-conscious thinking beings (how we are feeling or what we are intending to do), and we can also know ourselves through appearance (by looking at our bodies or in the mirror). But when it comes to *inanimate objects* in the world, we cannot know them in themselves, only as they appear to us. For Henry Allison, Kant's distinction is 'to point to the different epistemic or semantic relationships we establish (at the meta-level of philosophical reflection) with the *single ontological* set of empirical objects' (in Pablo Muchnik, 2008, p. 2, emphasis added). Kant himself does not intend this distinction to be read as two ontological realms; '[t]he division of objects into phenomena and noumena, and the world into a world of the senses and a world of the understanding' is, he writes, 'quite inadmissible' (B311). But Kant also uses the concept noumena as a *limiting* concept. He writes: 'The concept of a noumenon is thus a merely limiting concept, the function of which is to curb the pretensions of sensibility; and it is therefore only of negative employment' (B311). It is to show the limits of the senses, compared with the freedom of reason. We can 'think' anything, but to 'know' an empirical object, experience has to be added. Kant writes:

> To *think* an object and to *know* an object are thus by no means the same thing. Knowledge involves two factors: first the concept, through which an object in general is thought (the category); and secondly, the intuition, through which it is given. For if no intuition could be given corresponding to the concept, the concept would still indeed be a thought, so far as its form is

> concerned, but would be without any object, and no knowledge
> of anything would be possible by means of it. (B146)

We can think an object, but intuition—experience, receptivity,
sensibility—is needed for knowledge of one. Kant states that the
understanding 'cannot know these noumena through any of the
categories, and that it must therefore think them only under the title
of an unknown something' (B312). A noumenon is not one of two
selves or one of two ontological realms but is a concept Kant uses
to express the limitations of human sense perception.

Michael Friedman writes of this: 'the idea of a noumenon or thing
in itself is the idea of an object thought through pure understanding
alone, independently of sensibility' (2002, p. 34, footnote 51). He
translates Kant's words as follows (B309):

> the categories thus extend further than sensible intuition, for
> they think objects in general, without attending to the partic-
> ular manner (of sensibility) in which they may be given. But
> they do not thereby determine a larger sphere of objects, since
> one cannot assume that such can be given without presupposing
> another mode of intuition than the sensible as possible—which
> we are in no way justified in doing. (*Ibid.*)

This passage, Friedman says, 'seems to me to count decisively
against the "two-worlds" interpretation of Kant's distinction' (*ibid.*).

Like objectivity, *the general and the particular* form another
aspect of Kant's view that is obscured in typical educational
interpretations, but that is significant for a non-dualist understanding
of the capacities and for understanding the relationship between
subject and object as together. It also helps shed light on the
nature of categories, concepts and concept development for Kant.
'Categories', he says, are *general* concepts: 'concepts of an object in
general' (B128).[3] They are representations that are united according
to a 'rule', according to a concept. The unity of an object, he
explains, 'is no other than that which the category prescribes to the
manifold of a given intuition in general' (B145). In other words,
categories are not given by objects, rather they are the unity of
features or properties in a form—a concept. Rödl explains: 'One
does not receive the category *from the object*. In Kant's apt words,
the intellect supplies the category *from itself* (B1)' (2006, p. 347).
'From itself' meaning the power of mind, but categories still have to
be learnt as they are not innate. To unpack the idea of categories—of

concepts of an object *in general*—it is first helpful to say something about the categories extending further than sensible intuition, as in Friedman's quote above.

What does it mean to say that the categories extend further than sensible intuition? In traditional naturalist or empiricist epistemology (without the concept of spontaneity, or rational freedom), mind simply 'tracks reality' as it receives individual impressions or representations; it is limited to what it receives. As Kant says: '[e]xperience teaches us what is, but does not teach us that it could not be other than what it is' (B762). Dieter Henrich argues that, in empiricism, 'no means exist of consciously transcending the limits of the given. Yet every action, including the action of criticism, moves within a context of meaning that is concrete and motivated by a given set of conditions, and on whose basis alone one can attain something surpassing them' (1993, p. 112). On Kant's view, mind is dependent on what is given for content but not *limited* to it; it is intuition-dependent but can surpass what is given. McDowell also writes about this:

> a knowledgeable judgment enabled by an intuition has content that goes beyond the content of the intuition. The intuition makes something perceptually present to the subject, and the subject recognizes that thing as an instance of a kind. (2009a, p. 266)

What goes beyond the content of sensible intuition is the meaning of an object 'in general'. Meaning is derived not only from objects in experience but also from a concept's place in relation to other concepts, in a complex and dynamic network of concepts. This involves understanding concepts as interrelated, as forming a dynamic system of concepts. In using a particular concept, other concepts are entailed by it from their logical relations to it and to each other. In making empirical judgements, even in ordinary discursive activity, we are committing ourselves to more than what we actually see at that moment.

Rödl uses this Kantian insight to criticise empiricism, arguing that empirical thought always goes beyond all sensory evidence, and he provides the following example:

> When I say 'This is an apple' and only see the front of the apple, then what I say goes beyond what I see. It includes the back, which I do not see. Therefore it is possible that I walk around the ostensible apple and discover that there is no apple. Now,

no sum of perceptions can exclude that later perceptions will show that despite appearances there is no apple. Like a general judgment, the judgment 'There is an apple' goes beyond everything we will ever have perceived. From that, scepticism follows immediately ... If all empirical evidence is compatible with no apple being there, and if, therefore, all empirical evidence leaves open whether there is one, then we do not improve—do not in the least improve—our epistemic standing by obtaining more evidence. (2012, p. 12)

In saying 'this is an apple' we are committing ourselves to more than what we can see, for the meaning of apple is related to other concepts in the system of concepts which delineate what an apple is. Once learnt, this general knowledge of an apple is involved in how we pick one up and what to expect when we bite into one. As discussed in Part One, our *general* knowledge of objects is involved not only in perceiving particulars, but in how we use them and what we do with them—and exemplifies Kant's Copernican insight that objects conform to our knowledge.

As a subject acquires a new concept through an encounter with a *particular*, so she (spontaneously, unconsciously) adjusts and develops her dynamic network of conceptual capacities, her *general* knowledge. McDowell argues, 'we could not recognize capacities operative in experience as conceptual at all were it not for the way they are integrated into a rationally organized network of capacities for active adjustment of one's thinking to the deliverances of experience. That is what a repertoire of empirical concepts is' (1996, p. 29). And 'acquiring one's first conceptual capacities is necessarily acquiring many conceptual capacities, interlinked in such a way that the totality amounts to a conceptual repertoire that exemplifies the necessary forms of the understanding' (2009, p. 38, footnote 23). Forms of the understanding, general concepts, are interlinked, and the inferential linkages between them delineates their meaning.

Robert Brandom's enormously influential work on 'inferentialism' centres on the *use* of concepts and the inferential linkages between them. 'Contemporary thought about the use of concepts owes great debts to Kant', he writes, whose 'fundamental insight is that judgments and actions are to be understood to begin with in terms of the special way in which we are *responsible* for them' (1994, p. 8). In describing Kant's influence on Hegel, Brandom explains Kant's break with his inherited tradition:

Kant breaks with the tradition he inherits in taking judgment to be the minimal unit of apperceptive awareness because it is the minimal unit for which one can take responsibility, the minimal unit to which one can commit oneself ... At the center of what one is responsible for is having reasons for judging or acting as one does. Concepts are rules that determine what counts as a reason for (or against) applying them, and what applying them counts as a reason for (or against). In Kant's usage, 'discursive' means 'of or pertaining to the use of concepts'. Discursive activity is the application of concepts, which is undertaking doxastic and practical responsibilities or commitments by binding oneself by rules in the form of concepts. Where the Early Modern philosophical tradition had focused on our grip on concepts, Kant shifts attention to their grip on us, to the normative bindingness ('Verbindlichkeit') of these rules. (2019, p. 9)[4]

Judgements (and actions) are things we are responsible for and are subject to normative assessment. 'They are a kind of *commitment* we undertake', Brandom writes (2010, p. 2). Meaning, he argues, does not arise from relating a word directly to the object that word represents, as in traditional 'representationalism', but by its relations with other concepts in a dynamic network of concepts; and in using them we take responsibility for what we commit ourselves to. 'An essential part of what one is *doing* in committing oneself' to a particular content, Brandom argues, 'is taking responsibility for integrating it into a whole constellation of such commitments', and this is 'what Kant called "synthesizing the transcendental unity of apperception"' (2008, p. 18). An appreciation of the systematicity or interconnectedness of general concepts and knowledge helps an understanding of how particulars depend for their meaning on their place within the whole (and sometimes can only be understood as part of the whole).[5]

Jan Derry draws on Brandom's inferentialism for her extensive work in education, particularly the idea of the interrelatedness of concepts (for instance, 2011, 2013, 2014, 2017). She criticises Cartesian epistemology, which has 'led to a neglect of the question of knowledge and of the full extent of what is involved in bringing a learner into a knowledge domain' (2009, p. 150). Rather than approaching the meaning of a concept 'in terms of a relation between a representation and the thing that it represents', Derry argues, 'the emphasis needs to be on bringing the learner into the inferential relations that constitute a concept prior to its acquisition' (2014, p. 83). This means 'that representations learnt are already connected through reasons to other aspects of the knowledge domain to which they belong' (p. 84). On this way of thinking about knowledge, concepts and their meanings are not learnt individually, one by one, but gradually, through initiation into everyday social practices. Derry illustrates this piecemeal process:

> Take the example of a child using the word 'dog' in a domestic context where it is applied to the four-legged friend she shares her home with. On a trip out of town she applies the same term for the four-legged creatures in the field i.e. sheep. Her conception of dog as a quadruped has not yet excluded other four-legged creatures of similar height and size. The child is beginning to develop its application of concepts but this is as yet insufficiently refined; she is not yet committed to excluding the concept sheep from the concept dog, as Brandom might put it. However, as her word use develops, the concept dog is refined and its application restricted. (2014, p. 86)

This refers back to discussion in earlier chapters about the conceptual unity of an object being not simply 'Given' but grasped gradually, along with other conceptual connections and distinctions, through discursive activity with others. As well as Brandom, Derry draws on Hegel and McDowell to bring German Idealist thought into education, and her work is significant. When it comes to Kant however, Derry portrays Hegel in *opposition* to Kant by appealing to the dualist 'Kantian' picture of him, particularly in her work on Vygotsky (2013). In recognition of this she writes, 'this presumed Kantian framework should not be taken as a valid statement of Kant's work. Like other great philosophers Kant is open to a variety of readings, some of which fail to capture the richness and depth of his work' (p. 71). It is this 'presumed Kantian framework', so widely presupposed in educational theory, that I am attempting to challenge. German idealism has much to offer education, as Derry's work exemplifies, but the dualist 'Kantian' picture stands in the way of appreciating Kant's genuine insights. My argument, that runs through the chapters, is that, properly understood, Kant can be seen as a critic of this 'Kantian' picture.

How particulars depend for their meaning on their place within the whole is illustrated in the following practical example. In teaching history, Catherine McCrory asks 'How does knowledge of facts relate to understanding the import of those facts in answering history's "what", "how", and "why" shaped questions?'—a problem manifested, 'for example, when exam candidates deliver a narrow recitation of substantive information that is *related* to, but not *responsive* to what is actually asked?' (2015, p. 37). McCrory gives an example from her own experience. She was teaching about the different factors that culminated in Hitler becoming Chancellor, and she thought she had given the students the relevant information. But when she looked at the essays they subsequently produced, about the relative importance of these factors, she found that they knew the facts but did not know how to relate them to the question: they lacked the inferential connections. 'They interacted with the facts as if sorting coloured buttons into jars, with no conception that information was not simply there to be shuffled for content classification but rather to be interrogated for influence, interconnectivity and importance' (p. 41). The relative importance of the facts came not from the (isolated) facts themselves but from their place in the bigger picture. Inferring what was entailed by what—reasoning—was missing. Kant similarly talks of someone who has learnt and can repeat facts and proofs, but 'knows and judges only what has been given him. If we dispute a definition, he does not know whence to obtain another. He has formed his mind on another's, and the imitative faculty is not itself productive'; Kant concludes that he 'is merely a plaster-cast of a living man' (B864).

General concepts (that form a dynamic system of concepts) are what Kant also calls *a priori* (or pure) concepts. As noted previously, *a priori* in this context does not refer to statements that are tautologies—true in virtue of their logical relation, as they have come to mean in contemporary philosophy—rather, *a priori* concepts are concepts of objects *in general*. Andrea Kern writes that because *a priori* knowledge 'is not knowledge of this or that particular object, but knowledge of something in general that characterizes any object of experiential knowledge, as such, it is a kind of *general* knowledge of objects of experience' (2017, p. 255). McDowell similarly writes, 'In Kant's terms, a category, a pure concept of the understanding, is a concept of an object in general' (2009a, p. 265). Much of the knowledge taught in schools is general knowledge (not knowledge of this particular electric circuit, for instance, but knowledge of electricity in general). A subject's worldview (rational capacities, network of concepts) is constituted by such *a priori* general knowledge once it has been learnt. Rödl writes of *a priori* or pure concepts:

> pure concepts spring from the understanding: they are concepts that I, as a subject of thought, always already carry with me.

That does not mean that I represent all pure concepts clearly and distinctly. It means that in order thus to represent them I have to do nothing but *think*. (2012, p. 30)

As has been argued, concepts held *a priori* (that a subject always already carries with her) are involved in experience, in perceiving particular objects—the Copernican insight. 'In Kant's words, knowledge of the form [category or concept] is always encountered in the experience of the particular (Rödl, 2012, p. 204). We do not know a giraffe simply by seeing one, we first (*a priori*) need some idea of what a giraffe is in order to see it as a giraffe.

Stekeler-Weithofer also describes *a priori* statements, explaining that they 'function as presuppositions in our conceptual understanding of empirical claims. When I, for example, say that over there is a cat, you are entitled to suppose that it is a real cat and not a toy cat' (2010c, p. 19). Stekeler-Weithofer argues that without any *a priori* commitment to what is normally or *generally* the case, my assuming that what I perceive is a cat would be arbitrary and void of sense. Our general knowledge of cats is (implicitly) operative in perception, not only (explicitly) in judgements and claims. And Rödl writes that if an object is determined 'a priori, then the sensibility of a thinker is *always already* determined by the form of thought, and what is given in sensory intuition as such bears the unity expressed by the category' (2006, p. 354). This again illustrates Kant's view that objects conform to our knowledge and that we cannot escape subjectivity (but with a richer conception of subjectivity that is touch with the objects we perceive). However rudimentary or undeveloped our conceptual capacities are, they are still operative in experience, as illustrated in Derry's example of a young child referring to a sheep as a dog. It is through our *a priori* concepts and knowledge that empirical objects are perceived.

Kant's insight that objects conform to our knowledge is perhaps more clearly evident in relation to action and things that are moving; perceptions are conjoined according to a concept. This involves space and time as forms of intuition. As discussed in Part One, time itself cannot be perceived (Kant, B219): time is not a *content* of thought but a *form*. Rödl articulates this: 'I do not perceive that A is after B simply by first perceiving A and then perceiving B. A sequence of perceptions is not the perception of a sequence' (2006, p. 364). Rather, changes (of state) are united according to a concept, a general rule (general for the most part, that is, and not always the case). Kant talks of a ship moving downstream. 'Kant explains that we would not perceive that things are simultaneous with, or succeed one another, if the representation of time did not underlie this perception', Rödl writes (2012, p. 117). He explains:

> Perceiving something happening, we perceive not only that a ship is first higher up and then lower down the stream; we see the ship 'drifting down the stream'. What we perceive contains a state toward which the movement is progressing: the ship lower down the stream. This state is present in what we perceive, but not in such a way that the ship's drifting down the stream entails that it will be lower down the stream. It may run into a sandbank. The state that is yet to come is present as the state that the ship will reach if what is happening here and now conforms to *what happens in general*. (p. 184)

Perceptions of what is progressively happening depend on general or *a priori* concepts (the 'rule' that connects them), which say what happens in general. In other words, we use general knowledge to think that, being upstream at one time, the ship will be midstream later, and downstream after that, because we present these as serially—temporally and spatially—connected. And we can assert this by saying 'the ship is drifting downstream'. General concepts *'explain* the temporal reality that exemplifies them' (Rödl, 2012, p. 199) and 'by which we recognize a substance as the same through changes of its states' (p. 200). Rödl criticises empiricism: we do not arrive at concepts 'by repeatedly perceiving this and that happening'; rather it is through concepts 'that we perceive something happening' (p. 201). This illustrates the inseparable nature of the capacities on Kant's 'transformative' conception of sensibility.

Like changes of time, changes of aspect are also united according to a 'rule' or concept. Stekeler-Weithofer also talks of a moving ship, one that appears to be moving upstream, but is actually moving downstream, but slower than an observer walking in the same direction. We are only able to talk about this once we have acquired the relevant concepts that express such movement, and this involves our practical and spatial ability to change our own perspective relative to objects. The same Copernican idea is evident in actions too, which are understood and sometimes only make sense through reference to a concept or general knowledge (including knowledge of social practices). A helpful example comes from Michael Thompson, who quotes John Rawls:

> one can throw a ball, run, or swing a peculiarly shaped piece of wood ... [But no] matter what a person did he could not be

described as stealing a base or striking out or drawing a walk unless he could also be described as playing baseball, and for him to be doing this presupposes the rule-like practice which constitutes the game. The practice is prior to particular cases: unless there is the practice, the terms referring to actions specified by it lack sense. (in Thompson, 2008, p. 58)[6]

It is necessary to have some knowledge of the practice in order to refer to particular actions; it is in this way that general (*a priori*) knowledge and concepts are prior to particular determinations. And conversely, a 'particular' takes its meaning from its place within the whole, to reiterate the point made above.

Andrea Kern utilises Rawls's example to explain the constitutive nature of rational capacities, in that a capacity, like a practice, is logically prior to particular cases in which it is actualised (2012). The claim that the practice is prior to particular cases involves, she argues, three thoughts:

first, the claim holds that certain concepts do not make any *sense* independently of a reference to the practice. From that it follows, second, that some actions can only exist *as* instances of a praxis, because it is only by reference to the practice that the concepts under which they fall obtain their content. And it follows, third, that there are certain concepts that can only *exist* if that very practice exists on which their meaning depends. (p. 235)

This 'constitutive' character means that 'acts which fall under a certain capacity cannot be explicated without reference to the capacity in question', and also that 'a specific capacity cannot be explicated through acts prior to this capacity' (*ibid.*). This relates to Kant's insight that objects (and actions) conform to our knowledge or, conversely, that general knowledge is prior to determining particular actions or objects. *A priori* concepts provide context-dependent understandings of particulars through something general.

Interpretations of Kant in educational theory and in much philosophy often portray *a priori* concepts as something innate, ahistorical and fixed for all time. See for instance David Hamlyn (1970, p. 253) and Paul Hirst (1974, p. 93). Wolff-Michael Roth too interprets the insight that the category 'exists' before perception and experience to mean that 'Any action, any word, any piece of art has been completed in imagination before it is expressed in the world'

(2011a, p. 5). An assumption here is that if knowledge and concepts are required *a priori*, then they must be innate and therefore fixed and unchanging—part of the 'Kantian' picture. McDowell responds to such concerns:

> Kant surely would not suggest we master the forms of thought in advance of having any determinate empirical content to work with, and only subsequently derive content for empirical concepts from what is now, thanks to that supposedly prior mastery of the forms of thought, experience in the relevant sense. (2011b, p. 8)

Again, for Kant concepts are not innate but learnt; moreover, conceptual unity is *gradually* learnt, as children little by little learn what falls under a concept and what does not, what is entailed by the concept and what is not, as in Derry's example. In learning language children continually refine concepts as they develop the competence to identify objects and predicate something of them, refining what they are taking responsibility *for* as they make judgements about them. This is an ongoing process, not something that has an end, and it is in this ongoing process that concepts become changed. Kant holds that concepts are not *'axiomatic'* but subject to change, Howard Caygill writes. Indeed Kant revised and reinvented many philosophical terms himself:

> He reinvented philosophical language by introducing new terms and concepts from outside philosophy, as well as self-consciously redefining many of its traditional ones. The matrix for the linguistic and conceptual transformation lies in the lectures which he delivered for over four decades in a wide range of subjects. In these he explicated the traditional philosophical concepts of the officially prescribed textbooks by means of materials drawn from contemporary natural science, newspapers, novels and poetry, as well as from medical and travel books. (Caygill, 1995, pp. 1–2)

This shows Kant's creativity and innovation when it comes to concepts. It is not the innate and unchanging or ahistorical view we are familiar with.

To echo previous arguments, judging not only applies to actively coming to a decision about something but to everyday conversation about everyday objects too. In taking responsibility for what we say about things, we are subject to normative assessment, which comes from the norms and practices that make up the world in which we live. Another way to put this is that in saying something, referring to something, we take ourselves to be *correctly* referring to it—as in Stekeler-Weithofer's example above of a cat. 'She who judges' or asserts something, Rödl similarly argues, does so 'with the concept of correct judgment' (2017, p. 5). We take ourselves to be correct, but of course we may be wrong. To re-emphasise the objectivity that is lacking in the widespread 'Kantian' picture, I repeat Kern: 'we are by no means saying that one can judge and believe whatever one wants. Quite the contrary … [J]udging is "answering"' or "taking a stance on" the question of truth' (2017, p. 21), and judgements are objective because 'their truth is dependent on how things are in the world' (p. 53). Conant also argues that Kant is concerned with the question: 'What does it take to have thoughts that are vulnerable to how things are?' (2017, p. 83). Judging and referring to things involves taking responsibility for what one endorses, and this is answerable to how things are in the (already humanised) world for correctness.

Consider Derry's above example of the young child who calls a sheep 'a dog'. By living with a dog she has learnt that a four-legged animal, something alive, friendly etc. is captured by the word 'dog', and this is involved when spotting a similar sized animal. But her concept of a dog is not yet refined enough to distinguish it from that of a sheep. We can put this by saying that this youngster is making a judgement; her *a priori* knowledge is manifested in pointing out a sheep, but because her conceptual capacities as discriminating powers are still rudimentary, her assertion that this is 'a dog' will be judged incorrect. Through joint intuition and correct reference by others, she will come to distinguish more finely and judge more successfully what falls under a particular concept and what does not. She will similarly learn, for instance, that swans and geese do not fall under the concept duck, but share with ducks the concepts of swimming, feeding, living by water etc. and fall under 'things alive'. And of ducks, some of us might go on to distinguish between mallards, mandarins and merguses. As our conceptual capacities become more fine-grained, we learn to be better judges.

In further response to criticism of dualisms, I finish with re-emphasising the *unity* of the general and particular, thought and reality, subject and object by returning to Rödl. General empirical knowledge is acquired and developed through encountering particulars in experience; and particular knowledge is context dependent as it relies on intuition (which roots us in the here and now). Rödl talks of 'situational thoughts', which are context-dependent thoughts, and are distinguished from 'general thoughts', which do not relate directly to intuition. '2 + 2 = 4' and 'Water freezes at zero degrees Celsius' are general sentences that do not directly relate to intuition, whereas 'it is raining' is situational (2012, p. 65). 'We think situational thoughts by means of the time at which we think them', he writes, but 'as a *thought*, however, it is not tied to this time in such a way that it could not be thought at a different time' (*ibid.*). For instance, saying 'It is nice today' can be reasserted the next day with 'It was nice yesterday' (*ibid.*). Children learn deictic and tense reference at a young age, as previously discussed. The important point here is that *general* forms of thought (what happens in general) are developed through perceiving what is happening in *particular* instances—and what is happening in particular instances depends on *general* concepts and knowledge. Rödl writes: 'if we appreciate Kant's critique, we see how knowledge of general laws can, as it must, be based on experience. For we now recognize that experience is always already fraught with (perhaps implicit and inarticulate) general knowledge' (2007, p. 180). Knowledge of the particular is only possible through knowledge of the general because 'it is only through general knowledge that sense perception gives rise to knowledge of particulars' (2012, p. 13). This is not mind imposing structure or meaning onto a disenchanted world, but a subject embedded in the already meaningful world, to which she responds and acts in light of her knowledge.

This reading of Kant's mind-dependent view of knowledge thereby contrasts with constructivist interpretations of it. Rather than picturing mind as making and *imposing* meaning, it is pictured as embodied and his subject *encountering* meaning in experience. Kant's view is also far from empiricist epistemology, for, to repeat Rödl, '*empirical knowledge always already contains general knowledge, which therefore is not inferred inductively from the former*' (*ibid.*). Acquiring knowledge is not a causal process of impingements on the mind, even though acquiring knowledge is based on experience. Rödl writes: 'when Kant says that we can acquire specific generic [general] knowledge only with the help of experience, he does not want to resurrect the empiricist epistemology'; rather:

> Generic thoughts require experience because they contain concepts that would be empty did they not also figure in temporal thoughts representing something given in intuition. Thoughts of the form *This N is/was doing A* and thoughts of the form *Ns do A*

need each other. Temporal thoughts confirm and refute generic thoughts, not in spite of the fact, but *because* any temporal thought always already contains generic thought. (2012, p. 203)

In sum, general knowledge and *a priori* concepts are not innate but acquired: they are developed in ongoing experience and *Bildung*, as children are initiated into already established forms of life.

The richness that can be found in Kant's view becomes lost in the often simplistic characterisations of his work in education theory. In response to familiar criticisms of dualisms and a detached conception of mind, this chapter has emphasised the *unity* of the capacities, of the general and particular, of mind and world, subject and object. I finish by repeating some quotations I have used before to underscore this unity. Rödl argues 'we perceive the temporal only as we apprehend the general in it, and we apprehend the general only as we see it at work in the temporal' (p. 207). Henrich sees the unity of self-consciousness and the unity of the world as indissoluble (1994). McDowell insists that 'thought and the world must be understood together. The form of thought is already just as such the form of the world. It is a form that is subjective and objective together' (2009a, p. 143). Stekeler-Weithofer too argues, 'our social conceptual distinctions and our (joint) perceptual access to the object are "grown together", and embedded in our practices' (2010a, p. 15). There is no dualism in these readings of Kant. Mind is not detached from lived life. The next chapter continues with the theme of the embeddedness of Kant's subject, the subject who is at the same time a moral agent.

NOTES

1. Derry's work is discussed below.
2. R. S. Peter's appropriation of Kant for his influential work, particularly in *Ethics and Education* (1966), is briefly discussed in the following chapter.
3. Kant writes 'I shall introduce a word of explanation in regard to the categories. They are concepts of an object in general, through which its intuition is regarded as determinate in respect of one of the logical functions of judgment' (B128).
4. For a useful summary of Brandom's (2019) *A Spirit of Trust: A Reading of Hegel's Phenomenology*, see Stephen Houlgate's (2019) review in Notre Dame Philosophical Reviews, at: https://dpr.nd.edu/news/a-spirit-of-trust-a-reading-of-hegels-phenomenology/.
5. We return to this point below.
6. Thompson uses this to argue that, like a practice, a 'life-form' (such as that of a human) is a teleological unity that provides a standard or measure of good and bad.

10

Situated and Sensitive Agents

SHEILA WEBB

As noted in the Introduction, Kant's epistemology has been the focus of this book because his thinking in his first *Critique* (1787) shapes and informs his thinking on ethical and practical knowledge. That is, his second and third *Critiques* – the *Critique of Practical Reason* (1788) and the *Critique of the Power of Judgment* (1790) – are not stand alone works that depart from his first *Critique*, rather his initial theorems remain fundamentally 'unchanged and serve continuously as premises in all of Kant's subsequent work' (Dieter Henrich, 1992, p. 6). With alternative understandings of his epistemological terms, Kant's moral and practical philosophy can also be read in very different ways. Historically and more broadly, Kant's ethics have been a wellspring for normative ideas about moral education and upbringing. However, like his epistemology, in contemporary philosophy of education Kant's moral and ethical theories tend to be mocked more often than seriously studied. Almost always presented negatively, they are subject to the same critique as his epistemology: for their dualisms and a disembodied mind imposing rules or maxims, with no sensitivity to context. Such criticisms strengthen the familiar 'Kantian' picture in education, a picture I continue to challenge in this chapter.

I did not set out to write about Kant in relation to ethics or morality because a proper engagement with these would require far more space than a chapter. However, I do feel it is important to make the point that Kant's ethics *can* be read very differently, in a much more friendly and productive way. At the centre of Kant's conception of what it is to be human (as the concept-using beings we are) is a

Interpreting Kant for Education: Dissolving Dualisms and Embodying Mind, First Edition. Sheila Webb.
Chapters and editorial organization © 2022 Philosophy of Education Society of Great Britain.
Published 2022 by John Wiley & Sons Ltd.

capacity for knowledge, and this same capacity is exercised whether the perception, knowledge or judgements made are moral *or* empirical, practical *or* theoretical. In this sense, the discussions through the book are as relevant to Kant's ethics as his epistemology. Properly understood, his metaphysics can clear the conceptual barriers that give rise to dualisms in the first place, and this is most significant; it presents a new conceptual footing from which to theorise about ethical and moral education. Continuing the argument that Kant's work can be understood in a very different light, this chapter illustrates the mismatch between characterisations of Kant's ethics in the philosophy of education and some commentary by Kant scholars.

Contemporary characterisations of Kant's ethics in education theory come almost entirely from theorists who are advocating an alternative approach. For example, Nel Noddings and Michael Slote criticise 'the liberal-Kantian emphasis on the autonomous individual, individual rights and universal principles', and assert that recent virtue ethics casts doubt on 'the Kantian assumption that the highest morality and human excellence require a conscious and conscientious attention and obedience to universal moral principles' (2003, p. 342). They also write:

> communitarians would want to question the moral powers and potential of individual cognition and reason; they hold, contrary to Kant, that it is only in relation to community values, traditions, and good habits acquired in their context that we can become morally virtuous. Since communities obviously differ in their traditions and values, the communitarian typically holds, therefore, that there can be no universal enlightened morality grounded in an appeal to forms of reason or rationality that are the same for everyone everywhere. (*Ibid.*)

Communitarians (and many postmodern and feminist theorists) tend to present Kant, on the one hand, as a radical individualist, with his subjects 'in full autonomous control' with 'individual cognition and reason'; and, on the other hand, as following or obeying 'universal principles', 'the same for everyone everywhere'. Peter Fitzsimons similarly disapproves of Kant's unattainable realm of universal reason: 'Kant's moral reasoning had relied upon a structure of concepts and categories by means of which an active reason imposes order on the world. Kantian principles of practical reason were not natural objects capable of discovery, so much as the creation of individual reason and desire' (2007, p. 561). Principles are seen as a creation of individual reason and desire. Fitzsimons further argues that Kant's ethics is:

> a self-contained 'system' that can't be explained by empirical means, with its 'truth' dependent on an individual and private evaluation, and its ultimate driver in an unknowable realm. And such inaccessible incomprehensibility begets both the notion of 'duty' and the 'categorical imperative' that governs all moral thought and action. (2007, p. 564)

Again, on the one hand, truth is seen to be dependent on individual and private evaluation, by self-sufficient subjects—making for a subjectivist, indeed relativist, characterisation of reason. And, on the other hand, Kant's moral law is seen in absolutist terms, to be obeyed whatever the context, making for a universalism that communitarians see as problematic.[1] And again we find dualistic readings. John White writes, 'Kant's rationale for his view depends on his "two-world" view of man as consisting of a noumenal self and a phenomenal self', with reason divorced from emotions and detached from desire (2005, p. 34). And Wilfred Carr describes a 'transcendental, noumenal "self" stipulating absolute standards to which the earth-bound, phenomenal self should conform' (1995, p. 38). These are familiar characterisations in education.

Kantian scholars, however, present very different pictures. Allen Wood, for example, argues:

> The idea that Kantian ethics 'divides the heart from the head' is based largely on a traditional misreading of about two pages early in the Groundwork (G4:397-399). This passage is usually totally misunderstood, and the misunderstanding conditions the grotesquely distorted image of Kant's ethics most people (except those who have seriously studied Kant) carry around in their heads. (2016)[2]

Time constraints on educationalists make engagement with major philosophers somewhat prohibitive, but this lack of philosophical undertaking has left the crude 'Kantian' picture in place. Onora O'Neill also comments on dualist interpretations of the noumenal and the phenomenal distinction. Instead of two separate selves, she argues, Kant 'offers sustained arguments to show that we are dealing with two standpoints, that neither can be reduced to the other, that each is indispensable, that they are not inconsistent' (2000, p. 75). She writes:

> Much recent work has indeed been predicated on unvindicated idealizations, which undermine its applicability to human life. Kant's approach may be read in another sense, in which the finitude of human beings, of human rationality and the connectedness among human beings, is stressed rather than denied. (p. 80)

Readings by mainstream philosophers show that Kant's ethical agents, like his epistemological agents, are dependent on their relations with others to become moral and rational subjects at all, and are always embedded in a particular context with its particular set of conditions that cannot be separated from thought about what to do. Kant's ethics can be seen as much closer to Aristotelian, communitarian and virtue ethics than is widely portrayed.

As dualist presuppositions have already been discussed, I want to draw attention to some other presuppositions that are relevant to both Kant's ethics and his epistemology. First, there are individualist assumptions about Kant's subject, which are reflected in typical characterisations of the autonomous individual, self-sufficient or self-contained, with truth dependent on private evaluation, as we saw above. Such characterisations are negatively portrayed and often compared with social and communitarian positions. But they miss something important about Kant's conception of knowledge. Critiquing such readings of Kant, Alexandra Newton argues that the individualist narrative 'overlooks one of the most important lessons of Kant's first *Critique*. For the narrative is predicated on the *empiricist* assumption that the subject of judgment or knowledge is the individual; her acts of judging are *hers* because they belong to her individual mind' (2014, p. 272). Like others, Newton contrasts Kant's conception of reason with that of Hume. Following Hume, she argues that if judgement 'or "assent" is understood to be "an immediate impression of the senses, or a repetition of that impression in the memory," then the subject of the judgment must be a single individual (T85). For it is only the individual that can be affected or receive sensory impressions' (p. 273). As discussed in Part One, reason for Hume is inert, it is a series of individual impressions, with no power of mind to unite these ideas, or as Newton says 'to glue or hold' these ideas 'together in a whole, either in myself, or between myself and others' (*ibid.*, p. 276). In contrast, reason for Kant is:

> a capacity for *knowledge*. Knowledge, unlike sentiment, impressions, or affections, is not attached to an individual; its

consciousness of itself involves a consciousness that it can be communicated with any rational subject. Kant can thus be understood as reflecting on a universally shared capacity for knowledge from within the first-person perspective of judging and working down from there to awareness of the individual judgers who share it. (p. 277)

Kant's subject is not (in the first instance) the individual, he is reflecting on a universally shared capacity for knowledge that presupposes the communicability of knowledge, before working down to the individual. The enlightenment ideal, Newton argues, 'consists *not* in a harmonious community of impersonal anonymous judgments, where there is no disagreement among the individual subjects of those judgments, but in a culture of actual conflict and disputation among individuals through their public *use* of reason' (p. 286). Stephen Engstrom similarly writes that the unity of knowledge originates 'in the cognitive capacity we share in common', and 'self-consciousness, rather than being grounded in the individual subject alone must likewise originate in that same common capacity' (2015). Kant's first concern is with what a shared common capacity is or could be (a capacity *in general*) but an individual's capacity will be dependent on the life she shares with others and where and when this is. With charges of a universalist reason and absolutist moral law, the same for everyone everywhere, contemporary critics fail to recognise that Kant's moral agent *can* be understood as someone born into a particular community, who will learn its particular norms, traditions and moral values through *Bildung*, through relations with others.

Developing one's capacity for moral knowledge and judgement takes place, and can only take place, from *within* a community, which again is what communitarians and Aristotelians hold. Engstrom talks of 'standard misreadings' of Kant's ethics, which 'have calcified in more recent times, particularly within anglophone philosophy, where for much of the last century preoccupation with utilitarianism and noncognitive approaches ensured that comparatively little notice was taken of the practical-cognitivist tradition' (2009, pp. x–xi). In educational theory though, Aristotle's practical-cognitivist tradition *has* been drawn on quite widely, but as previously discussed this tends to be presented in *opposition* to Kant. An example of this comes from David Carr, who over the years has written on Kant as a point of comparison with his own.

Carr's impressive work is influential in ethics and character education, and its importance derives from his drawing attention to the ethical dimensions of teaching and professionalism (2000, 2003, 2007, 2012, 2015). As with other theorists, I comment not on this work but on his interpretation of Kant. Carr has some strong criticisms of Kant, including his depiction of Kant as postulating a detached mind that imposes maxims, and he goes so far as to take Kant's view 'to be a potentially dangerous line of thought about the moral upbringing, training and education of children' (2012, p. 17). Carr sees the Cartesian problem as responsible for the instrumentalist culture in education; he writes, 'it is the Cartesian idea of a person as an inner, private and dissociated psychological entity' that haunted the heirs of Descartes. And Carr attributes this to Kant:

> Indeed, a particularly virulent form of Cartesianism seems deeply implicated in Kant's idea of the moral agent as a non-empirical subject of an other-worldly moral law ... For Kant the real person is not the empirical self of familiar everyday association, but rather the metaphysical *noumenal* self of transcendent practical rationality. (2003, p. 6)

Again Kant is read as if there were a dualism at the heart of his philosophy. Carr writes, 'it seems hard to deny that Kant's epistemology is bedevilled by a dichotomy of reason and experience', and the 'trouble precisely is that if mind and body are ontologically distinct entities, how might any kind of empirical story about the evolution of human theoretical or rational capacities be possible?' (p. 92). My argument has been that we need not attribute this dualism to Kant; mind and body should not be understood as 'ontologically distinct entities', nor a dichotomy read between reason and experience. Kant's noumenal self and empirical self are the same 'self'. As previously discussed, Kant's point is that a subject *not only* is an empirical subject (of familiar everyday association) but is also *self-conscious*: the self is one and the same; what is distinguished are two ways of knowing our 'self'. Kant's argument (against the empiricist) is that a subject knows herself to be a self-conscious and thinking subject not through experience but through spontaneity. Rödl writes about the concept of a 'thinking subject':

> Kant says the representation of a thinking subject cannot arise from experience, but only through self-consciousness. He does

not mean that the representation of a thinking subject does not involve experience, but rather that experience alone is not the source of the representation of a thinking subject. When I abstract everything I know from spontaneity, I shall not find a thinking subject in anything given to me by the senses. So Kant not only says that a self-conscious subject can be known through self-consciousness; he says, a self-conscious subject can be known *only* in this way. (2007, p. 181)

In saying that the 'I think' must be able to accompany all my representations (B131), Kant is formulating a description of self-consciousness (a power that unites representations or thoughts into a unity, a worldview) and that differentiates his view from that of Hume (according to whom reason lacks this power). As previously argued, this 'I' need not be read as *separate* from the empirical self; we can say that the 'I' (mind, self-consciousness) has a different 'mode of existence', as Stekeler-Weithofer puts it. That is, Kant's empirical self is at the same time a self-conscious and intentional agent; the distinctions he makes, which are conceptual and not ontological, are in service of fine-tuned explanation.

Carr sees Kant as the 'key philosophical influence on cognitivist attempts to explain learning in terms of the active construction and imposition of principles or rules on experience' (2003, p. 90). This is a familiar interpretation in education, as we have seen. Carr also writes of Kant:

> his moral philosophy is just about as thoroughgoingly *constructivist* as it is possible to be: to the extent that moral judgements constitute a type of prescription that is utterly dissociated from the normal workaday motives, wants or inclinations of agents, they are entirely innocent of empirical content or any necessary connection with sensible experience. For Kant, then, morality requires to be understood in terms of the rational *imposition* of rules or principles or pure practical reason on the rough and tumble of human practical experience. (p. 94)

This is reaffirmed later: moral judgements, having no empirical content, are simply 'a matter of active imposition of meaning-constitutive rules and principles on the brute data of sensory perception' (p. 100). Such 'imposition' interpretation presupposes empiricism's conception of sensibility, as brute sense data, and the layer-cake conception of mindedness, 'according to which the forms of the understanding are taken to be exogenous to the inner character of that which is given to us in sensibility' (Conant, 2016, p. 88). Carr's influential reading reflects the empiricist presuppositions that have shaped interpretations of Kant's terms and led to the widespread 'Kantian' imposition picture. In contrast to this, on the reading developed through the chapters, a judgement, whether moral or empirical, is *dependent* on sensible experience for content, and Kant provides for content with his conceptions of sensibility, intuition and receptivity. For Kant, the rough and tumble of practical experience *is* the content of thought and judgements, and of practical knowledge.

In arguing that Kant's moral and practical philosophy is rationalistic and his subject disembedded, Carr reflects other interpretive issues already considered. For instance, he writes:

> Kant's epistemology maintained that if the subjective experiences of agents were to be sources of genuine knowledge, such knowledge claims would need to correspond to an objective reality lying beyond experience which he called the *noumenon* or thing-in-itself. (2003, p. 187)

Again, Kant's use of thing in itself is understood as objective reality, and this as 'lying beyond experience'. Carr also argues:

> it is because Kant fails to question the empiricist idea that all perception is of the *appearances* of things—their observable properties of size, shape, colour, odour, texture, and so on—that he feels compelled to say that something 'behind' appearance is needed to secure the complete objectivity of accurate perceptions. (p. 104)

If, however, as previously urged, we understand things themselves and the way they appear as the *same* things (again with a conceptual, not a ontological distinction), the picture changes. That is, the compulsion that Carr attributes to Kant dissolves if we do not presuppose appearances to be something mental but instead understand appearances as the very world we know: appearances *themselves* secure the objectivity of experience; there is not something 'behind' experience, providing it. Kant's distinction between *mundus sensibilis* and *mundus intelligibilis* is a conceptual distinction not an ontological one. Observable properties of size, shape, colour, etc. *are* what we perceive through sensory consciousness.

Carr acknowledges that Kant's *epistemology* is less radically constructivist, as it involves rational principle *and* sensory input, suggesting that sensory input is not involved in moral knowledge. But Kant's ethical works should not be read as stand-alone texts, at odds with his epistemology, but located within it as part of a systematic whole. A subject's capacity for knowledge is the same capacity for both moral *and* theoretical knowledge, united in one consciousness, one 'I', which is to say that concepts used in ethical thinking and in deciding what to do *involve* empirical concepts. As Dieter Henrich writes, 'we certainly cannot claim that the world of objects and the world seen from the moral viewpoint are totally separate. For moral action has as its domain the very situations and circumstances we regard as part of the physical world' (1992, p. 4). It is incorrect to sever Kant's ethics, the forms through which we think ethically, from the forms of thought involved in empirical cognition; his thinking about moral and practical agency grow out of his reflecting on our distinctively human capacity for knowledge that constitutes his first *Critique*.

When it comes to the categorical imperative, there is of course a huge literature on this, as with all of Kant's work, but in educational theory it is usually negatively characterised and frequently derided. Carr (more seriously but still negatively) reads Kant's categorical imperative as 'a matter of the purely "cognitive" or intellectual inference of valid moral conclusions from true premises', and with a 'disconnection' between inner thought and outer reality (2003, p. 82). He similarly writes: 'the unconditional good will that drives moral conduct has its source not in any natural human desires or feelings, but in a rationally detached ("noumenal") grasp of the ethically self-justifying principles of the categorical imperative' (2007, p. 392). Reason and principles are routinely presented as divorced from desires, emotions and behaviour, as we saw with John White and Wilfred Carr above. This changes with non-dualist understanding of the capacities, and while much could be and has been said about dualist characterisations, given space limitation I want to draw attention to another presupposition that affects interpretation. The categorical imperative is typically characterised unsympathetically, as something external to the subject, like a list of what to do, universal principles to be obeyed no matter the context, or an unconditional command to be followed despite our desires and inclinations. Understanding the moral law in this absolutist way is part of 'Kantian ethics' in education, but, like his other terms, the categorical imperative can be understood very differently.

Karl Ameriks writes of misunderstandings that correspond 'to readings of Kant as a rigoristic rationalist who invokes a wholly transcendent "metaphysical self" that demands we act in a "Prussian" fashion and serve any law that is commanded simply for the sake of uniformity and obedience to what is "higher"' (2019, p. 87). In education, James Scott Johnston similarly takes issue with typical interpretations of the categorical imperative; he argues that:

> the Categorical Imperative is not a simple rule deployed from on high to judge the rightness or wrongness of our moral acts. I believe it is this misreading of the Groundwork—Kant's prefatory text to a metaphysics of morals—that is central to the ignorance, even contempt, of Kant in education scholarship. Kant wrote the Groundwork as a prologue to a fuller account of the metaphysics of morals, not as a stand-alone guide to constructing moral judgments. The view of moral judging as a detached, isolated, spectator making moral decisions in a supposed vacuum by calling on a commandment (the Categorical Imperative) is the single greatest reason for education passing over Kant. (2013, pp. 4–5)

This is similar to Wood's criticism (2016, quoted above) of the 'distorted picture' of Kant that abounds. Johnston critiques what he calls 'ossified' readings of Kant's ethics, those that privilege

> an autonomous rule-maker that brings all moral decisions to the final arbiter of the Categorical Imperative, with no accounting of the rich contexts and situations in which our ethical lives unfold and operate. In fact, Kant emerges as sensitive to contexts in moral decision-making; he is concerned with humanity and peoples (not simply individuals) and is well aware that reason has its limits in matters of human conduct. (2013, p. 4)

Johnston portrays Kant's moral philosophy in a very different light, as do other philosophers including Wood, Ameriks, Allison, Engstrom, Velleman, O'Neil, Korsgaard and Ameriks, and I recommend engagement with any of these.[3]

It has been argued that the objectivity of Kant's view (such as the 'ideal' world to which thought and judgement are 'answerable' for correctness) is obscured in the 'mind imposing meaning and maxims' pictures illustrated through Part Two. These characterisations tend to be made by theorists rejecting what are seen as Enlightenment ideals and absolutist ideas about reason (and turning to more postmodern, constructivist and social epistemology). But it would be a mistake not to acknowledge here Kant's influence on the powerful restatement of the idea of a liberal education provided by R. S. Peters, Paul Hirst and Robert Dearden in the 1960s and 1970s. These influential authors understood their project to have a Kantian orientation in salient respects, and one feature of this is a commitment to a conception of universal reason, with truth and objectivity understood in its light. The weight they gave to truth and objectivity, particularly in ethics, can be found in Kant, but this has, however, changed over time to become (through various avenues of critique) the kind of caricature illustrated above—a universal command deployed from on high to be obeyed by everyone everywhere. Suspicion of the very idea of universal reason and absolutist truth was aimed at their theories as well as at Kant's, but to repeat McDowell, it is 'the deformations to which the vocabulary of objectivity [and truth] has historically been prone' that is the problem (2000, p. 121)—with which Peters *et al.* would likely agree. Different conceptions of objectivity, reason etc. have been discussed through the chapters.

But while the objectivity that permeates their theories, and that they attribute to Kant, stands in contrast to the 'mind-makes-nature' interpretations of contemporary theorists, their readings uphold dualisms in several ways. The first is the idea, which was particularly powerful at the time of their writing, of a separation of reason and the passions, with reason given the role of ordering or governing the latter, and with the good will given pride of place. (This idea is reflected in criticisms of Kant by White and Carr above.) Furthermore, the choice of language used to express Kant's view is telling of the same presuppositions so often encountered. For instance, Peters writes of Kant:

> In the history of philosophy Kant rightly achieved fame for outlining this structure of concepts and categories by means of which order is imposed on the flux of experience; this he attributed to an active reason at work in the experience of all individuals. (1966, p. 49)

That order is imposed on the flux of experience, through an active reason at work, reflects the layer-cake conception of mind in the familiar 'Kantian' picture (presupposing empiricism's blind sense data that the mind then goes to work on). As argued, this misses the passive nature of most of our experience and the objectivity of seeing experience as *already* structured, not something that needs active ordering. Peters also writes that, for Kant, thought of the moral laws 'was inseparable from that of the autonomous rational beings who created them', and principles of practical reason 'were the creation of individuals possessed of reason and desire' (p. 209). While this can be understood in an objective way, the very language of individuals creating moral laws is more suggestive of constructivist interpretation. There was also at that time an absorption of the idea of a separation between pure and practical reason, in which the fact–value dichotomy appeared in a hardened form. In these senses, the appropriations of Kant by Peters, Hirst and Dearden are quite different to the reading being presented.

The conception of objectivity that has been developed, as something within thought rather than external to it, is related to understanding the moral law or categorical imperative also as something to be grasped from within, and not as something *external* to the subject (such as a universal command to be followed). It is related to Kant's conception of autonomy. The ideal of autonomy is Kant's third formulation of the categorical imperative. Again there is a vast literature on autonomy, especially as it has become such a key term in modern thought. I comment on autonomy only with reference to the presuppositions I am attempting to make explicit from characterisations in education theory: the individualism and the externalising of the categorical imperative as something to be obeyed from on high. Engstrom argues, '[w]hat is crucial to appreciate here is that the autonomy expressed in this requirement is precisely opposed to the individualism' that is often the target of criticism (2015). He explains:

> Autonomy is self-rule, but not the self-rule of an isolated rational individual. The autonomy invoked is the autonomy of practical reason not what is nowadays usually understood under the rubric 'personal autonomy'. Reason is the common discursive cognitive power that we all share as persons, and practical reason is a use of that same power, the use in which, by determining, in accordance with reason's conditions of unity, what we should do, we can move ourselves to do what we should do. (*Ibid.*)

Autonomy can be seen as a *capacity* for morality, a practical use of the common discursive cognitive power we share. 'Kant's own notion of autonomy', Ameriks similarly argues, should 'be defined in terms of an altogether higher notion of deciding on one's own', more like 'a free will that functions as a unique cause that is not at all externally determined in its causing' (2019, pp. 89–90). McDowell too writes of the normative force of reasons:

> to exercise autonomy is to subject oneself to the normative force of reasons. That is a self-subjection that is at the same time a self-determination. If one conforms to the authority of a reason one appreciates as such, one's thought or action is determined by the power in one by virtue of which one is able to recognize that authority and think or act accordingly. And it is in exercising that power that one is truly oneself. (McDowell, 2011b)

Moral and practical knowledge are not divorced from behaviour and action; quite the contrary, the imperative for action comes from knowledge itself. That is, when acting well we do not follow a command, or act merely in *accordance* or conformity with a moral law, but from our *knowledge* of it. This relates to discussions of autonomy in Part One.

Stephen Engstrom's work is helpful in explicating Kant's practical knowledge, knowledge of the good. He argues that 'the one great impediment to understanding how knowledge can be practical is the assumption that reason, the cognitive capacity itself' is passive and 'determined from without, by conditions external to its own conscious activity', so that 'only something separate from it can ever move us to act' (2009, p. 14); this reflects Kant's critique of Hume's empiricism. Engstrom explains that Kant does not depart from the Aristotelian conception of practical reason as a *capacity* for knowledge of the good. However, where Kant does differ is in reconceiving 'the good', which was previously seen as something *external* to reason, and apprehended *by* reason (presupposed in educational characterisations of the categorical imperative). Engstrom writes:

> Kant breaks sharply with the received view that reason's function in the practical sphere is to guide us in action on the basis of its antecedent apprehension of a final end that has an independent footing in nature. Kant rejects this picture, claiming that practical reason's most basic imperatives, those of morality, are categorical rather than hypothetical in form. Human reason must accordingly be conceived as autonomous, as the sole source of its principle of action. (2009, p. ix)

For Kant, as previously discussed, mind or thought alone can be the source, the 'causality', of our actions: we are not merely pushed around by external forces (determined from without); rather the power of thought *itself* can move us to act. This relates to Kant's distinction between 'cause' as heteronomous (one thing acting on another from outside) and as autonomous (self-determining). To repeat Sebastian Rödl from Part One: 'Thought or action in the light of reasons has a cause in virtue of, and only in virtue of, its conceiving that cause as its cause. Thus thought and action resting on reasons are not determined by a cause outside them … to act in the light of reasons is to be autonomous' (2016, p. 85).

Andrea Kern similarly argues that the 'causality' is not external on Kant's self-determining conception of mind as a capacity for knowledge, rather the capacity is the 'cause' of actions that manifest the capacity in question. She says that 'when Kant describes a teleological causal connection as a cause "whose efficacy is determined through concepts", what he has in mind, in this context, is a rational subject capable of intentional action' (2017, p. 242). This is the case whether a subject's knowledge is theoretical, practical or ethical; what is significant is that the 'obligation derives from the dictate of the agents own mind', as Christine Korsgaard also describes it (1996, p. 31).

But to repeat a point from above, this does not mean Kant's ethics is grounded in the individual or isolated minds. In discussing 'Kant's universalism about the subject of judgement', Newton explains that the subject of judgement may be understood 'as a universal subject, or a "consciousness in general" (B134n)' (2014, p. 278). This is because reason's 'perfection and realization in the individual' can 'be achieved only in sociality and culture' (p. 286). Like Engstrom above, she writes:

> This idea of a universal subject of judgment and knowledge should not invite the fantasy of a 'homunculus' that mysteriously underlies the judgments of different individual subjects. The idea is not a *metaphysical* one, but a *reflective* one. Kant's point … is precisely to deny that a universal consciousness exists (or persist through time) independently of our consciousness of it. The universal I is not a hidden metaphysical subject or substratum of judging, but is the unity of any judgment of which we are self-conscious in actively judging. (2015, p. 278)

Obligation (intentional action) derives from the cognitive capacity we share in common, 'consciousness in general'. This was illustrated in Chapter Eight with McDowell's example of a signpost: it relates to the normative bindingness of concepts discussed in Chapter Nine and the normative demands of an 'ideal' world considered in Chapter Four. Knowledge of a signpost will prompt normative action when encountering one. While in this case we are acting from our knowledge (of a signpost) in response to an empirical object, practical knowledge involves a different relation between subject and object.

Engstrom explains the difference: in the case of theoretical knowledge, 'the knowledge depends for its actuality on the actuality of its object', whereas in the practical case, 'the relation is the reverse: here the actuality of the object … depends on the actuality of the knowledge' (2009, p. 119). That is, unlike empirical knowledge, the object known *practically* (what to do) does not (yet) exist but is brought into existence through our activity. Engstrom describes the 'existential dependence' of theoretical knowledge on its object; but with practical knowledge, our experience of the object (the good) depends on it being produced by our (practical) knowledge. Taking the example of a promise, if I promise you something (that I will take care of your sick mother while you are away), the object (the good, taking care of your sick mother) does not yet exist but is brought into existence by my actions. At the same time, moral knowledge (of a promise) is kept in existence through such actions. Another way to put this is:

> the conceptual connection between the capacity to recognize a certain action to be something it would be good to do and the capacity to be moved by that recognition to do it (or perhaps to help another to do it) reflects the efficacy of practical knowledge, whereby it works to bring its object into existence or to maintain it in existence. (Engstrom, 2009, p. 14)

Shared knowledge (joint consciousness) of what a promise is prompts action and expectation of others, as self-conscious subjects reciprocally relate themselves to one another. (Of course, a promise can be broken, but this also involves shared comprehension—i.e., that it is broken). Kant's subjects can be read as situated and sensitive to others. They relate themselves to each other discursively and their actions spring from shared consciousness of their situation. There is not a separate act of reasoning, an imposition of rules, or inference to conclusions from premises *before* they act. The 'will' for Kant is our capacity for knowledge of the good, but 'the good' (practical knowledge) here is not *independent* of our knowledge of it: rather the existence of 'the good' *is* our knowledge of it. Moreover, a community is required for the realisation of practical knowledge of the good.

Autonomy (Kant's third formulation of the categorical imperative) can be seen as a capacity for knowledge of the good, a capacity that is 'possessed by all well-functioning human beings', Ameriks argues (2019, p. 102). Acknowledging that 'the opportunity to realize this capacity varies significantly', Ameriks writes, 'one can endorse O'Neill's deeply anti-Luciferian understanding of Kant's main idea: "autonomy is not the special achievement of the most independent but the property of any reasoning being"' (*ibid.*). Like Engstrom, Newton and the other theorists mentioned above, Ameriks presents a rich picture of Kant's ethics and again I recommend engagement with any of these.

In contrast to the often simplistic and negative caricatures of Kant's ethics found in the philosophy of education, I have attempted to show in this chapter that they can be understood entirely differently, with Kant's ethical subjects sensitive to context and always situated in a shared world written through with norms and values. 'As human beings', Johnston says of Kant's ethics, 'belonging to families, to institutions, to culture, we are always already in contact with norms, rules, conventions, beliefs, and traditions ... We love, hate, envy, enjoy, and wish to please others. These facts of the matter are shared bases for our moral conduct' (2013, p. 16). They are the shared bases we are born into and that shape our moral development – the *bildung* that, for Kant, makes us human.

NOTES

1. This puzzling contradiction tends not to be unpacked in such communitarian critique. We return to this below.
2. Wood tells us that his own work 'on Kant has been largely an attempt to provide a more accurate picture of what Kantian ethics really is, freeing it from many misunderstandings due to its 19th century reception and its invidious depiction by consequentialist critics' (2016).
3. For an in-depth discussion of the categorical imperative in particular, see Engstrom's *The Form of Practical Knowledge* (2009).

11

Contrasting Readings of Kant

SHEILA WEBB

In this final chapter I again contrast readings of Kant in order to revisit and expand on some of the main differences in interpretation that have been discussed through the chapters. It looks at some readings of Kant by Anglophone theorists for a sense of the source of the familiar 'Kantian' picture in education. Presuppositions about mind and an external world can be seen at work in these influential readings. But the difficulty of setting aside preconceptions when interpreting unfamiliar work (particularly from a different time and tradition) is considered. Discussion draws together strands from the book to review key differences in translations, further clarifying the reading being presented.

I start with H. A. Prichard's influential interpretation of Kant at the start of the 20th century in Oxford, for this reflects presuppositions from mind-independent epistemology about the relation between mind and world that underlie different readings. In *Kant's Theory of Knowledge* (1909), Prichard criticises Kant intensely. His central argument is that on Kant's view we cannot know things in themselves but only as they appear to us, and this is a problem.[1] Prichard writes of the 'opposition between things as they are in themselves and things as they are as perceived' (p. 71). Note the rewording of 'things in themselves' as 'things *as they are* in themselves', which he sees as distinct from 'things *as they are* as perceived', leading him to interpret a 'distinction between two different realities' (p. 75). This is an early example of Kant's conceptual distinction being read as an ontological distinction, positing two different realities.[2] Furthermore, interpreting appearance

Interpreting Kant for Education: Dissolving Dualisms and Embodying Mind, First Edition. Sheila Webb.
Chapters and editorial organization © 2022 Philosophy of Education Society of Great Britain.
Published 2022 by John Wiley & Sons Ltd.

as 'being necessarily something mental', Prichard writes that it 'cannot possibly be said to be extended' and therefore 'access to a non-mental reality is excluded' (p. 76). This reflects the empiricist assumptions identified in Chapter One: assuming mind as separate from material reality, appearances are read as something mental and therefore access to non-mental reality is excluded. However, Chapter Two introduced different understandings of Kant's capacities, which were continually revisited to emphasise their *unity* in perception (and experience). With sensibility understood as 'transformed' by rational capacities, we can say that reality is accessed by anyone with the requisite capacities. And with appearances understood as the ordinary empirical world (ideality was discussed in Chapter Four): it is appearances themselves that provide objectivity.

In tandem with the familiar picture in education, a dualism is identified between Kant's capacities. Prichard writes that Kant 'by his distinction between the sensibility and the understanding, sets himself another problem ... He has to determine what *a priori* judgements are related to the sensibility and to the understanding respectively' (p. 34). And, 'For Kant, the conformity is not between something within and something without the mind, but between two realities within the mind' (p. 15). Two realities within a mind separate from reality. 'If in perception we apprehended reality as it is, no difficulty would arise. But we do not', Prichard writes of Kant (p. 77); and he concludes that 'in the end the realities perceived are merely our perceptions' (p. 139). This reflects both appropriations and criticisms of Kant in education for subjectivist 'mind-makes-nature' pictures with the world seen as unknowable and objectivity becoming completely lost. With non-dualist understandings of the capacities, by contrast, we can say that in perception we apprehend reality as it is.

Another example illustrates the mind-independent assumptions about knowledge that Prichard brings to interpreting Kant. This is what he says of Kant's 'impossible anti-thesis':

> To take Plato's example, suppose that we are looking at a straight stick, partially immersed in water. If we have not previously seen the stick, and are ignorant of the laws of refraction, we say that the stick is bent. If, however, we learn the effect of refraction, and observe the stick from several positions, we alter our assertion. We say that the stick is not really bent, but only looks or appears bent to us. But, if we reflect at all, we do not express our meaning by saying that the

stick *is* bent to us as perceiving, though not in reality. The word 'is' essentially relates to what really is. (1909, p. 72)

Using Plato's example, Prichard reduces to absurdity Kant's claim that we can know only appearances and not things in themselves. Again, this is because he interprets appearances as something, to use his words, 'from the side of the perceiving subject as opposed to that of the object perceived' (p. 73). A dualism is identified between subject and object. However, the absurdity dissolves if, again, appearances are understood not as something mental but as the object perceived. As argued, on Kant's Copernican view, correctness does not come from comparison with a mind-external reality; rather, we make sense of things from a human standpoint *within* an already up-and-running system of concepts, an already meaningful world, 'without needing to break out through a boundary that encloses the system of concepts', as McDowell puts it (1996, p. 36). That our general knowledge is (unreflectively) exercised in perception means we can say that our knowledge of sticks (as straight and inflexible) and our knowledge of refraction (water can distort the appearance of things) means that (if we know these things) we will judge that the stick is not really bent but looks that way in water.

The argument from illusion, a concern for theorists over many years, exemplifies the scepticism inherent in traditional empiricist epistemology. With his Copernican insight, Kant changes the way perception is understood, as involving subjectivity, our rational capacities. As McDowell argues, 'we cannot suppose that intelligible order has completely emigrated from the world' (1998b, p. 178), the 'cognitive faculty needs to be in the picture not just to account for the unity with which certain content figures in an intuition, but also, in the guise of the productive imagination, to provide for part of the content itself' (2009a, p. 262). As discussed in Chapter Nine, general concepts go beyond sensible intuition; 'a knowledgeable judgment enabled by an intuition has content that goes beyond the content of the intuition. The intuition makes something perceptually present to the subject, and the subject recognizes that thing as an instance of a kind' (p. 266). In similar vein, Rödl articulates this in terms of the general and particular: 'we perceive the temporal' (*this* stick looks bent in water) 'only as we apprehend the general in it' (sticks look bent in water), 'and we apprehend the general' (sticks look bent in water) 'only as we see it at work in the temporal' (2012, p. 207). If, however, we have not learnt about refraction, that water distorts the way things look, then we may well judge that the stick we see partially immersed in water is bent (until we learn otherwise from knowledgeable others). Our general knowledge is involved in encountering particulars. Prichard's characterisation of Kant's 'problem' relates to discussion in Chapter Three: the empiricist Hume takes the senses to deliver individual representations that have no connections among them; that is, 'the unity of a substance, which holds together changeable states', Rödl explains, 'cannot be found in what is given to the senses' (2007, p. 179). This is because for Hume, 'the discursive capacity lacks any spontaneous power of combination' (Engstrom, 2015, p. 21). Prichard's argument to absurdity about appearances stems from his Humean presuppositions about knowledge. In contrast to Hume, Kant's conception of reason is of a power that spontaneously *unites* representations into a body of knowledge (a worldview that I can call 'mine', self-consciousness); otherwise, Kant writes, 'I should have as many-coloured and diverse a self as I have representations of which I am conscious to myself' (B134). To repeat Rödl: 'Thoughts of the form *This N is/was doing A* and thoughts of the form *Ns do A* need each other. Temporal thoughts confirm and refute generic thoughts, not in spite of the fact but *because* any temporal thought always already contains generic thought' (2012, p. 203).[3] Again, the *unity* of the general and particular, thought and reality, mind and world has been emphasised throughout the chapters for marking a significant difference from dualist interpretations.

Like Prichard, Bertrand Russell and G. E. Moore read Kant as holding that the objects of perception and objects of knowledge are constituted by our mental activity. Thus, Kant's view is taken to be a subjectivist and relativist position. Fundamental to their rejection of this view is again the desire for mind-independent knowledge. Prichard argues that our desire is to know things 'as they are, i.e. as they are independently of perception' (1909, p. 77). The desire to know things independently of perception is incoherent on Kant's view, for it is through perception that we know things. The desire to shed or exclude the first person—subjectivity and mind—for what is taken to be a totally objective account of knowledge was discussed in Chapter Five. It is this deep-seated desire—the possibility of *mind-independent* perception and knowledge—that both Rorty and McDowell are concerned to expel (as discussed in Chapter Six), for this embeds a Cartesian dualism. Unlike Rorty, however, McDowell acknowledges the appeal of traditional empiricism and recognises that unless presuppositions that give rise to this dualism are exposed or 'exorcised', they will continue to creep back into our thinking.

I agree with McDowell, and this is why much philosophic work in every chapter of this book has been aimed at trying to dislodge them, for they not only stand in the way of non-dualist understanding of the capacities and therefore a more fertile reading of Kant, but stand in need of 'exorcising' from much educational theorizing that continues to give them life.

Moore's influential *Refutation of Idealism* (1903) reflected 'a prejudice that was imported to the United States', a prejudice that arose, according to Italo Testa, 'with the arrival of logical empiricism between 1933 and 1940 and [that was] historiographically canonized by Bertrand Russell's *A History of Western Philosophy* (1946)' (2016, pp. 7–8). Scepticism towards Kant and German Idealism stemmed from the dominance of empiricist suppositions about knowledge. David Pacini was a student at Harvard University in the 1970s and talks of the reception of Dieter Henrich, who offered a course on the philosophy of Kant and his successors. Pacini writes:

> The analytic mindset of the [Harvard philosophy] department at that time harbored a skepticism, deriving in part from G.E. Moore and Bertrand Russell, toward the tradition Henrich was interpreting: their wariness deemed such thinking little more than a pastiche or metaphysical phantasmagoria. (Pacini, 2003, p. x)

It was precisely this scepticism that Henrich had sought to address.[4] Pacini continues:

> More focused opposition arose from those for whom even the mere hint of these topics caused more chill than Cambridge's winters, and who were bemused that students would endure either of these elements merely to hear Henrich. So encumbered, Henrich's hopes for dialogue were not substantially realized. (*Ibid.*)

The students however were enthusiastic and, as Henrich worked mainly from memory, they made transcripts of his lectures; these were circulated and kept, and later put together for a book, *Between Kant and Hegel: Lectures on German Idealism* (2003), from which the above quotations are taken.[5]

Kant for Richard Rorty is the primary target of his whole critique of philosophy. As demonstrated in Chapter Six, Rorty associates Kant with the foundationalism of the empiricist tradition because he sees them as sharing the idea of mind as mirror of a mind-external nature, a picture he rejects entirely (1979). Rorty's antagonism was such that while at Princeton University he thought of introducing a new course called 'An Alternative History of Modern Philosophy' that would bypass Kant; but he had to abandon it because the history could not be told *without* Kant (Geuss, 2008). For, as discussed in Chapter Three, Kant completely changed the course of philosophy with his Copernican insight, re-describing what it means to be human and revolutionising what it is to have a mind, with those after him responding to or developing his work in various ways. James Tartaglia points out, 'Kant was the principal target of Rorty's career, but the antidote to Kantianism he recommended was essentially Kantian' (2016, p. 2).

Peter Strawson's (1966) *Bounds of Sense: An essay on Kant's Critique of Pure Reason* was and continues to be an enormously influential reading and critique of Kant. Strawson acknowledges the power of Kant's philosophy and is sympathetic to Kant's project of investigating mind in terms other than those of the natural sciences: '[Kant] knew very well that such an empirical inquiry was of a quite different kind from the investigation he proposed into the fundamental structure of ideas in terms of which alone we can make intelligible to ourselves the idea of experience of the world' (1966, p. 2). But Strawson goes on to reject much of Kant's philosophy, objecting mainly to what he refers to as Kant's transcendental subjectivism and idealism, 'according to which the whole world of Nature is merely appearance' (p. 6). Strawson writes:

> The doctrines of transcendental idealism, and the associated picture of the receiving and ordering apparatus of the mind producing Nature as we know it out of the unknowable reality of things as they are in themselves, are undoubtedly the chief obstacles to a sympathetic understanding of the *Critique*. (1966, p. 6)

Reading 'things as they are in themselves'[6] as objective reality, and with mind's 'receiving and ordering apparatus' producing Nature out of this, Strawson gives life to the (layer-cake) 'Kantian' picture still dominant in education. He also writes of 'the forms imposed by our sensibility and our understanding' (*ibid.*), strengthening the 'imposing' characterisations that are familiar. Interpreting mind as making Nature leads Strawson to argue that Kant is close to British empiricist Berkeley, whose subjectivist view doubts the existence of reality.

Kant's rejection of this view and his careful distinction between his 'transcendental idealism' about forms and Berkeley's 'material idealism' about matter were discussed in Chapters Seven and Eight.[7]

Strawson's reading of Kant can be described as a 'two-worlds' reading. Robert Greenberg explains that 'two-world' theorists

> hold that Kant was ontologically committed to two distinct types of object—appearance and thing in itself—with no single type of object spanning the two types in some way—a way in which appearance and thing in itself can be considered as mere aspects of one and the same object. (2008, p. xv)

Characterisations of Kant's view in educational theory are overwhelmingly 'two-world' readings. Like other Kantian commentators, Rüdiger Bubner responds to dualist readings: 'Spontaneity is not some synthesizing or ordering power that stands opposed to an anonymous sphere of sense data, contingently impinging on us from the outside and thereby providing the basis for all empirical knowledge' (2002, p. 209). What McDowell is driving at in *Mind and World*, Bubner writes, is 'the Kantian discovery of *spontaneity*, that specific achievement of subjectivity whose beginning and ground lies not outside but within itself' (*ibid.*). Again, the unity of the capacities has been emphasised throughout Part Two in response to frequent criticisms of dualisms and a detached conception of mind. To repeat Engstrom, 'a proper understanding' of the capacities not only 'eliminates the appearance of dualism', but also alleviates concern about 'an unacceptable subjectivism' (2006, p. 2).

Andrea Kern also is concerned to emphasise the unity of the capacities, and her remarks on Strawson's reading help further clarify the main difference in interpretations. She argues that 'receptivity and spontaneity do not characterize two distinct capacities, but are *two aspects of a single capacity*', a capacity for knowledge (2006, p. 157). She explains that 'the faculty of sensibility is not a different faculty from the understanding, but rather that sensibility and understanding are one faculty, which one can only pick apart for the purposes of analysis' (p. 158). She explains the distinction:

> When Kant calls understanding and sensibility 'faculties' or 'capacities', then he represents them as something general that *explains* the acts that actualize them ... What these characterizations have in common is that they describe the relation of a

capacity to its acts as one of *explanation* … The understanding explains acts of the understanding, sensibility explains acts of sensibility, etc. (p. 153)

Kern sees Strawson as the epitome—in a sense, the best expression—of two-world readings. She quotes him: 'The doctrine of synthesis rests firmly on the distinction of faculties. What is given in sense alone, in mere receptivity, is one thing; what is made out of it by the understanding, the active faculty, … is quite another' (quoted in Kern, 2006, p. 154). On such readings, Kern points out, 'a representation springs from *either* the receptive *or* the spontaneous faculty, it is ruled out that a receptive representation *as such* be self-conscious' (*ibid.*). And with the tendency to interpret two distinct capacities, cognition is seen as the result of *two steps*. Kern describes this:

In the first step, an object actualizes the subject's faculty of sensibility: the subject has a sensible representation, which does not yet belong to the unity of self-consciousness. In the second step, the subject produces a spontaneous representation by which it brings the given sensible representation inside the unity of self-consciousness. (*Ibid.*)

Interpreting sensibility as empiricism's raw sense data and mind as going to work on this was shown to be inherent in readings of Kant as a constructivist throughout Part Two and reflects the 'layer-cake' conception of mind discussed in Chapter Eight. It was argued that with the activity of mind prioritised—ordering experience and imposing meaning and maxims—the objective roles of intuition and receptivity in providing content become lost.

James Conant also comments on the Anglophone tendency to dualistic interpretation of the capacities. 'It is standard in Anglophone Kant commentary', he argues, to speak 'of a concept "imposing" a certain form of unity on a manifold', and the various forms of imposition terminology 'naturally encourage a certain picture of the relation between sensibility and understanding' (2016, p. 88). Again, 'imposition' terminology is all pervasive in characterisations of Kant's view in educational theory. For instance, David Carr talks of the 'active imposition of meaning-constitutive rules and principles on the brute data of sensory perception' (2003, p. 10). Conant argues that this misconceives the relation between sensibility and understanding, which is one of deep *unity*: one depends on its relation to the other to be the capacity it is (Conant, 2016, p. 80). Conant reminds us that:

> For Kant mere intuitions without concepts must remain blind: without some understanding of its internal relation to a possible concept, there would be nothing that could constitute the apperceiving subject's self-consciously recognizing some putative 'intuition' as a re-occurrence of the 'same' intuition in consciousness. And mere concepts without intuitions must remain empty: without some internal relation to intuition, there would be nothing that could constitute the apperceiving subject's self-consciously taking herself to be employing the same concept across a series of objectively valid acts of judgment. And we saw that Kant's opposition to both empiricism and rationalism flows from a single source: his conception of the interrelation of the perceptual and intellectual dimensions of our single unitary capacity for knowledge. (2020, p. 863)

Intuitions and concepts, sensibility and the understanding, are aspects of a single unitary capacity for knowledge, as has been continually stressed. 'Our *Erkenntnisvermoegen* is a unified capacity that is thus *in energeia* in each and every exercise of its ingredient capacities of perception, imagination, understanding, judgment, and reason', Conant writes (2016, p. 116). As we have seen, portrayals in education put all the focus on the activity of mind and intuition is hardly mentioned.

The rich notion of intuition has been discussed in many chapters. Importantly, Stekeler-Weithofer highlights its objectivity and talks of the social and practical aspects of intuition, as it socially grounds joint reference to things and their features in actual experience. Learning deictic reference, for instance, involves complex social activity, always embedded in context. Our 'social conceptual distinctions and our (joint) perceptual access to the object are "grown together" and embedded in our practices', he writes (2010a, p. 15). Objectivity comes from this joint perceptual access to objects in the world through subjectivity. This shows mind as situated and connected with things perceived, which is in contrast to widespread criticisms of the 'Kantian' detached mind. As a child develops the ability to jointly refer to things with others, she expands her conceptual capacities through which the world is disclosed. As discussed, this does not mean disclosure is always clear or the world is fully in view; at any time our concepts are partial, opaque, underdetermined and subject to error. But that the meaningful world is disclosed in perception is different to a disembedded mind imposing meaning. Rödl too stresses the unity of the capacities. 'The power of thought transforms human sensibility', he argues (2007, p. 70), and further: 'that we apprehend substances and their movement through the senses, and forms and their laws through the intellect, are two sides of a coin' (2012, p. 207). Understanding their unity shapes conceptions of experience, which has also been repeatedly discussed. As Stekeler-Weithofer writes, experience 'as Kant uses the word is already conceptually formed' and 'must always already be seen as taking part in complex and joint practice' (2010a, p. 19); moreover, 'Kant's whole analysis is misread if we do not keep this in mind' (p. 5).

That experience comes as already structured, as already meaningful, contrasts with mind having to order or make sense of it. David Jardine, for instance, holds that reason 'actively constructs orderliness out of the chaos of experience' (2006, p. 23). Understanding experience as already meaningful comes from intuition having the same kind of content or 'logical form' as possible judgements. Kern quotes Kant on this[8]: 'The same function which gives unity to the various representations *in a judgment* also gives unity to the mere synthesis of various representations *in an intuition*' (B104-105). 'If we take this passage seriously', Kern argues, 'then receptive and spontaneous representations are not to be distinguished according to the kind of faculty from which they spring'; she explains:

> Receptive representations involve an actualization of the understanding. It is not that sensible intuitions are distinguished from judgments in that the former have non-conceptual content … Rather, sensible intuitions and judgments are distinguished in that, in the case of sensible intuitions, the conceptual content is the result of the object's *acting on* the subject, whereas, in the case of judgments, the conceptual content is the result of the *self-activity* of the subject. (Kern, 2006, p. 155)

This contrast illustrates the passive nature of receptivity compared with the self-activity involved in judgement, reflection, conversation etc. As argued in Chapters Eight and Nine, constructivist 'mind imposes meaning' interpretations do not make this distinction, which loses objectivity and the idea that judgement is answerable to how things are.

Karl Ameriks also emphasises the objective and passive aspects of experience and perception for Kant. He argues, 'the *Critique* proper begins, in its step one, with an objective statement', namely, 'that "objects (*Gegenstände*) are *given* to us" (A19/B33)' (2019, p. 140). He continues: 'Kant emphasizes the term "given," to stress that we are in part passive beings rather than creative intuitors, but the implications of all the other terms in his statement are also very important: that we are dealing with concrete *Gegenstände* (rather than mere abstract *Objekte*), that the objects are plural, that they are actual and not merely hypothetical, and that they are asserted with respect to a plurality of subject ("us")' (*ibid.*). The plurality of Kant's subject was discussed in Chapter Ten, and the objectivity and passivity involved in much of our contact with the world have been a continual theme, for again they are obscured in the widespread imposition characterisations. But it was also noted that while objectivity is obscured in contemporary interpretations, earlier theorists of education, such as R. S. Peters, Paul Hirst and Robert Dearden, were committed to a Kantain conception of universal reason, with truth and objectivity very much central. This objective strand of Kant's view was rightly emphasised in response to moves towards more relativist theories, particularly in ethics. But as argued, their theories, like Kant's, became subject to critique with growing suspicion of Enlightenment ideas and universalism about reason. And these theorists, too, use language of mind actively ordering experience and imposing structure, thus exaggerating the activity of mind and obscuring the passive aspects of most of our sense experience.

McDowell gives voice to these aspects of experience. In talking about the 'authority' of conceptual constraint, he writes:

> In the thick of experience, the conceptual capacities we currently have are drawn into operation in a way that is not up to us. But for them to be intelligible conceptual capacities in the relevant sense, capacities that belong to the spontaneity of the understanding, it must be that in having them drawn into operation we find ourselves answerable to the authority of norms for thought that constitute the content of the capacities. And this subjection to authority comes within the scope of the self-determination idea. So, though our experience at any time is determined, outside our control, by concepts we find ourselves with at the time, we have a responsibility over time to ensure that our acquiescence in the concepts we find

ourselves with is not a matter of subjecting ourselves to an alien authority, exercised by dogma or tradition. (2009a, p. 97)

That our conceptual capacities are drawn into play 'in a way that is not up to us' in experience again illustrates the passive nature of much of our contact with the world. We are bound by 'the authority of norms for thought that constitute the content of the capacities' from shared consciousness, layers of historically evolved social practices embodied in concepts and language. To repeat McDowell:

> In being initiated into a language, a human being is introduced into something that already embodies putatively rational link-ages between concepts, putatively constitutive of the layout of the space of reasons, before she comes on the scene. This is a picture of initiation into the space of reasons as an already going concern … [T]he language into which a human being is first initiated stands over against her as a prior embodiment of mindedness, of the possibility of an orientation to the world. (1996, p. 125)

'Ideality' and the idea of an already meaningful world that we are born into were discussed in Chapter Four; as we learn a language we are bound by 'the authority of norms for thought'. But as also argued, norms and concepts are continuously revised (maintained, altered, rejected), through participation in our everyday discursive and social practices, discussed in Chapter Five. As McDowell insists, '[t]here must be a standing willingness to refashion concepts and conceptions if that is what reflection recommends' (1996, pp. 12, 13).

In this book I have attempted to refashion concepts and conceptions for a richer understanding of Kant's insights. The difficulty of setting aside familiar understandings has been a continual theme. For this McDowell has been most valuable, particularly in helping to 'dislodge' empiricist understandings of mind and world (and other concepts) and think of them in a different way. But McDowell too has not been immune to the prevailing influence of dualist metaphysics; working in the analytic tradition, he was influenced by two-world readings, particularly those of Strawson and Sellars. This led him to write in *Mind and World* that Kant spoils his picture with his transcendental story and that we should look instead to Hegel to correct this aspect of Kant's framework (1966, pp. 40–45). This characterisation of Kant prompted objections. For instance, Günter

Zöller wrote a paper entitled 'Of Empty Thoughts and Blind Intuitions: Kant's Answer to McDowell', in order 'to demonstrate the limitations of a selective appropriation of Kant and the philosophical potential of a more comprehensive and thorough consideration of his work' (2010, p. 1). McDowell responded by rereading Kant's first *Critique* in 'a collaborative enterprise that I am privileged to be engaged in with my colleagues James Conant and John Haugeland' (2009a, p. 4).

Since rereading Kant, McDowell acknowledges a change, writing that he 'corrects the picture I gave, meaning it to be Kantian, in *Mind and World*': 'There I took it that "object", in the Kantian idea that intuitions are of objects, just mean "objective somewhat", including, for instance, states or affairs. I now think it means something much closer to what "object" means in the standard translations of Frege' (p. 37, footnote).[9] When Kant implies that thought without intuitions would be empty, McDowell writes, he means they must have *content*, a subject matter. This is Kant's transcendental requirement, McDowell explains:

> The transcendental requirement is that it must be intelligible that conceptual activity has a *subject matter*. And Kant's thought is that this is intelligible only because we can see how the very idea of a conceptual repertoire provides for conceptual states or episodes in which a subject matter for conceptual activity is sensibly present, plainly in view in actualizations of capacities that belong to the repertoire. (p. 37)

Intuition provides content, a subject matter that can be thought or referred to. Stekeler-Weithofer writes, 'It seems to me also that in his recent papers and books McDowell adopts a "Kantian" position as I have defended it for quite some time, namely that a proper understanding of the notion of *Intuition* is of highly systematic importance for understanding the possibility of reference and of world-related content not only of judgments about things present to us but all things in the real world at large' (2010c, p. 2). The role of intuition is another aspect that has been repeatedly highlighted through the chapters because of its lack in the widespread 'Kantian' imposition picture.

McDowell points out a misleading translation problem, even within some 'one-world' readings. This is regarding understandings of Kant's appearances and things in themselves, which we have so often come across. McDowell writes:

I here correct the two-worlds picture of Kant that I presupposed in *Mind and World.* But note that what Kant insists on, in passages like Bxxvii, is an identity of things as they appear in our knowledge and 'those same things as things in themselves'; not 'those same things as they are in themselves'; (This latter wording pervades, e.g., Henry E. Allison's non-two-worlds reading, in *Kant's Transcendental Idealism*). Things in themselves are the very things that figure in our knowledge, but considered in abstraction from how they figure in our knowledge. That is not to say: considered as possessing, unknowably to us, other properties than those they appear as possessing in our knowledge of them. With this latter construal of things in themselves, the non-two-worlds reading might as well be a two-worlds reading. The picture still involves two realms of fact, one knowable by us and one unknowable by us; it does not undermine the damage this does to say that the same objects figure in both. (2009a, p. 42 footnote)

As this illustrates, small differences in translation can result in significant differences to the overall picture. The length of McDowell's collaborative reading, over many years, indicates the difficulty of engaging deeply with unfamiliar and complex texts; Kant had himself similarly engaged deeply with the ideas and issues of his predecessors, from the ancients up to his contemporaries. In the process of articulating his own position in relation to these, Kant redefined and reinvented many existing philosophical concepts and introduced new ones. The complexity and intricacy of his terms make interpretation difficult, Howard Caygill writes, for '[n]ot only are many terms defined disjunctively, but they also participate in a network of related terms which further enrich and complicate their meaning' (1995, p. 2). For Kant (contrary to typical portrayals in education), concepts are never fixed but always up for change. 'In Kant's own terms, philosophical concepts were *acroamatic* and not *axiomatic*,' Caygill writes, 'by which he meant that they were the discursive outcome of an open-ended process of reflection upon philosophical problems' (1995, p. 2).

Readings and commentary on Kant continue today in many languages across the globe as the significance of his work continues to be relevant and fruitful. There are of course many different readings and interpretations of Kant as his insights are used to throw light on an enormous range of philosophical problems. I have drawn on some of these readings in order to question the intellectualist and dualist picture of Kant that prevails in educational theory and to show the possibility of interpretations that are of much greater value. While there is no one correct reading of Kant, some readings are more credible than others. Stekeler-Weithofer argues:

> There are widespread misreadings of Kant's philosophy, especially in Anglophone traditions, that stem from prevalent empiricist prejudices on one side, some underestimations of Kant's terminological distinctions on the other. A third problem results from the time-bound and idiosyncratic ways in which Kant tried to articulate the things he wanted to say. But instead of complaining about possible misleading connotations and perhaps still vague metaphors in Kant's writings—such complaint is rather an attitude of beginners—we should always give his texts the best interpretation *de re* possible. (2010b, p. 5)

A *de re* interpretation, as opposed to a more literal *de dicto* interpretation, means articulating Kant's arguments using not only reliable translations from German into English, but from Kant's language into our own. This is why I have quoted less of Kant's own text and more of recent commentary, for this uses contemporary language that makes Kant's insights more accessible. The mainstream theorists I draw on all present Kant in a positive light, without a dualism or detached mind, and give philosophical authority to this unfamiliar reading aimed at theorists of education. I recommend engaging with their work, not only for an understanding of Kant but for the rich insights and resources they offer for thinking about a range of educational issues.[10]

Robert Brandom says that Kant's status for contemporary philosophers is 'what the sea was for Swinburne: the great, gray mother of us all' (2013, p. 107). However, in contemporary educational theory, as we have seen, Kant's status remains far from revered, with more criticism than acclamation. This book has tried to improve his status. Rather than being responsible for dualisms and a detached conception of mind, Kant gives us valuable resources for seeing that such a dualism is an illusion, and he shows the conceptual inconsistencies in empiricist epistemology in which that illusion is embedded. But this book is not only about Kant. As Cigman and Davis point out: 'What is really at stake are questions about the nature of knowledge and how we learn, of what constitutes human being and the good life.

These are of profound importance for our culture as a whole' (2009, p. ix). And as Standish also writes:

> Rigorous, ethically charged epistemological enquiry uncovers presuppositions of a metaphysical kind, disturbing those primary categories in which the world is understood (such as subject and object, cause and reason). This effects shifts in the understanding of the way that the world comes to light, even in the understanding of what the world is; and, in finding new bearings in the philosophy of mind, it modifies the idea of human being itself. Inevitably these shifts in understanding affect what education can be. (2020, p. ccliii)

The content of these pages – uncovering metaphysical presuppositions, disturbing understandings of familiar concepts and comparing interpretations of Kant's terms – are at the same time exploring different ideas about the nature of knowledge and concepts, about cognition and rationality, about how we learn, and what it is to be minded and to be human. In this way, the discussion through the chapters can be seen as contributing to the open-ended process of developing these profound and rich ideas in the philosophy of education, as well as a critique of the impoverished conceptions inherent in the 'performativity' culture that presently shapes too much of education. Delving into Kant's philosophy or engaging with the now flourishing literature generated by renewed interest in it, provides a wealth of fascinating resources for exploring these ideas so fundamental to education.

NOTES

1. Discussing Kant's conception of space, Prichard writes 'Kant's conclusion (and also, of course, his argument) presupposes the validity of the distinction between phenomena and things in themselves. If, then, this distinction should prove untenable in principle, Kant's conclusion with regard to space must fail on general grounds' (1909, p. 70). And he argues that it fails.
2. Prichard does acknowledge that Kant *begins* with 'the distinction between things as they are in themselves and things as they appear to us' which relate 'to one and the same reality regarded from two different points of view', but he continues, '[Kant] ends with the distinction between two different realities, thing-in-themselves, external to, in the sense of independent of, the mind, and phenomena or appearances within it' (p. 75). It is the latter that Prichard assumes in his ongoing translation and criticisms of Kant's *Critique*.
3. For a refutation of the argument from illusion see Rödl (2007, pp. 157–158); and for a Kantian response to the sceptic, see Andrea Kern (2014, pp. 81–104).

4. Henrich had wanted to convince sceptics 'of the importance of conversation that might begin to bridge the divide between the so-called "Anglo-American" and "Continental" traditions of philosophy' (Pacini, 2003, p. x).
5. Henrich's sustained effort to 'bridge the divide' has in recent years (since McDowell and Brandom) resulted in theorists from both German and Anglophone traditions working on joint projects, workshops, conferences etc. and as discussed in the Introduction, there is now a flourishing literature on German Idealist ideas and issues.
6. Again, note the (re)wording: 'things *as they are* inthemselves'.
7. Kant writes, 'I have also, elsewhere, sometimes entitled it *formal* idealism, to distinguish it from *material* idealism, that is, from the usual type of idealism which doubts or denies the existence of outer things themselves' (B519, footnote).
8. McDowell too often draws attention to this quote for its significance.
9. In this paper, McDowell is differentiating his reading of Kant from that of Sellars; he writes 'I think a fully Kantian vision of intentionality is inaccessible to Sellars, because of a deep structural feature of his philosophical outlook' (2009a, p. 34.)
10. As previously noted, some of the contemporary work on Kant and Hegel in analytic philosophy is making its way into the philosophy of education, for instance David Bakhurst draws on McDowell (2009, 2011, 2014, 2016, 2020) and Jan Derry draws on Brandom and McDowell (2009, 2011, 2013, 2014, 2016, 2017). And both Sebastian Rödl and Andrea Kern contribute directly to educational theory, emphasising the centrality of education. Kern says, 'the concept of education describes the distinctive form of development of what, from its first minute, is a self-conscious being' (2020, p. 287). And education for Rödl is the child's growth into itself (2016, 2020).

References

Allison, H.E. (2015) *Kant's Transcendental Deduction. An Analytical-Historical Commentary* (Oxford, Oxford University Press).

Ameriks, K. (1982) *Kant's Theory of Mind* (Oxford, Clarendon Press).

Ameriks, K. (2019) *Kantian Subjects: Critical Philosophy and Late Modernity* (Oxford, Oxford University Press).

Bakhurst, D. (1991) *Consciousness and Revolution in Soviet Philosophy: From the Bolsheviks to Evald Ilyenkov* (Cambridge, Cambridge University Press).

Bakhurst, D. (2009) Mind, Brains and Education, in Cigman, R., Davis, A. (eds.) *New Philosophies of Learning* (Sussex, Wiley-Blackwell), pp. 57–74.

Bakhurst, D. (2011) *The Formation of Reason* (Oxford, Wiley-Blackwell).

Bakhurst, D. (2014) Learning from Others, in Kotzee, B. (ed.) *Education and the Growth of Knowledge: Perspectives from Social and Virtue Epistemology* (Oxford, Wiley-Blackwell).

Bakhurst, D. (2016) Exploring the Formation of Reason. *Journal of Philosophy of Education*, 50 (1): 76–83, 123–129.

Bakhurst, D. (2020) Teaching, Telling and Technology. *Journal of Philosophy of Education*, 54 (2): 305–318.

Bennett, M.R., Hacker, P.M.S. (2003) *Philosophical Foundations of Neuroscience* (Oxford, Blackwell Publishing).

Bennett, M.R., Hacker, P.M.S. (2007) *Neuroscience and Philosophy, Brain, Mind, and Language* (Chichester, Columbia University Press).

Bird, G. (1962) *Kant's Theory of Knowledge* (London, Routledge, Kegan Paul).

Bird, G. (2006) *The Revolutionary Kant: A Commentary on the Critique of Pure Reason* (Chicago and La Salle, Illinois, Open Court, a division of Carus Publishing Company).

Blackburn, S. (2006) Julius Caesar and George Berkeley Play Leapfrog, in *McDowell and his Critics* (Oxford, Blackwell Publishing).

Blackburn, S. (2010) *Practical Tortoise Raising: And Other Philosophical Essays* (Oxford, Oxford University Press).

Blake, N., Smeyers, R., Smith, R.D., Standish, P. (2003) *The Blackwell Guide to the Philosophy of Education* (Oxford, Blackwell Publishing Ltd).

Boghossian, P. (2006) *Fear of Knowledge* (Oxford, Oxford University Press).

Brandom, R. (1994) *Making It Explicit* (London, Harvard University Press).

Interpreting Kant for Education: Dissolving Dualisms and Embodying Mind, First Edition. Sheila Webb.
Chapters and editorial organization © 2022 Philosophy of Education Society of Great Britain.
Published 2022 by John Wiley & Sons Ltd.

Brandom, R. (2000) *Articulating Reasons* (London, Harvard University Press).

Brandom, R. (2006) Kantian Lessons about Mind, Meaning, and Rationality. *Philosophical Topics*, 34 (1/2): 1–20.

Brandom, R. (2008) *Between Saying and Doing: Towards an Analytic Pragmatism* (New York, Oxford University Press).

Brandom, R. (2008) How Analytic Philosophy Has Failed Cognitive Science. Available at: https://www.ucd.ie/philosophy/normativityconference/resources/How_Analytic_Philosophy_Has_Failed_Cognitive_Science.pdf. accessed 03.04.2018.

Brandom, R. (2010) From German Idealism to American Pragmatism – and Back. William James Lecture, Harvard University, 03.12.2010. Available at: http://lms.ff.uhk.cz/pool/download_14.pdf. accessed 20.04.2017.

Brandom, R. (2013) From German Idealism to American Pragmatism – and Back, in *Kant und die Philosophie in weltbürgerlicher Absicht: Akten des XI. Internationalen Kant-Kongresses* (Berlin, Walter de Gruyter GmbH).

Brandom, R. (2019) *A Spirit of Trust. A Reading of Hegel's Phenomenology* (London, The Belknap Press of Harvard University Press).

Bruner, J. (1973) *Beyond the Information Given: Studies in the Psychology of Knowing* (USA, W.W. Norton & Co).

Bruner, J. (1983) *In Search of Mind: Essays in Autobiography* (New York, Harper & Row Publishers).

Bruner, J. (1986) *Actual Minds, Possible Worlds* (London, Harvard University Press).

Bruner, J. (1990) *Acts of Meaning* (London, Harvard University Press).

Bruner, J. (1996) *The Culture of Education* (London, Harvard University Press).

Bubner, R. (2002) Bildung and Second Nature, in Smith, N.H. (ed.) *Reading McDowell* (London, Routledge).

Calvin, W. (1997) *How Brains Think: The Evolution of Intelligence* (GB, Weidenfeld & Nicolson).

Card, C. (1996) *The Unnatural Lottery: Character and Moral Luck* (Philadelphia, Temple University Press).

Carr, D. (2000) *Professionalism and Ethics in Teaching* (London, Routledge).

Carr, D. (2003) *Making Sense of Education: An Introduction to the Philosophy and Theory of Education and Teaching* (London, Routledge Falmer).

Carr, D. (2007) Moralized Psychology or Psychologized Morality? Ethics and Psychology in Recent Theorizing about Moral and Character Education. *Educational Theory*, 57 (4): 389–402.

Carr, D. (2012) *Educating the Virtues: An Essay on the Philosophical Psychology of Moral Development and Education* (first edition 1991) (London, Routledge, 2012 edition).

Carr, D., Harrison, T. (2015) *Educating Character Through Stories* (Exeter, Imprint Academic).

Carr, W. (1995) *For Education: towards Critical Educational Inquiry* (Buckingham, Open University Press).

Carr, W. (2001) Confronting the Postmodern Challenge, in Paul Hirst, Patricia White (eds.) *Philosophy of Education: Major Themes in the Analytic Tradition* (London, Routledge, London).

Carr, W. (2006) Education without Theory. *British Journal of Educational Studies*, 54 (2): 136–159.

Cavell, S. (1969) *Must We Mean What We Say?* (New York, Charles Scribner's Sons).

Caygill, H. (1995) *A Kant Dictionary* (Oxford, Blackwell Publishers Ltd.)).

Caygill, H. (2007) *Introduction to Kant's Critique of Pure Reason* (1787). (trans. Kemp Smith, N.) (revised 2nd edition 2007) (New York, Palgrave Macmillan).

Cigman, R., Davis, A. (2009) *New Philosophies of Learning* (Sussex, Wiley-Blackwell).

Clark, A. (1997) *Being There: Putting Mind, World, and Body Back Together* (Cambridge, MIT Press).

Clark, A., Chalmers, D. (1998) The Extended Mind. *Analysis*, 101: 401–431.

Code, L. (2005) Ecological Naturalism: Epistemic Responsibility and the Politics of Knowledge. *Dialogue and Universalism*, 15 (5–6): 87–102.

Code, L. (2006) *Ecological Thinking: The Politics of Epistemic Location* (Oxford, Oxford University Press).

Conant, J. (2016) Why Kant Is Not a Kantian. *Philosophical Topics*, 44 (1), Spring 2016: 75–125.

Conant, J. (2017) Kant's Critique of the Layer-Cake Conception of Human Mindedness in the B Deduction, in O'Shea, J. (ed.) *Kant's Critique of Pure Reason: A Critical Guide* (Cambridge, UP), pp. 120–139.

Conant, J. (2020) Reply to Gustafsson: Wittgenstein on the Relation of Sign to Symbol, in Sofia Miguens (ed.) *The Logical Alien: Conant and His Critics* (USA, Harvard University Press).

Crane, T. (1992) *The Contents of Experience* (Cambridge, Cambridge University Press).

Davidson, D. (1986a) A Nice Derrangement of Epitaphs, in LePore, E. (ed.) *Truth and Interpretation: Perspectives on the Philosophy of Donald Davidson.* (Blackwell Publishing), pp. 433–446.

Davidson, D. (1986b) A Coherence Theory of Truth and Knowledge, in LePore, E. (ed.) *Truth and Interpretation: Perspectives on the Philosophy of Donald Davidson* (Blackwell Publishing), pp. 307–319.

Davidson, D. (1991) Three Varieties of Knowledge, in Griffiths, P.A. (ed.) *Royal Institute of Philosophy Supplement* (New York, Cambridge University Press), pp. 153–166.

Davidson, D. (2000) Truth Rehabilitated, in Brandom, R. (ed.) *Rorty and His Critics* (Oxford, Blackwell Publishing Ltd).

Davidson, D. (2001) On the Very Idea of a Conceptual Scheme, in: *Inquiries into Truth and Interpretation* (Oxford, Clarendon Press).

Davis, D. (1998) *The Limits of Educational Assessment* (Oxford, Blackwell).

Davis, A. (2004) The Credentials of Brain-based Learning. *Journal of Philosophy of Education*, 38 (1): pp. 21–36.

Davis, A. (2009) Examples as Method? My attempts to Understand Assessment and Fairness (in the Spirit of the Later Wittgenstein), *Journal of Philosophy of Education*, 43 (3): 371–389.

Davis, A. (2011) Interpreting Student Responses in High Stakes Standardized Quantitative Learning Assessment. *Philosophy of Education Society*: 186–189.

Davis, A. (2013) How far can we aspire to consistency when assessing learning? *Ethics and Education*, 8 (3): 217–228.

Davis, A. (2015) Is It Really Possible to Test All Educationally Significant Achievements with High Levels of Reliability? *Ethics and Education*, 10 (3): 372–379.

Davis, A. (2018) *A Critique of Pure Teaching Methods and the Case of Synthetic Phonics* (London, Bloomsbury Academic).

De Caro, M., McArthur, D. (2004) Introduction: The Nature of Naturalism, in *Naturalism in Question* (USA, Harvard University Press).

Dennett, D. (1991) *Consciousness Explained* (London, Little, Brown & Co).

Derry, J. (2009) Technology-Enhanced Learning: A Question of Knowledge, in *New Philosophies of Learning* (Chichester, Wiley-Blackwell).

Derry, J., Bakker, A. (2011) Lessons from Inferentialism for Statistics Education, in *Mathematical Thinking and Learning*, 13 (1): 5–26.

Derry, J. (2013) *Vygotsky and Education* (Chichester, Wiley Blackwell).

Derry, J. (2014) Can Inferentialism Contribute to Social Epistemology? in Kotzee, B., (ed.) *Education and the Growth of Knowledge* (Chichester, Wiley Blackwell).

Derry, J. (2016) From Disembodied Intellect to Cultivated Rationality, *Journal of Philosophy of Education*, 50 (1): 117–122.

Derry, J. (2017) An Introduction to Inferentialism in Mathematics Education. *Mathematics Education Research Journal*, DOI: 10.1007/s13394-017-0193-7. Available at: http://discovery.ucl.ac.uk/1541289/1/Derry-2017-Mathematics_Education_Research_Journal%20published%20version.pdf. accessed 01.05.2017.

Dennett, D. (1991) *Consciousness Explained* (London, Little, Brown & Co).

Donaldson, M. (1978) *Children's Minds* (London, Fontana Press).

Dunne, J. (1993) *Back to the Rough Ground: Practical Judgment and the Lure of Technique* (USA, University of Notre Dame).

Dreyfus, H.L. (2005) Overcoming the Myth of the Mental: How Philosophers Can Profit from the Phenomenology of Everyday Expertise. *Proceedings and Addresses of the American Philosophical Association*, 79 (2): 47–65.

Einstein, A. (1916) Stanford Encyclopedia of Philosophy. Available at http://plato.stanford.edu/entries/einstein-philscience/. accessed 05.04.2017.

Elkind, D. (1989) Developmentally Appropriate Practice: Philosophical and Practical Implications. *The Phi Delta Kappan*, 71 (2): 113–117.

Engstrom, S. (2006) Understanding and Sensibility. *Inquiry*, 49 (1): 2–25.

Engstrom, S. (2009) *The Form of Practical Knowledge: A Study of the Categorical Imperative* (London, Harvard University Press).

Engstrom, S. (2013) Constructivism and Practical Knowledge, in Bagnoli, C. (ed.) *Constructivism in Ethics* (Cambridge, Cambridge University Press), pp. 133–152.

Engstrom, S. (2015) Reflection and Reason in Hume and Kant, *Hegel Bulletin*, 36 (1): 15–32.

Evans, G. (1982) *The Varieties of Reference* (Oxford, Oxford University Press).

Fitzsimons, P. (2007) The 'End' of Kant-in-Himself: Nietzschean difference. *Educational Philosophy and Theory*, 39 (5): 559–170.

Fodor, J. (1998) The Trouble with Psychological Darwinism. *London Review of Books*, 20 (2): 11–13.

Freeman, W. (1999) *How Brains Make Up Their Minds* (New York, Columbia University Press).

Friedman, M. (2002) Exorcising the Philosophical Tradition, in Smith, N.H. (ed.) *Reading McDowell on Mind and World* (London, Routledge), pp. 25–57.

Geake, J., Cooper, P. (2003) Cognitive Neuroscience: Implications for Education? *Westminster Studies in Education*, 26 (1): 7–20.

Geuss, R. (2008) Richard Rorty at Princeton: Personal Recollections. Available at: https://www.bu.edu/arion/files/2010/03/Geuss-on-Rorty.pdf. accessed 18.02.2018.

Gilligan, C. (1982/1993) *A Different Voice* (Cambridge, Harvard University Press).

Glasersfeld, E. von (1984) An Introduction to Radical Constructivism, in Watzlawick, P. (ed.) *The Invented Reality* (New York, Norton & Co), pp. 17–40.

Glasersfeld, E. von. (1989) Cognition, Construction of Knowledge and Teaching. *Synthese*, 80 (1): 121–140.

Glasersfeld, E. von. (1990) An Exposition of Constructivism: Why Some like it Radical, in Davis, R.B., Maher, C.A., Noddings, N., (eds.) *Monographs of the Journal for Research in Mathematics Education*, No.4 (National Council of Teachers of Mathematics, Virginia, Reston), pp. 19–29.

Glasersfeld, E. von. (1991) Knowing without Metaphysics: Aspects of the Radical Constructivist Position, in Steier, F. (ed.) *Research and Reflexivity* (London, Sage), pp. 12–29.

Glasersfeld, E. von. (1995a) *Radical Constructivism: A Way of Knowing and Learning* (London, RoutledgeFalmer). Available at: http://www.univie.ac.at/constructivism/archive/fulltexts/1462.html. accessed 15.04.2017.

Glasersfeld, E. von. (1995b) A Constructivist Approach to Teaching, in Steffe, L.P., Gale, J. (eds.) *Constructivism in Education* (Hillsdale, Erlbaum), pp. 3–15.

Glaserfeld, E. von. (2001) The Radical Constructivist View of Science, in Riegler, A. (ed.) *Foundations of Science. Special issue on 'The Impact of Radical Constructivism on Science'*, Volume 6 (1–3), pp. 31–43.

Goswami, U. (2004) Neuroscience and Education. *British Journal of Special Education*, 74 (4): 175–183.

Goswami, U. (2008) *Cognitive Development: The Learning Brain* (Hove, Psychology Press).

Green, J. (2011) *Education, Professionalism and the Quest for Accountability: Hitting the Target but Missing the Point* (Oxon, Routledge).

Greenberg, R. (2001) *Kant's Theory of a Priori Knowledge* (USA, The Pennsylvania State University).

Greenberg, R. (2008) *Real Existence, Ideal Necessity: Kant's Compromise, and the Modalities without Compromise* (Berlin, Walter de Gruyter).

Hacking, I. (1999) *The Social Construction of What?* (Cambridge, Harvard University Press).

Hamlyn, D. (1970) *The Theory of Knowledge* (London, Macmillan Press Ltd.).

Hanna, R. (2016a) Kant, the Copernican Devolution, and Real Metaphysics. Available at: https://phil.hse.ru/data/2016/04/22/1129978006/hanna_1.pdf. accessed 24.04.2017.

Hanna, R. (2016b) Directions in Space, Non-Conceptual Form, and the Foundations of Transcendental Idealism, in Jiménez, R.V.O., Hanna, R., Louden, R., de Rosales, J.R., Madrid N.S. (eds.) *Kant's Shorter Writings: Critical Paths Outside the Critiques* (Newcastle, Cambridge Scholars Publishing).

Henrich, D. (1992) *Aesthetic Judgment and the Moral Image of the World: Studies in Kant* (Stanford, Stanford University Press).

Henrich, D. (1993) On the Meaning of Rational Action in the State, in Reiner, R., Booth, W.J. (eds.) *Kant and Political Philosophy: The Contemporary Legacy* (London, Yale University Press).

Henrich, D. (1994) *The Unity of Reason* (London, Harvard University Press).

Henrich, D. (2003) *Between Kant and Hegel: Lectures on German Idealism* (London, Harvard University Press).

Herdt, J.A. (2019) *Forming Humanity: Redeeming the German Bildung Tradition* (Chicago, University of Chicago Press).

Hirst, P.H. (1963) Philosophy and Educational Theory, *British Journal of Educational Studies*, 12 (1): 51–64.

Hirst, P.H. (1973) Forms of Knowledge – A Reply to Elizabeth Hindess, *Journal of Philosophy of Education*, 7 (2): 260–271.

Hirst, P.H. (1974) *Knowledge and the Curriculum: A Collection of Philosophical Papers* (Oxon, Routledge and Kegan Paul).

Hirst, P.H. (2008) In Pursuit of Reason, in Waks, L.J. (ed.) *Leaders in Philosophy of Education: Intellectual Self Portraits* (Rotterdam, Sense), pp. 113–124.

Hotam, Y. (2019) *Bildung*: Liberal Education and its Devout Origins, *Journal of Philosophy of Education*, 53 (4): 619–632.

Houlgate, S. (2005) *An Introduction to Hegel: Freedom, Truth and History* (Oxford, Blackwell Publishing).

Houlgate, S. (2019) Review of Robert Brandom's A Spirit of Trust: A Reading of Hegel's Phenomenology, in *Notre Dame Philosophical Reviews*. Available at: https://ndpr.nd.edu/news/a-spirit-of-trust-a-reading-of-hegels-phenomenology/. accessed 30.11.2020.

Hume, D. (1739) *A Treatise of Human Nature* (reprinted 1985) (London, Penguin Books).

Jardine, D.W. (2005) "Cutting Nature's Leading Strings": A Cautionary Tale About Constructivism, *Canadian Journal of Environmental Education*, 10 (spring 2005): 38–51.

Jardine, D.W. (2006) *Piaget and Education* (New York, Peter Lang Primer).

Jensen, E. (2008) *Brain-based Learning: The New Paradigm of Teaching* (California, Corwin Press).

Johnston, J.S. (2013) *Kant's Philosophy: A Study for Educators* (London, Bloomsbury Publishing plc).

Kant, I. (1787) *Critique of Pure Reason* (trans. Kemp Smith, N.) (revised 2nd edition 2007) (New York, Palgrave Macmillan).

Kant, I. (2002) *Critique of Practical Reason* (trans. Pluhar, W.S.) (Indianapolis, Hackett Publishing Company).

Kant, I. (2000) *Critique of the Power of Judgment* (trans. Paul Gower, Eric Matthews) (New York, Cambridge University Press).

Kern, A. (2006) Spontaneity and Receptivity in Kant's Theory of Knowledge. *Philosophical Topics*, 34 (1&2): 145–162.

Kern, A. (2012) Knowledge as a Fallible Capacity, in Tolksdorf, S. (ed.) *Conceptions of Knowledge* (Berlin, Walter de Gruyter).

Kern, A. (2014) Why Do Our Reasons Come to an End? In: Conant, J., Kern, A. (eds.) *Varieties of Skepticism; essays after Kant, Wittgenstein, and Cavell* (Berlin, De Gruyter).

Kern, A. (2017) *On the Concept of a Rational Capacity for Knowledge* (London, Harvard University Press).

Kern, A. (2020) Human Life, Rationality and Education. *Journal of Philosophy of Education*, 54.2: 268–289.

Kohlberg, L. (1973) The Claim to Moral Adequacy of a Highest Stage of Moral Judgement. *Journal of Philosophy*, 70 (18): 630–646.

Kohlberg, L. (1981) *Essays on Moral Development. Volume One: The Philosophy of Moral Development* (CA, Harper & Row).

Korsgaard, C.M. (1996) *The Sources of Normativity* (2003 edition) (Cambridge, Cambridge University Press).

Kukla, A. (2000) *Social Constructivism and the Philosophy of Science* (London, Routledge).

Lavin, D. (2004) Practical Reason and the Possibility of Error. *Ethics*, 114 (3): 424–457.

Levant, A. (2012) E.V. Ilyenkov and Creative Soviet Marxism: Introduction to Dialectics of the Ideal. *Historical Materialism,* 20 (2): 128–129.

Longuesse, B. (2005) *Kant on the Human Standpoint* (Cambridge, Cambridge University Press).

Løvlie, L., Standish, P. (2002) Bildung and the Idea of Liberal Education, *Journal of Philosophy of Education*, 36 (3): 317–340.

Malik, K. (2000) *Man, Beast and Zombie* (London, Weidenfeld & Nicolson).

Meyer, D. (2008) The Poverty of Constructivism. *Educational Philosophy and Theory*, 41 (3): 332–341.

McCrory, C. (2015) The Knowledge Illusion: Who Is Doing What thinking? *Teaching History*, (issue 161): 37–47.

McDowell, J. (1996) *Mind and World* (London, Harvard University Press).

McDowell, J. (1998a) *Mind, Value, and Reality* (London, Harvard University Press).

McDowell, J. (1998b) *Meaning, Knowledge and Reality* (London, Harvard University Press).

McDowell, J. (2000) Towards Rehabilitating Objectivity, in Brandom, R. (ed.) *Rorty and his Critics* (Oxford, Blackwell Publishing), pp. 109–123.

McDowell, J. (2004) Naturalism in the Philosophy of Mind, in de Caro, M., Macarthur, D., (eds.) *Naturalism in Question* (London, Harvard University Press).

McDowell, J. (2006) *McDowell and his Critics* (Oxford, Blackwell Publishing Ltd).

McDowell, J. (2009a) *Having the World in View* (London, Harvard University Press).

McDowell, J. (2009b) *The Engaged Intellect* (London, Harvard University Press).

McDowell, J. (2011a) *Perception as a Capacity for Knowledge* (Wisconsin, Marquette University Press).

McDowell, J. (2011b) *Autonomy and Community: Some Remarks on the Second Movement of Brandom's Sonata*. Chicago University. Available at https://voices.uchicago.edu/germanphilosophy/files/2011/04/Autonomy-and-Community.pdf. accessed 05.04.2017.

McDowell, J. (2012) Why Sellars's Essay is called 'Empiricism and the philosophy of Mind'. Dublin Conference on Wilfred Sellars, June 2001, p. 1. Available at: https://voices.uchicago.edu/germanphilosophy/files/2011/04/Autonomy-and-Community.pdf

McGinn, M. (2009) McDowell's Minimal Empiricism. *Philosophical Topics*, 37 (1): 77–94.

Misawa, K. (2013) Education as the Cultivation of Second Nature: Two Senses of the Given. *Educational Theory*, 63 (1): 35–50.

Misawa, K. (2017) Humans, Animals and the World We Inhabit – On and Beyond the Symposium 'Second Nature, Bildung and McDowell: David Bakhurst's The Formation of Reason', *Journal of Philosophy of Education*, 51 (4): 744–759.

Moore, A.W. (1997) *Points of View* (Oxford, Oxford University Press).

Moore, G.E. (1903) The Refutation of Idealism. *Mind*, 12 (48): 433–453.

Muchnik, P. (2008) in Muchnik, P. (ed.) *Introduction to Rethinking Kant, Volume 1* (Newcastle, Cambridge Scholars Publishing).

Mulder, J. (2018) The Limits of Humeanism. *European Journal for Philosophy of Science*, 8 (3): 671–687.

Mulder, J. (2019) The Limits of Reductionism: Thought, Life and Reality. Available at https://kurtgoedel.de/cms-83FO/wp-content/uploads/2020/01/The_limits_of_reductionism.pdf. accessed 03.04.2020.

Nagel, T. (1986) *The View from Nowhere* (Oxford, Oxford University Press).

Newton, A. (2014) Kant on Testimony and the Communicability of Empirical Knowledge. *Philosophical Topics*, 42 (1): 271–290.

Noddings, N., Slote, M. (2003) In: Blake, N., Smeyers, P., Smith, R. and Standish, P., (eds.) *The Blackwell guide to the Philosophy of Education* (Oxford, Blackwell Publishing).

O'Neill, O. (2000) *Bounds of Justice* (Cambridge, Cambridge University Press).

Pacini, D. (2008) Introduction, in Henrich, D. (ed.) *Between Kant and Hegel* (Cambridge, Harvard University Press).

Peacocke, C. (1992) *A Study of Concepts* (Cambridge, MIT Press).

Peters, R.S. (1966) *Ethics and Education* (Oxon, Routledge).

Phillips, D.C., Siegel, H. (2013) Philosophy of Education, in *The Stanford Encyclopedia of Philosophy* (Fall 2013 edition).

Piaget, J. (1928) *The Child's Conception of the World* (London, Routledge and Kegan Paul Ltd).

Piaget, J. (1936) *Origins of Ilntelligence in the Child* (1953 edition) (London, Routledge and Keegan Paul).

Piaget, J. (1955) *The Construction of Reality in the Child* (London, Routledge and Kegan Paul).

Piaget, J. (1971) *Genetic Epistemology* (New York, W.W. Norton).

Prichard, H.A. (1909) *Kant's Theory of Knowledge* (Oxford, Clarendon Press).

Pring, R. (2000) The 'False Dualism' of Educational Research, *Journal of Philosophy of Education*, 34 (2): 247–260.

Pring, R. (2004) *The Philosophy of Education: Aims, Theory, Common Sense and Research*.

Pring, R. (2007) Reclaiming Philosophy for Educational Research. *Educational Review*, 59 (3): 315–330.

Pring, R. (2013) *The Life and Death of Secondary Educational for All* (Oxon, Routledge).

Pring, R. (2014) What counts as an educated person in this day and age? in *The EBOR Lectures*, September 2014 (York, St. John University).

Prichard, H.A. (1909) *Kant's Theory of Knowledge* (Oxford, Clarendon Press).

Putman, H. (2004) The Content and Appeal of "Naturalism", in de Caro, M., and Macarthur D., (eds.) *Naturalism in Question* (London, Harvard University Press).

Redding, P. (2010a) Two Directions for Analytic Kantianism: Naturalism and Idealism, in *Naturalism and Normativity* (New York, Columbia University Press), pp. 263–288.

Redding, P. (2010b) The Possibility of German Idealism after Analytic Philosophy: McDowell, Brandom and beyond, in Chase, J., Mares, E., Williams, J., and Reynolds, J., (eds.) *Postanalytic and Metacontinental: Crossing Philosophical Divides* (New York, Continuum), pp. 191–202.

Reichenbach, R. (1999) Postmodern Knowledge, Modern Beliefs, and the Curriculum. *Educational Philosophy and Theory*, 31 (2): 237–244.

Rietveld, E. (2010) McDowell and Dreyfus on Unreflective Action, *Inquiry*, 53 (2): 183–207.

Rödl, S. (2005) Transcendental Deduction and Predicative Structure in Kant and Brandom, *Pragmatics and Cognition*, 13 (1): 91–107.

Rödl, S. (2006) Logical Form as a Relation to the Object. *Philosophical Topics*, 34 (1&2), spring and fall 2006.

Rödl, S. (2007) *Self-Consciousness* (London, Harvard University Press).

Rödl, (2011) Reason and Nature, First and Second, in Hindrichs, G., Honneth, A. (eds.) (Freiheit, Stuttgarter Hegel-Kongress 2011) (Frankfurt/Main, Klostermann 2013). Available at: http://www.stuttgart.de/img/mdb/item/435842/66938.mp3. accessed 01.04.2017.

Rödl, S. (2012) *Categories of the Temporal* (London, Harvard University Press).

Rödl, S. (2014) *Self-Consciousness and Knowledge*. University of Chicago, available: https://lucian.uchicago.edu/blogs/objects/files/2014/05/Sebastian-Self-Consciousness-and-Knowledge-annotated.pdf. accessed 01.04.2017.

Rödl, S. (2016) Education and Autonomy. Journal of Philosophy of Education, 50 (1): 84–97.

Rödl, S. (2017) Self-Consciousness, Negation, and Disagreement. Proceedings of the Aristotelian Society, 138th Session, issue 3, volume CXVII, Senate House, London.

Rödl, S. (2020) Teaching, Freedom and the Human Individual. *Journal of Philosophy of Education*, 54 (2): 290–304.

Rorty, R. (1979) *Philosophy and the Mirror of Nature* (New Jersey, Princeton University Press).

Rorty, R. (1982) Contemporary Philosophy of Mind. *Synthese*, 53 (2): 323–348.

Rorty, R. (1989) *Contingency, Irony and Solidarity* (Cambridge, Cambridge University Press).

Rorty, R. (1990) Solidarity or Objectivity?, in *Objectivity, Relativism and Truth* (Cambridge, Cambridge University Press).

Rorty, R. (1998) The Very Idea of Human Answerability to the World: John McDowell's Version of Empiricism, in *Truth & Progress* (Cambridge, Cambridge University Press).

Rorty, R. (1999) *Philosphy and Social Hope* (London, Penguin Books).

Rorty, R. (2000) *Rorty and his Critics*, in Brandom, R. (ed.) (Oxford, Blackwell Publishing Ltd).

Roth, W.-M. (2005) *Talking Science: Language and Learning in Science Classrooms* (Langham, MD, Rowman and Littlefield Publishers).

Roth, W.-M. (2006) *Learning Science: A Singular Plural Perspective* (Rotterdam, Sense Publishers).

Roth, W.-M. (2009) *Dialogism: A Bakhtinian Perspective on Science and Learning* (Rotter-dam, Sense Publishers).

Roth, W.-M. (2011a) *Possibility: At the Limits of the Constructivist Metaphor* (London, Springer).

Roth, W.-M. (2011b) *Geometry as Objective Science in Elementary School Classrooms: Mathematics in the Flesh* (London, Routledge).

Roth, W.-M. (2013) From Information Processing to the Whole Person. *AVANT,* IV (1): 398–415.

Roth, W.-M. (2017) *The Mathematics of Mathematics: Thinking with the Late, Spinozist Vygotsky* (Rotterdam, Sense Publishers).

Royer, D. (2006) Genre, Relationality, and Whitehead's Principle of Relativity: How We Write, in Allan, G., and Evans, M.D. (eds.) *A Different Three Rs for Education: Reason, Relationality, Rhythm* (Amsterdam, Rodopi), pp. 61–74.

Russell, B. (1905) On Denoting, *Mind,* 14: 479–493.

Russell, B. (1914) *Our Knowledge of the External World: As a Field for Scientific Method in Philosophy* (London, The Open Court Publishing Company).

Ryle, G. (1949) *The Concept of Mind* (London, Penguin Books Ltd).

Schear, J.K. (2013) *Mind, Reason and Being-in-the-World: The McDowell-Dreyfus Debate,* in Schear, J.K. (ed). (Oxon, Routledge).

Sedgwick, S. (1997) Can Kant's Ethics Survive the Feminist Critique? in Schott, R.M. (ed.) *Feminist Interpretations of Immanuel Kant* (Pennsylvania, The Pennsylvania State University Press), pp. 77–100.

Sellars, W. (1967) *Science and Metaphysics; Variations on Kantian Themes* (California, Ridgeview Publishing Company).

Sellars, W. (1997) *Empiricism and the Philosophy of Mind* (1st edition 1956) (London, Harvard University Press).

Siegel, H. (2006) Epistemological Diversity and Educational Research: Much Ado About Nothing Much? *Educational Researcher,* 35 (2): 3–12.

Siegel, H. (2007) Review of Paul Boghossian's 'Fear of Knowledge', in *Notre Dame Philosophical Reviews* (1st January). Available at: http://ndpr.nd.edu/news/fear-of-knowledge-against-relativism-and-constructivism/. accessed 5/4/2017.

Siegel, H. (2010) Knowledge and Truth, in Bailey, R., Barrow, R., Carr, D., McCarthy, C. (eds.) *The SAGE Handbook of Philosophy of Education,* pp. 283–296.

Siljander, P., Sutinen, A. (2012) Introduction, in Siljander, P., Kivelä, A., Sutinen, A. (eds) *Theories of Bildung and Growth* (Rotterdam, Sense Publishers).

Smeyers, P., de Royter, J., Waghid, Y., Strand, T. (2014) Publish Yet Perish: On the Pitfalls of Philosophy of Education in an Age of Impact Factors, in *Studies in Philosophy and Education* (Springer, July 2014, issue 33), pp. 647–666.

Smith, R. (2016) The Virtues of Unknowing. *Journal of Philosophy of Education,* 50 (2): 272–284.

Sousa, D. (2005) *How the Brain Learns to Read* (California, Corwin Press).

Sousa, D. (2007) *How the Special Needs Brain Learns* (California, Corwin Press).

Sousa, D. (2008) *How the Brain Learns Mathematics* (California, Corwin Press).

Sousa, D. (2011) *How the Brain Learns* (California, Corwin Press).

Standish, P. (2007) Claims of Philosophy, Education and Research. *Educational Review,* 59 (3): 331–341.

Standish, P. (2010) Calling to Account, in Smeyers, P. and Depaepe, M., (eds.) *The Ethics and Aesthetics of Statistics* (London, Springer).

Standish, P. (2011) Transparency, Accountability, and the Public Role of higher Education, in *Higher Education as a Public Good: Critical Perspectives* (Oxford: New College).

Standish, P. (2020) Preface. *Journal of Philosophy of Education*, 54 (2): 789–790.

Stanford Encyclopedia of Philosophy. (2013) Philosophy of Education. Available at https://plato.stanford.edu/entries/education-philosophy/. accessed 17.3.2017.

Stekeler-Weithofer, P. (2005) Formal Truth and Objective Reference in an Inferentialist Setting, *Pragmatics and Cognition*, 13 (1): 7–37.

Stekeler-Weithofer, P. (2008) Formal Truth and Objective Reference in an Inferentialist Setting, in Stekeler-Weithofer (ed.) *The Pragmatics of Making it Explicit* (Amsterdam, John Benjamins Publishing Company).

Stekeler-Weithofer, P. (2010a) Intuition and Inference, in *Second Graduate International Summer School in Cognitive Sciences and Semantics, on 'Robert Brandom's Analytic Pragmatism'*, July 19–29 (Riga, University of Latvia).

Stekeler-Weithofer, P. (2010b) Perception and Intuition in a Kantian 'Philosophical Anthropology'. Conference on Kant and Intuition, University of Chicago.

Stekeler-Weithofer, P. (2010c) On the role of Anschauung as a Logical form in Kant's Transcendental Analytic. Conference on Kant and Intuition, University of Chicago, 2010.

Stern, R. (2016) Does Hegelian 'Ethics Rest on a Mistake? in Testa, I., Ruggiu, L. (eds.) *'I, That Is We, We That Is I'*: *Perspectives on Contemporary Hegel: Social Ontology, Recognition, Naturalism, and the Critique of Kantian Constructivism* (Leiden, Brill), pp. 109–206.

Strawson, P. (1966) *The Bounds of Sense: An Essay on Kant's Critique of Pure Reason* (edition 2002) (London, Methuen).

Stroud, B. (2000) *The Quest for Reality: Subjectivism & the Metaphysics of Colour* (Oxford, Oxford University Press).

Tartaglia, J. (2016) Rorty's Ambivalent Relationship with Kant. Available at: http://www.jamestartaglia.com/publications/RortyKant.pdf. accessed 17.02.2018.

Taylor, T. (2001) Bruner and Condillac on Learning How to Talk, in Bakhurst, D., Shanker, S.G. (eds.), *Jerome Bruner: Language, Culture and Self* (London, SAGE publications Ltd).

Testa, I. (2016) Hegelian Resources for Contemporary Thought. Introductory Essay, in Testa, I., Ruggiu, L. (eds) *"I That Is We, We That Is I"*. *Perspectives on Contemporary Hegel. Social Ontology, Recognition Naturalism, and the Critique of Kantian Constructivism* (Boston, Brill Books), pp. 1–28.

Thompson, M. (2008) *Life and Action: Elementary Structures of Practice and Practical Thought* (London, Harvard University Press).

Usher, R., Edwards, R. (1994) *Postmodernism and Education* (London, Routledge).

Velkeley, R.L. (1994) Introduction, in Dieter Henrich (ed.) *The Unity of Reason* (London, Harvard University Press), pp. 1–15.

Vygotsky, L. (1934) Thinking and Speech. Available at: https://www.marxists.org/archive/vygotsky/works/words/Thinking-and-Speech.pdf. accessed 1.5.2017.

Vygotsky, L. (1987) in Reiber, R.W., & Carton A.S. (eds.) *The Collected Works of L. S. Vygotsky: Volume 1: Problems of General Psychology* (New York, Plenum Press).

Vygotsky, L. (1998) in Reiber, R.W. (ed.). *The Collected Works of L. S. Vygotsky: Volume 5, Child Psychology* (New York, Plenum Press).

Warnock, M. (1992) Higher Education: The Concept of Autonomy, *Oxford Review of Education*, 18 (2): 119–124.

Warnock, M. (2006) Cultural Relativism and Education, in *Research and Method in Education* (Oxford, Routledge), pp. 35–44.

Wertsch, J.V. (1997) *Vygotsky and the Formation of the Mind* (Cambridge, Harvard University Press).

White, J. (2005) *The Curriculum and the Child* (Oxon, Routledge).

Williams, B. (1985) *Ethics and the Limits of Philosophy* (Cambridge, Harvard University Press).

Williams, B. (2002) *Truth and Truthfulness: An Essay in Genealogy* (Princeton, Princeton University Press).

Williams, B. (2005) *Descartes: The Project of Pure Enquiry* (Oxon, Routledge).

Wilson, E.O. (1994) *Naturalist* (USA, Island Press).

Wilson, E.O. (1975) *Sociobiology: The New Synthesis* (Cambridge, Harvard University Press).

Wittgenstein, L. (1958) *Philosophical Investigations*, 129 (Oxford, Basil Blackwell).

Wittgenstein, L. (1967) *Zettel* (Berkeley, University of California Press).

Wood, Allen W. (2016) Interview on 3am [online]. Available at: http://www.philosophy.uncc.edu/mleldrid/SAAP/USC/pbt1.html. accessed 5/4/2017.

Young, M. (2008) *Bringing Knowledge Back In: From Social Constructivism to Social realism in the Sociology of Education* (Oxon, Routledge).

Zoller, G. (2010) Of empty thoughts and blind intuitions. *Kant's Answer to McDowell. Trans/Form/Ação*, 33 (1): 65–96.

Zull, J.E. (2002) *The Art of Changing the Brain: Enriching Teaching by Exploring the Biology of Learning* (Virginia, Stylus Publishing).

Index

Interpreting Kant for Education: Dissolving Dualisms and Embodying Mind, First Edition. Sheila Webb.
Chapters and editorial organization © 2022 Philosophy of Education Society of Great Britain.
Published 2022 by John Wiley & Sons Ltd.